S0-AJX-312

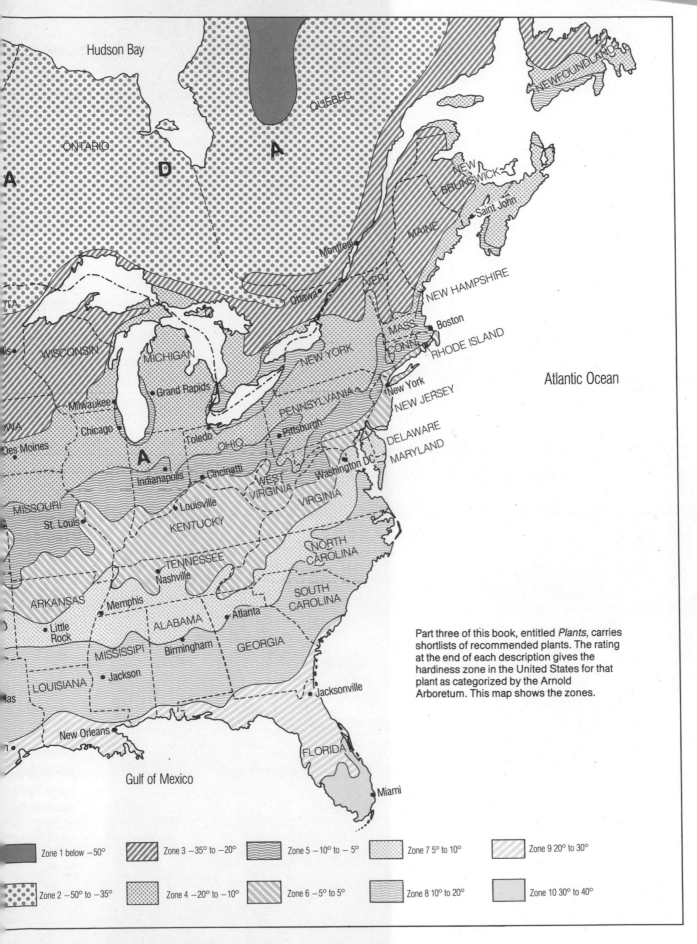

Hudson Bay

QUÉBEC

ONTARIO

A

D

A

NEWFOUNDLAND

NEW BRUNSWICK

Saint John

MAINE

Montreal

Ottawa

VER.

NEW HAMPSHIRE

WISCONSIN

MICHIGAN

Grand Rapids

Milwaukee

Chicago

Toledo

Des Moines

IOWA

MISSOURI

St. Louis

NEW YORK

MASS

CONN.

Boston

RHODE ISLAND

New York

NEW JERSEY

PENNSYLVANIA

Pittsburgh

DELAWARE

MARYLAND

Washington DC

OHIO

A

Indianapolis

Cincinatti

WEST VIRGINIA

VIRGINIA

Louisville

KENTUCKY

TENNESSEE

Nashville

NORTH CAROLINA

ARKANSAS

Memphis

SOUTH CAROLINA

Little Rock

ALABAMA

Atlanta

MISSISSIPI

Birmingham

GEORGIA

LOUISIANA

Jackson

Jacksonville

New Orleans

FLORIDA

Gulf of Mexico

Miami

Atlantic Ocean

Part three of this book, entitled *Plants*, carries shortlists of recommended plants. The rating at the end of each description gives the hardiness zone in the United States for that plant as categorized by the Arnold Arboretum. This map shows the zones.

Zone 1 below −50°

Zone 3 −35° to −20°

Zone 5 −10° to −5°

Zone 7 5° to 10°

Zone 9 20° to 30°

Zone 2 −50° to −35°

Zone 4 −20° to −10°

Zone 6 −5° to 5°

Zone 8 10° to 20°

Zone 10 30° to 40°

THE
WEEKEND
GARDENER

THE
WEEKEND
GARDENER

*Peter McHoy
and Roger Swain*

**All you need to know to plan and
make a good-looking, low-maintenance
and fast-maturing garden**

1817

Harper & Row, Publishers, Inc.

New York, Cambridge, Philadelphia, San Francisco, Washington,
London, Mexico City, San Paulo, Singapore, Sydney.

Contents

For information address
Harper & Row, Publishers, Inc.
10 East 53rd Street
New York, New York 10022
Published simultaneously in Canada
by Fitzhenry & Whiteside Limited,
Toronto.

Library of Congress Cataloging-in-Publication Data
McHoy, Peter.
   The weekend gardener.
   Previously published as: The garden making manual. 1985.
   Includes index.
   1. Landscape gardening. 2. Gardens-Designs and plans. 3. Plants, Ornamental. I. Swain, Roger B. II. Title.
SB473.M376   1987   712.6   86-12059
ISBN 0-06-015674-0

Title page: Suburban London garden

Below: A 'Japanese style' garden

Origination by
RCS Graphics Ltd, Leeds, England

Conceived and produced by
Swallow Publishing Limited
Northdown House, Northdown Street,
London N1

Editor Aston Keele
Editorial assistant Angie Doran
Art director David Young
Designer Malcolm Smythe
Studio Del and Co
Illustrations Steve Cross,
Rob Stone and David Tetley
Picture research Liz Eddison

INTRODUCTION

Every weekend, garden centres are teaming with people buying plants and garden materials. We spend a great deal of money, time and energy on our gardens, and yet too often they end up looking very ordinary and unimaginative. This is because not enough thought has gone into their design. Often only a little planning could make them more interesting and attractive, and would not necessarily cost more to run.

The book has been written in the belief that you can improve your garden, no matter how modest its size or how restricted your purse, if you plan carefully and think constructively about what you want and how to achieve it.

This book shows a cross-section of garden sizes, from the simple to the grand, reflecting different gardening styles, but in all cases, the gardens present real problems to which there are practical solutions. I hope that it will not only provide ideas and inspiration, but above all move you to get out and really do something with your garden.

The biggest hurdle is knowing how to make a start, and I hope to give you the confidence to have a go. I have tried to make it easy, and a special help here is the section of the book which gives planning symbols, starting on page 182. These will help give your plans a professional touch, and since the same symbols are used on the finished plans included, you can easily follow or adapt any features that you like. You can photocopy or trace the symbols and move them around to refine your plan; so that the mistakes are made on paper instead of in the garden.

Part One deals with garden planning and design, and advises on how to make the best of the limitations (whether it is poor soil or the presence of a factory at the end of the garden). In Part Two there are some garden plans to provide ideas on which you can build, and perhaps inspire you to look creatively at your garden layout. The plants themselves come in Part Three, and have been arranged according to use.

In Part Four we tell you how to put the plan into practice. Garden construction is hard work if you are not used to it, and even buying the right materials can be confusing if you are not used to dealing with them. This section acknowledges the difficulties and points out the pitfalls as well as the pleasures of garden construction.

Having decided on the sort of garden that you would like, it is natural to want to see results quickly. However, no matter how much you feed, water and otherwise try to coax your plants, you cannot buy time. Any garden that depends largely on trees and shrubs for effect, will take several years to look respectable. Planting fast-growing plants is not necessarily a solution – trees like eucalyptus grow extremely fast, but they carry on growing and may become far too large. You also need a variety of trees and shrubs in your garden and not simply those that grow the fastest.

If you want 'instant' results you will have to depend more on hard landscaping, containers, ornaments, and bedding plants or bulbs.

A garden that is all paving and potted plants will lack the vital 'backbone' trees and shrubs that help to make a garden look mature as well as beautiful. The answer is to plant for the long term, but use plenty of gap fillers in the meantime.

Gardens do not come 'off the shelf'; they have to be tailor-made to suit the site and your individual taste. If you have the money you could employ a professional garden designer to do the planning for you, and then employ a contractor to carry out the work. But doing it yourself is both cheaper, and much more satisfying.

It would be easy simply to let the garden evolve, rather than work to a design, yet with a few tips, some ideas to fire the imagination and a little encouragement, you have the key to a more impressive garden that will be greatly admired.

Making a new garden from scratch, or even modifying an existing garden, can take many weeks or months of hard work and will probably be expensive, too. Quite simply, you have to get it right the first time, for although you can modify a garden later in modest ways, you probably will not want to face a major reconstruction. Even if you do feel inclined to redesign your garden frequently, the result will be that the plants never have a chance to become established. It will take some seasons for most plants to begin to fill out and put flesh on the skeleton of your design, and if you uproot them every time you have second or third thoughts, they will not thrive or do any of your designs justice.

It is far better to spread the work over several seasons and get it right, than to rush the design and construction and have to live with wrong decisions, made in haste.

Making a start
On the page opposite there is a checklist of features you might want to include. Before you put pen to paper to start sketching your design or looking at what other people have done, go through the list and tick those elements that are important to you. It will probably be impossible to incorporate everything – either because of space or cost – so place your ticks in order of importance to you: very important; important; desirable; nice but could do without. Unless you are very fortunate you will probably have to compromise on some of these, but it always helps to be clear about what you want from your garden.

Do not forget to plan for the future, especially if you intend to remain in your present home for some years. A young couple might be worried about including a pond because of the danger to young children, but if a water feature really appeals to you, and the children will be responsible, in say, four or five years time, you can plan for it now. In the meantime the pond could be used as a sand-pit, or a raised pool could be turned into a flower bed for a couple of years, as long as you don't put the liner in at this stage. Even if the ground is not excavated initially, the design should allow for the feature to be constructed later. If you ignore it in the initial plan you will probably find it very difficult to work in your water feature later.

If the children have left home you may have plenty of time and energy for the garden at first, but as you get older jobs like weeding, grass mowing, and hedge trimming can all become increasingly difficult. A minimum-maintenance garden need not be dull or uninteresting; you can design it to give greater variety now provided there is the possibility of adapting it later. You could, for instance, design it so that a grass area, or a vegetable plot that needs a lot of digging and regular care, could be paved over or converted to gravel later.

Planning the garden as a whole
With a small garden, you have little choice but to treat the design as an integrated whole; with larger gardens, however, it can be difficult to integrate the various parts of the garden. For simplicity of design, as well as making the project easier to manage, it makes sense to treat the back and front gardens as separate designs. The same applies if you have a large area at the side of the house. If you try to design all the parts at once, the task is likely to be overwhelming, but you will need to make sure that the sections link together effectively. That does not mean that each part of your garden has to follow the same theme or style, but if you want several styles it is better to design your garden in definite sections with clear breaks between them, perhaps using hedges or walls as dividers. This way, the different areas resemble outdoor rooms.

If your garden is large enough for this, take it into account when trying to incorporate the features in the check-list on the opposite page. If you can avoid trying to cram them all into one part of the garden, say the back or front plot, the design will almost certainly be better for it. The simpler you can make your design, the more successful it is likely to be. If you can design and construct your garden in sections, try to resist the urge to put all the most desirable features into the first part that you tackle.

It is worth looking at the garden as a whole when you are working out where to put utilities such as dustbins (known as trash cans in the USA), bonfires, and the compost heap, as well as the greenhouse and garden shed. Again, if you try to find room for all of them in the first part of the garden you design, the chances are it will look cluttered and unattractive.

By the clever use of a suitable screening, the dustbin could even go into the front garden. This might make a difference to the design of the back plot if you do not feel that you have to fit everything into the one section.

Although in practical terms it is sensible to design and construct one part of the garden before you start on the next as it will spread both cost and effort, it is sensible to have a rough plan for the *whole* garden. Do not spend a lot of time producing detailed plans for those sections that you will not be starting this year, but make a very rough sketch of what you might want to do, and note which features you want to incorporate.

Making a check-list

Below is a check-list that includes most of the popular garden features, but when you come to draw up your plan it is also worth bearing in mind how you might be able to incorporate them. Often, a feature that you want to find a place for but seems hard to incorporate can be worked in easily if you look at the problem from a slightly different angle.

Decorative features

Flower beds do not have to be at ground level. If space is tight and you want to introduce changes of level, consider raised beds or even a sunken area, though you must ensure adequate drainage.

A herb garden should be convenient: the nearer to the kitchen, the more likely you are to use it. Herbs can make a very attractive ornamental feature, so do not feel that they have to be grown in the kitchen garden. If space is really tight, grow them in among the flowers; they will not look amiss.

Herbaceous borders need to be reasonably large to be effective. Unless you can make a real feature of a border, the space is probably best used for something else. Sometimes a small island bed can be as effective as a large single-sided border.

Lawns form the backbone of many gardens, but unless you are prepared for the maintenance they require it is best to keep them small if all you want is a decorative feature. If the lawn is for playing games, then make sure it is large enough or the surrounding beds will suffer, as well as the lawn itself from concentrated wear on a small area.

Ornamental trees should not be excluded just because the garden is small, but always choose them very carefully (see page 112). Think longer and harder about trees than other plants you buy. They will have a major impact and could make or mar your design.

A pergola or rustic work can add charm, but it needs to be well made. Avoid arches without a purpose. Make them join sections of hedge or divisions within the garden. Have a *reason* for walking through a pergola – towards a focal point or another part of the garden. If you have a patio, timber can be used to form an attractive open 'roof' to give it a more enclosed atmosphere.

One person's idea of a good garden will include a lot of paving, walls, raised beds, and so on, while another person will want the emphasis to be on plants, such as here. Even the path is informal.

Think clearly about the 'mood' and image of the garden you want to create, as well as about individual features.

Check-list *(tick as appropriate)*

Decorative features	Very important	Important	Desirable
Flower beds			
Herb garden			
Herbaceous border			
Lawn			
Ornamental trees			
Pergola			
Rock garden			
Shrub border			
Soft fruit			
Terrace/patio			
Top fruit			
Vegetables			

Check-list *(tick as appropriate)*

Practical features	Very important	Important	Desirable
Barbecue			
Clothes line/rotary drier			
Dustbin (trash can) area			
Garage			
Greenhouse			
Play area			
Change of level			
Sandpit			
Summerhouse			
Swimming Pool			
Tank/shed camouflage			
Water feature			

A rock garden is one of the most difficult features to incorporate into a small modern plot. It really needs an open, sunny, sloping site. If you are unable to provide a suitable setting, you can still grow most of the same plants successfully in dry walls, stone sinks or troughs, in a gravel area, or in a scree if you are ambitious.

Shrub borders need space, but in a large garden will provide a real sense of permanence, adding 'height' and 'texture' in a way that few other plants will. If you do not have room for shrub borders, have a mixed border instead so you get the best of both worlds. If space is at too much of a premium even for this, grow a few choice shrubs as specimen plants in the lawn.

Soft fruit gives a good return for the space, but it is best to grow the plants in an area that you can net easily. A fruit cage is ideal, but it adds to the expense, and the cage really needs to be screened from the ornamental area. If all you want is strawberries, you could grow them in strawberry pots or other containers.

Terrace/patio. A small paved area outside the house is useful but try to make a paved area large enough to be a feature — and do not be afraid to construct it away from the house.

Top fruits such as apples and pears can be grown in a small garden, but choose varieties of dwarfing rootstocks and compact shapes such as a cordon, fan or espalier. Wall-trained fruit can be decorative, so do not feel that the fruit has to be banished to the kitchen garden or orchard.

Vegetables are not easy to accommodate attractively. Though some can be very pretty for a short period, most of the time the ground will look either bare or unappealing. For that reason the temptation is to tuck them out of sight. But is is also convenient to have the kitchen garden close at hand, and the best compromise is to have an area that is convenient but screened, without casting too much shade.

Practical features

A barbecue sounds attractive, but may be used for comparatively few days of the year, so it does not make sense to hinge your design around this feature. Consider using a portable or temporary barbecue, then during the winter you can replace it with containerized plants.

A clothes line/rotary drier is one of the most difficult elements to incorporate when designing a small garden. It is not only the space needed for the line or rotary drier that you have to allow for, but also the area that has to be kept clear of tall plants, as large items such as sheets will damage them when they billow out in the wind. If you have enough space, set aside a screened area.

A dustbin area has to be convenient for the home, and, ideally, well screened. If you have a fuel bunker or tank, it usually makes sense to group these together.

A garage is not usually a problem if it is integrated into the house. If it is not, consider moving the drive to a different position, or putting it at the end of the back garden if there is access.

Below: If this small front garden had been hedged in, it would have looked commonplace and would have involved a lot of maintenance. Instead the owner decided that this first priority was minimum maintenance, but at the same time wanted it to have a fairly spacious look. These aims have been achieved by the combination of paving and dwarf conifers.

Below right: This garden reflects the strong personality of the owner and a 'feel' for plants and design. Beach pebbles have been used to add 'texture' to the garden while at the same time providing a wonderful background for suitable plants.

A greenhouse can be a decorative feature in its own right. If a traditional greenhouse does not fit into the design easily, consider one of the more decorative dome or pinnacle greenhouses, or a conservatory or attractive modern lean-to with curved eaves. Remember that if you want to install a power supply or water, the nearer the greenhouse is to the house, the cheaper this will be.

A play area should always be within sight of the house if the children are young. Older children usually prefer a certain amount of seclusion.

A change of level can be achieved by lowering the ground or raising it. A bit of both is the easiest solution: you will have less soil to excavate and the soil removed can be used to form the raised areas. If your garden is on a flat site, keep the changes of level small — a step 1 ft (300mm) down, and a few raised beds may be all that is necessary.

A sandpit can form an important element of your design, but you will almost certainly regret it when the children get older! Either make sure it can be converted into a flower bed or a pool, or use a temporary portable 'pit'.

A summerhouse can form a focal point within the garden, as well as being pleasant to sit in and capable of storing garden furniture.

A swimming pool is a mammoth undertaking, and professional advice is essential. If you want to incorporate a swimming pool, discuss your ideas with a specialist firm before you attempt to design the rest of the garden.

Tank/shed camouflage will be dictated by the position of the shed or tank. If it is in a position where a living screen would be difficult, do not overlook the possibility of using wattle panels or even screen walling blocks, both of which can be very effective.

A water feature will add a great deal of interest to your garden. If you have plenty of room and the right site, consider a pool, even a stream, and perhaps cascades. If you are unable to manage this, consider a small bubble fountain; it will take up very little room yet you will have the sight and sound of running water. Most designs are safe even for small children.

Above: The pond in this garden provides a natural focal point.

Below left: A patio need not be a geometrical area separated from the plants, but can integrate well with them.

Below: If you lack the space for a proper pond there are still ways to enjoy a water feature. This old beer barrel holds liquid again.

Every garden has its limitations. A town garden may have good soil and a mild climate but an unpleasant outlook; a country garden may have a superb vista but difficult soil and a windswept site. There is almost certain to be *something* that will make either the design difficult or the growing hard. But if you accept the limitations and adapt your design to minimize them, sticking to those plants most likely to thrive, you should have a successful garden.

Difficulties will arise if you try to ignore a design problem or persist in trying to grow plants that are unsuitable for the soil or climate. If you acknowledge the handicaps you are already part way to overcoming them.

The site

The problems you are likely to encounter fall into two categories: those within the garden and those outside it. Occasionally, of course, the difficulty may lie in both areas — a large building that blocks or dominates the view from the garden may also cast shade within it.

Ouside the garden the most common difficulty is likely to be the *view* or lack of it. If you live in a city the garden may be penned in and overlooked by other buildings. Sometimes the view is just a brick wall; occasionally a garden will overlook a really unattractive site, like a factory or warehouse, in which case a wall might be preferable.

Even in suburban and rural areas there may be eyesores that you will have to hide or live with. Sometimes it is impossible to hide them and the most you can do is minimize their effect.

A distant eyesore, like a railway or factory chimney, can often be screened successfully from ground level by using suitable trees and shrubs to divert the eye to a more attractive focal point as shown in the illustration below.

Sometimes the impact of a fairly close structure can reduce by dropping the level of the main part of the garden by say 1-2 ft (300-600mm). If there is a fence or wall, this has the same effect as raising them by 1-2 ft (300-600mm). This is often preferable to raising the height of the fence because it gives you a chance to introduce a change of level. A combination of lowering part of the garden and increasing the height of the wall or fence with an extension trellis may be all that is necessary.

Ugly structures exist *within* gardens too, of course. Old, neglected sheds that you do not want to pull down; tree stump that are too difficult or expensive to remove; a garage that simply has to stay in a conspicuous position — all these and many more will need to be considered.

Most ugly sights inside the garden can be covered or screened with suitable plants (see page 94), but if the problem is an old tree stump or a fallen tree, it can be made into quite a dramatic feature or focal point.

Shade from trees can be eliminated if you are prepared to sacrifice the tree, but shade from buildings is a handicap you will have to learn to live with. Before you fell a large tree (or preferably have it felled for you, because this is a job for professionals), make sure that you are able to cut it down. In some countries, like Britain, there are tree preservation orders that forbid felling certain trees without permission (except under certain circumstances where it is dangerous). If this is likely to apply, your local government authority will be able to advise you.

Never remove a tree without a lot of thought first. Any tree will give your garden a sense of maturity that only comes with time. Wherever possible, try to retain good, healthy trees, and if they cast shade, try to grow plants which will tolerate lack of sun in that area (see page 108). Sometimes, though, there are simply too many trees, or they may be too large and too close to buildings, and you may have to remove some of them.

Shade from buildings is something that you have to incorporate into your design. There are plenty of plants which flourish without direct sun-

Below: Limitations in gardening are not only caused by the site. Physical disability can be even more restraining, but gardens for the disabled do not have to be dull or uninteresting.

Above left: Garages are functional buildings, and their looks rarely enhance a garden. They can, however, be screened off, as here by a bamboo.

Above: A sloping corner needs bold treatment to make it interesting. Here staggered, interlinking circular beds provide variety of shape and level.

Above: This small garden in Holland shows how with imagination even a small area can be made interesting.

light, but the trouble with shade close to buildings is that the ground is usually very dry too, and where buildings are too close together there could be a 'wind tunnel' effect that makes the area even more inhospitable. Try to use the very worst areas for items such as dustbins for storage, or for hanging out the washing, rather than for growing plants. Otherwise grow some of the tough, shade-tolerant plants listed on page 108.

Shelter will reduce the effect of wind, and a hedge or permeable screen will be a more efficient filter than a solid wall or fence as these cause too much turbulence. Between two close buildings, though, it will probably be difficult to grow many plants successfully even with a screen. For these places it is best to use the area for storage and perhaps the garden shed, or to choose only the toughest plants. Certainly avoid these areas for a patio or terrace.

Frost pockets can be a particular problem if you grow early-flowering fruit trees or early-flowering ornamental shrubs. The problem is worse on an open, sloping site where the cold air flowing downhill gets trapped by a hedge or wall at the low point of the garden. If this is likely to be a problem, simply have a fairly open fence at the lowest point so the cold air is not dammed up.

You cannot do much about the shape of your site, but there are several ways of dealing with a *slope*. The main choice is whether to leave it as it is, or whether to level sections of it and create terraces. If you want a formal garden, there is much to be said for terracing, but a natural garden that uses the slope as a natural backdrop is much less effort to make. If you leave a steep slope, though, keep lawns to a minimum as in this case mowing will be difficult and may even be dangerous.

No matter how good the garden design, a poor or difficult soil often means a poor display of plants unless you choose them to suit the soil and not simply for their visual appeal. Even for difficult soils, there are so many plants to choose from that there are bound to be some that suit both your taste and the soil.

Difficult soils can be improved, but if you persist with plants that are not happy on a particular soil, the results are likely to be disappointing. The illustrations below show the results you can expect if you try to grow susceptible plants in the wrong soil. If you really do have a passion for plants that love an acid soil, such as rhododendrons, then it is probably better to content yourself with a few superb pot-grown specimens that you can grow in acid compost, rather than have a garden filled with ailing and unhappy plants.

Difficult soils

A soil that is low in nutrients is relatively easy to improve with fertilizers. The intractable problems are soils that are too acid or too alkaline for most plants, or those that have a physical characteristic that makes them difficult to work or manage. A clay soil, for instance, is heavy to work, whereas a sandy soil is usually dry and 'hungry'.

There are no miracle cures for any of these conditions. But there are plenty of plants that will grow well in them, and you can make the conditions more tolerable for the others.

Testing soil

There are soil testing laboratories that will analyze your soil for you. They will tell you the pH (a measurement of how acid or alkaline the soil is), and levels of the major nutrients such as nitrogen, phosphorous, and potash. You will then be able to tell how *fertile* the soil is.

Alternatively you can buy do-it-yourself test kits. Some consist of meters, others are chemicals that you mix with the soil then compare the resultant colour of the solution against a colour card. Many of the chemical pH test kits are perfectly

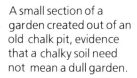

satisfactory, but tests have indicated that the amateur soil pH meters (which have a probe that you push into the soil) can be misleading and may not reveal a high or low pH.

The significance of pH

The pH scale runs from 0-14; 7 is neutral, numbers below indicating increasingly acid and numbers above indicating increasingly alkaline soil. What is confusing about the scale is that it is not linear: pH8 is *10* times more alkaline than pH7; pH6 is *10* times more acid than 7. So even a seemingly small difference on the scale can make a large difference to the plants. In horticulture, few soils fall outside the range 5 to 8.

Most plants prefer 6.5 to 7, but many of them will grow satisfactorily in quite acid or alkaline soils. In the Tables on pages 92 to 129 it is indicated if a plant needs acid or alkaline soil.

Once you know the pH of your soil, you can modify your planting list so it does not include any that will clearly not do well. Then try to adjust the more extreme soils to make them acceptable to a wider range of plants.

An acid soil can be improved by applying lime. How much you need depends on the type of lime and soil, but to increase the pH by one step you will probably have to apply about 10 oz of ground limestone per sq yd (300g per sq m) or 7oz of hydrated lime per sq yd (200g per sq m). This is best applied in the autumn or after winter digging.

Alkaline soil is much more difficult to make acid, but use as much peat as you can afford when planting, and use acidic fertilizers such as sulphate of ammonia. Flowers of sulphur at about 4oz per sq yd (140g per sq m) will increase acidity, and aluminium sulphate can be used for ornamentals. But remember that alkaline soil-water will constantly seep in and gradually reverse the process, so these are not complete answers.

Chalk soils (which are usually the most alkaline) are often very shallow in upland areas. If this is the problem, increase the depth of useful soil by breaking up the chalk as much as possible when you plant, and add plenty of compost.

If your soil is very shallow, be careful not to make matters worse if you change levels in the garden. It is better to add height in the form of raised beds than to take soil away.

Clay soils are very hard to work. In winter they are often waterlogged, and in summer they are usually baked hard. But many plants do well on clay

once they are established. Be generous with the compost and manure, and if the ground is very poorly drained, consider installing land drains before you lay your lawn or start construction.

Sandy soil is wonderful to dig, but it is usually impoverished and dries out very quickly. Try to include plants that will tolerate dry soil (see pages 106-107). Be prepared to feed regularly, and add plenty of compost or manure to beds.

Buying-in soil

If you have a problem soil it may seem a good idea to buy-in topsoil, but in practice this can be fraught with difficulties. If you answer newspaper advertisements you may be buying soil that you have not seen and almost certainly have not tested. You need to be sure that it is fertile topsoil, and not just earth excavated from some building site, containing subsoil as well.

If your garden is relatively weed-free to start with you may end up bringing millions of weed seeds into your garden. And the soil may contain pests and diseases, some of which (such as clubroot) could be devastating.

Finally, if you simply spread the new topsoil over the existing problem soil, the roots of most plants will probably soon penetrate the 6in (150mm) or so that you have added (more than this may mean you have to excavate some to the old soil and you will be no better off than before).

An acid soil is not suitable for many plants, but it does provide a good home for rhododendrons and azaleas, amongst others. This photograph shows the famous Leonardslee garden in Sussex, England, where many beautiful rhododendrons have been raised on its acid soil.

If you have moved into a newly built home, you may be starting a garden from scratch. But far more people move into a home with an existing garden, which is almost sure to have its good and its bad aspects.

If you try to create your new garden around the existing features that you like, do so with great care or you are likely to end up with an uneasy compromise.

Keeping existing paths and drives is a natural temptation and it will be a considerable saving in cost, effort, and time if you can avoid having to re-make them. Unfortunately, they will inhibit your design unless, by good fortune they are already in the right place. Paths are usually solid, dominant features and, if left in place, will dictate the form and general shape of the garden, so it may be necessary to steel yourself to dismantle those paths that impinge on your new plans.

Saving trees and shrubs

The positive side of starting with an existing garden is that there is bound to be much that you can *save* and incorporate into the new design. Trees and specimen shrubs in particular should not be uprooted and discarded until you are sure they cannot be used. They will give your garden a sense of maturity and unity that would take years to re-create with new plants. And, of course, the more you can incorporate from the old, the less you will have to buy.

Leave as much as you can where it is already growing, provided it does not compromise the new design too much. Then see what plants you can make use of by moving them. You should

Clematis montana rubens used to make a focal point out of an old tree stump.

have little trouble with herbaceous and rock plants, and you could even try moving reasonably large trees and shrubs – if they die you will have to buy new plants, but if they survive you will have saved money and several years of growth. It is quite feasible to move shrubs and trees 6-8 ft (1.6-2.4m) high, provided you lift them in the dormant season and replant immediately, keeping them well watered until they are re-established.

Always take out a trench around the plant first, then start to undercut the roots, leaving on as much root and soil as you can. Have the new planting hole ready, and a couple of helpers on hand to assist. First water the plant thoroughly and allow the moisture to soak the root-ball. Then lift the plant onto a sheet of sacking or thick polythene. Tie the sacking or polythene around the plant to keep as much soil as possible intact; then move smoothly and speedily to the new position. If you water the plant thoroughly whenever the ground becomes dry – for weeks or months if necessary – there is a good chance it will survive the shock. It may, however, be necessary to provide stakes and support until the roots have grown enough to anchor the plant again.

Saving a lawn

An existing lawn is always worth trying to incorporate into your new design if the quality of the turf is adequate. If you want it as a play area or as part of a fairly 'wild' part of the garden, even a poor lawn can be good enough especially if you try to restore it to better condition. But if you want a high quality, 'putting-green' type of lawn, there is no point in trying to salvage turf with coarse grasses such as rye grass; it is better to start again.

Be wary of trying to extend an existing lawn, or to fill in and grass over beds cut into the turf. It will be extremely difficult to match the grasses and they usually show as distinct areas for many years. If you do try to patch up or extend the lawn to fit your own design, decide whether the grasses are coarse or fine and buy grass seed that contains similar grasses.

Sometimes it is possible to remove the turf from one area and use it in another part of the garden. This can be a successful way of making use of an existing lawn without being totally restricted by its position.

Modify and disguise

Sometimes a major feature can be modified to make it more acceptable. A dull, precast concrete path could be made wider and more interesting by adding a different paving material at the sides such as bricks, cobbles, gravel or even timber. An extension to an established lawn could be edged with a suitable path or, perhaps, a gentle change of level emphasized with brick edging, so the appearance of different grass mixtures will not be so noticeable.

Greenhouses and sheds in the wrong place can sometimes be screened with suitable plants (see pages 92-94), or by a strategically-placed screen wall. But be particularly careful that the greenhouse is not in too much shade.

A pond lying in the way of a new path can sometimes look very attractive if it is divided by stepping stones. This solution can, in fact, add a great deal of visual interest.

An old, or perhaps not very attractive, fence could be expensive to replace. A simple solution is to screen it with climbers or quick-cover shrubs such as bamboos.

A tree in the wrong place can be among the most intractable problems to solve, especially if you do not want the job of removing it entirely. You could leave the stump and cover it with a suitable climber, or perhaps cut it down to a height at which you can make a garden table or seat from it. But in the end there may be no alternative to having it felled and removing the stump.

Left and below:
This garden posed a problem. An existing path of concrete slabs bedded into concrete spoilt the informal and more natural look wanted, though the owner did not want the mammoth job of breaking up the old path (which to make matters worse also incorporated a drain inspection cover).

The problem was overcome by laying natural stone crazy-paving (slate was used) over the existing path. It was also possible to lay a removable section over the inspection cover.

Occasionally, good gardens just 'happen'; they evolve in stages without lots of advance planning and trial and error on paper. But this is a gamble and not a course to be recommended. A three-dimensional, living garden can be difficult to visualize from a plan, however it is really the only way to design your garden methodically.

It is far better to make your mistakes on paper than on the ground. Plotting everything carefully also makes you think through exactly what you want to include; it ensures that you look at the garden as a whole, in terms of shapes and patterns, before you deal with the detail.

Measuring the plot
The starting point is an accurate plan of the garden. An existing plan, perhaps with the deeds of the house, could save you a lot of time. Although it is unlikely to show detail, this is easily added using the method described below.

The rough plan
It is worth drawing a rough freehand sketch of the garden *before* you go out to make measurements, and include on it arrows to show which dimensions you need to add (see illustration left). This is usually easier than sketching the shape and details as well as taking dimensions as you work, and will serve as a reminder of what you will have to measure once you are outside.

Most homes are rectangular in outline, with 90 degree angles, so it is sensible to start from the building and take as many measurements as possible in straight lines from there. You can then plot many more positions at 90 degree angles form these lines, and you will probably be left with only a few that have to be determined by 'triangulation' – a procedure described below that is not as complicated as it sounds.

Sketch in all the major features that you want to include, such as trees and paths to be retained, shed and greenhouse, that are going to stay put. Do not overlook large trees just the other side of your boundary that might affect your plan.

The views from windows may be important, so it is always worth including their position on the plan. Then you will be ready to take the slightly more difficult measurements

Measuring up
For a small plot you might be able to manage with a measuring stick, but it will be easier with a proper surveying tape measure. You will also need a length of string or twine, and skewers or pegs to hold it in position. If you already have a traditional, wind-up garden line you could use this. Even if you use a surveyor's tape, it will often be necessary to lay a line so you can then use the tape to measure off 90 degree angles from this.

Start by measuring off as many angles as you can from the corners of the house, noting the measurements as you go along. If there are any readings to be taken off these lines, take these before moving.

Continue to fill in as many other dimensions as you can by measuring at right angles then use

Make a rough sketch of your garden first, then go out into it and measure it up, recording the measurements on your drawing.

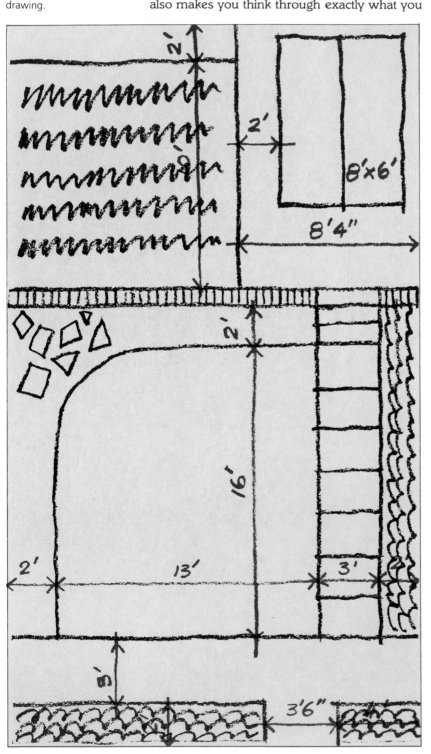

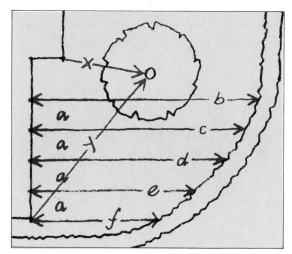

Fixing the position of an object by triangulation (x and y), and plotting a curved border (a to f)

triangulation to fill in the remaining measurements.

Triangulation is a method of arriving at a position by measuring from two known fixed points. Choose two convenient positions, perhaps two corners of the house, and measure from these to the object that you are plotting (see illustration). By setting your compasses to the right scale you can determine the position on your finished plan by noting where the two arcs intersect.

A curved border or drive can be measured fairly accurately by taking measurements about 6ft (1.8m) apart at right angles from a straight line (see illustration above).

Making a finished copy
The rough freehand sketch should now contain all the measurements you will need to produce a proper plan. Transfer it neatly to a clean sheet of paper – graph paper will make the job easier.

You will have to decide on the scale. The symbols and shapes on pages 182-9 are drawn to a scale of 1:50, whcih is easy to work with. These were used for the plans shown in Section Two, although to fit some of the larger gardens into the page some have been reduced.

If the garden is very large, you could use a smaller scale to produce a rough plan so you can see how the various elements relate; then use the 1:50 scale for details of the various sections. You will probably find it easier than trying to work with a very large plan.

Before you start to draw your finished outline, check the largest dimensions to make sure the plan will fit on the paper. If it is too large, simply join two pieces together.

Draw the house or bungalow to scale on your plan, indicating the windows, then use the measurements from your rough sketch to complete the drawing.

You might find it useful to photocopy this basic outline of your garden, so that you always have a clean master copy if you draw on the working copy. Alternatively, you can simply lay tracing paper over the top for rough sketching.

Either way, it is best to attach your finished outline to a clipboard because it is important to be able to take your plan into the garden to view things from the actual spot if necesssary.

Work on tracing paper overlay to plan your new design.

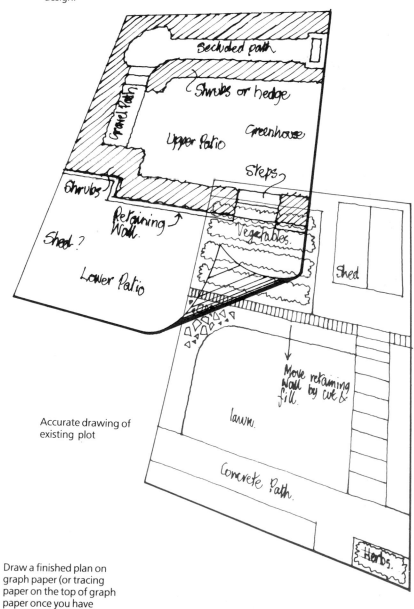

Accurate drawing of existing plot

Draw a finished plan on graph paper (or tracing paper on the top of graph paper once you have collected all the measurements from the plot itself.

If you have drawn the outline of your garden, together with the features that you would like to retain, as described on the previous two pages, you are ready to try your hand at designing your own, special garden.

Although the plan will already contain a lot of detail, the process you are embarking on is rather like starting a novel on a blank sheet of paper. You probably have plenty of vague ideas, but making a start and structuring the ideas so that they make sense, can be extremely difficult.

If you are to do this unaided two skills are needed in good measure: a creative mind and some degree of draughtsmanship. Fortunately there are some short-cuts if you don't feel completely confident.

Start by looking at the garden in terms of overall patterns and shapes. Once the basic patterns have been conceived, use the checklist on page 9 to make sure as many priority features as possible are included in your scheme.

The garden designs on pages 52-89 will provide some ideas for gardens of various types. The germ of an idea from part of an existing design can often be developed to suit your own preferences and garden. Maybe you know that you want a barbecue but need ideas about different types and how they can be integrated into the garden. One of those in this book may give you the lead that you need. Do not be afraid to take various ideas from different designs and illustrations and work them into your own unique plan; you will almost certainly find it more rewarding than following someone else's ideas too closely, no matter how good they are.

The ideas then have to be put on paper, which creates another barrier for anyone not blessed with a steady, as well as creative, hand. A professional's garden plan will almost always look much more impressive than your own efforts because of its presentation.

To help overcome this problem, we have produced a collection of key symbols, patterns, and shapes on pages 182-9, which you can use to help produce a more polished and easy-to-visualize result. These have also been used for the plans in Section Two, so you can easily reproduce sections of plans that you like.

If you are happy to do your plans in rough freehand first, all you need to do is trace the various design elements to produce your finished garden plan.

Normally, however, it is difficult to get the plan right first time, and you may prefer to photocopy the symbols (or trace them) then cut them out so they can be moved about on the outline plan. This way you can indulge in endless permutations to see which work best.

The elements of design

Start by looking at the design as a series of shapes. Do not worry about individual plants or other, small-scale details at this stage.

It will be much easier if you divide your garden into a grid on which you can base your patterns. The exact nature of the grid must depend on the site, but a fence with posts at 6 ft (1.8m) intervals would suggest a grid of this size. There may be some feature of the house that suggests a grid. Either way, you can draw these grid lines on an overlay to put over your basic outline, drawing lines at 90 degree angles to the first to make a series of squares.

Try to use these as the basis for divisions and boundaries within the garden, but do not feel that you have to treat them inflexibly; it will often be necessary to deviate slightly. But even curves can work to the basic grid, using the grid lines as a guide for radii. This will work not only for 'classic' gardens but for 'informal' gardens too.

Try to incorporate the patio, terrace, or sitting out area at an early stage because you will want this to be in the most favourable position. It must be in a sheltered, sunny spot, and although you will probably need shade at the height of summer, you can always provide it artificially – whereas there is not a lot you can do to overcome a shady or cold position.

The paved area may, in fact, suggest an overall pattern for the garden, but if not, you should look at shapes, then modify your sitting area to link with the rest of the garden.

If you are going to keep, basically, to straight lines, decide at an early stage whether the emphasis will be along the garden, across it, or diagonally. Lines that run away from you will have the effect of making the garden look longer; lines running across the view will give breadth to the site. A strong diagonal emphasis can be very effective, or a horizontal and diagonal emphasis can be useful if you want to divert the eye from some unpleasant view ahead.

A design based on circles and curves can be very effective, especially if one intersects another, perhaps combined with a change of level.

Do not be too hasty in marking in the paths as they will immediately inhibit a free flow of further design ideas for that area. Make sure the overall shapes and features are right first, then you can think about the mechanics of access and paths; the latter will usually emerge naturally simply because you have designed to a grid in the first place.

Once you are happy with the design, mark in key trees and shrubs, though you do not need to name them at this stage.

Make it three-dimensional

Any design has to work on the ground. Unless you are experienced at visualizing garden plans, it is best to peg it out in the garden before you make any final decisions. Use string stretched between pegs to mark out the various features, and if possible insert stakes and canes to suggest key trees and large shrubs.

Look at the marked-out plot from various angles, and leave it for a day or two so you can see it in different lights and at different times of day. Note where shadows fall: although shadow lengths will be different at a different time of year, at least you will have some idea of potential shade problems. Consider, too, potential privacy if that is important to you.

When you have drawn up the finished plan of your garden you can experiment with different arrangements by using the symbols given on pages 182–9.

1. GARDEN ELEMENTS

Your dream garden may be no more than that: a dream that never becomes a reality because it is not practical and does not meet the day-to-day demands of an ordinary household. For a garden to be attractive in the real world and not only in your imagination, it has to be planned according to your circumstances. For example, if you have children they will want to play in it, and young children do not have much respect for beds and borders. Moreover, you will probably have to find somewhere for the refuse, somewhere for the washing to hang out, and somewhere for all the mundane but valuable garden items such as a compost heap and a site for bonfires. All these will impinge on your dream design, before you even let it be shattered by the problems of cost and maintenance. Designing a garden is infinitely more problematic than dreaming of one by the fireside.

Nevertheless, these restraints should not be allowed to get in the way of producing an interesting and attractive garden, which in the end will give you far more satisfaction than fantasizing about what will never be. This applies however small and limited your plot. If you assume that you have to wait until you have a larger garden, a better aspect, or a nicer setting, then you will always be missing wonderful opportunities. You can make any garden a success, providing that you make the most of what you have, designing well and planning carefully, and holding realistic expectations.

Section Two of this book contains ideas for different garden designs. Some of them are relatively simple; others are more complex ones for which the only short-cut would be to hire a team of professionals for a couple of weeks, at the cost in labour and materials of about half the price of a new family car, even if the garden is of modest size. If you want to follow these designs you can, however, reduce the expense by doing the job yourself, and this will give you a much greater sense of achievement and satisfaction in the end. The skills needed are not special and the rewards are great but these designs do take a long time. However, there are also plenty of other schemes for satisfying ways of building or improving your garden. And whether you incline to the elaborate or the simple, there are only two rules: decide what you want to do, and *make a start*.

This section of the book is designed to guide you on both of these points — to help you decide what kind of garden you want, and to tell you how to make your plans.

It is tempting to skip to the finished designs for ideas, but it is well worth reading this section carefully first; it will help you to decide what is right for *your* garden, *your* family, *your* budget, and *your* ability. If you rush into copying or modifying a plan simply because it appeals visually, the chances are that enthusiasm and energy will wane if you have not understood clearly what is involved.

Never be afraid to adapt or modify other good designs that work — the chances are that those, in turn, evolved from someone else's efforts. But always make sure that they work for your garden.

Remember that time spent listing your aspirations, detailing your priorities, and then trying to work it all out on paper is never time wasted. Experimenting with various designs at this stage will cost you nothing (use the symbols on pages 182-189 to 'juggle' the various features until they are right). Some improvisation may be necessary during construction, but *never* plan your garden as you go along. Always work to an overall framework which has been thought out beforehand.

An unusual stepped wall brings additional character to the corner of this garden.

Paths and drives divide and define a garden very clearly. Unimaginatively placed or constructed, they will spoil a garden, but tastefully positioned and built with 'sympathetic' materials they can be an important feature in their own right.

Resolve the overall design before you consider paths in detail, unless you have to incorporate a driveway, which could dictate the scale and grid upon which the rest of that part of the garden is based.

Choosing the right material
Other aspects of the design may suggest suitable materials. The paving used for a patio or terrace is usually a good choice for the connecting paths – or a material which at least blends with the paved area.

If the retaining walls for raised beds are brick, it is generally best to use bricks or clay pavers for adjoining paths.

Curved paths will be easier to construct in gravel or perhaps a mixture of a regular paving module and a more flexible material, such as cobbles to infill the curves.

Paths should be practical
The *purpose* of the path should always be borne in mind. A single-width path, about 1½ ft (45cm) wide, may be perfectly adequate as a 'strolling' path to connect different parts of the garden, and a narrow path can be particularly effective where it leads to a gate or through an opening in a hedge, as it creates a sense of exploration. On the other hand, such a narrow path leading to your front door would be woefully inadquate. Any hindrance is annoying for all concerned. People must be able to carry things up the path easily without it becoming like a tightrope act, and it is more pleasant for a couple of visitors to be able to approach the house side by side instead of having to walk single file.

Always make sure your paths are practical. Stepping-stone paths through a lawn or a flower bed are fine for effect and occasional use, but they are not a sensible approach to a garden shed, which you would probably want to use in all weathers, and maybe negotiate with a wheelbarrow or lawnmower.

If you like the look of gravel for a front drive, bear in mind that it will not be easy to wheel a pram or pushchair over it. You may, however, be able to incorporate a smooth surface at the edge for pedestrians.

Give it a purpose
A path should always have a purpose, even if you have to create one. It should *lead* somewhere, if only to the compost heap behind a screen, or to a pond, or garden seat. Failing all else, let it lead to a focal point, such as a statue or ornament.

Avoid needless curves and bends. If you make the route too tortuous, people will start to take short-cuts, and these will soon become obvious whether they are across the lawn or a flower bed.

Curves should always have gentle sweeps, both to make construction easier and to provide a more restful design.

A drive for the car will usually dominate all but the largest front gardens, so pay particular attention to choosing suitable materials. If you want to use paving slabs, consider softening the hard lines by leaving out sections at the edges, in which you can set suitable, low-growing plants. Think about replacing some slabs with an alternative material, such as cobbles. If you do this, try to arrange for some of these to be positioned beneath where the engine will be when the car is parked. Even with a well-maintained car, there will be an occasional oil drip, and stains will be less conspicuous on cobbles than on paving slabs.

On the following two pages there are plenty of ideas for different paving materials – with the pros and cons for each. The permutations are almost endless and you should not be afraid to try different ideas and combinations if these suit your design. But remember that they should always be practical; bear in mind how you are going to lay the path, and how suitable it will be *in use*.

Drain inspection covers
Drain inspection covers, or manholes, can be a problem anywhere in the garden. Fortunately there are many positions where they can be disguised quite easily with low, prostrate, plants. In a path, however, this option is closed unless the cover happens to be at the side of a wide path or drive.

The problem is compounded if the inspection cover does not lie at the same angle as the path. It may be possible to angle the path slightly so that the paving slabs can be butted to the cover end on.

You may be able to buy a tray, or have one made, that will fit over the area, so that you can lay your paving material in this. It will have to be shallow of course, and even so, its level will dictate the height of the rest of the path. Whatever solution you decide on, it must remain easy to gain access to the inspection cover.

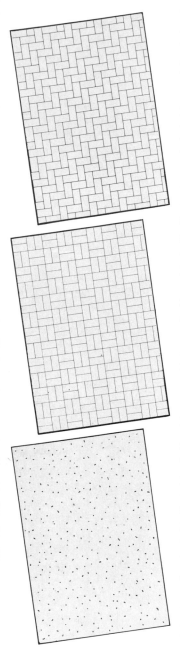

Top and middle: Two brick path patterns – herringbone and basket-weave.

Bottom: Gravel is a material that blends well in a garden setting, and presents no problem in laying curves.

If at all possible, try to align the path so that it misses any inspection cover; it will be less of a problem alongside a path than actually in it.

The choice of paving

All the paving materials mentioned on these two pages have their uses, but in any particular situation some are going to be preferable to others, whether on cost or aesthetic grounds, or for practical reasons.

Before finally deciding on a particular type of path, examine its drawbacks as well as its advantages. Consider the alternatives to see whether another material might be more effective or more suitable.

Do not overlook the possibilty of mixing materials; you could end up with a path that is more attractive and distinctive than either material on its own. Be careful, though; the borderline between good taste and bad is, unfortunately, a thin one, and can easily be breached when it comes to mixing paving materials that may look attractive individually but overfussy or incompatible when combined.

The choice

Brick paths have much to recommend them: the permutations for laying them are enormous and some patterns are illustrated on page 163 to 167. Consider laying them on edge if you want variety, but bear in mind that this method will cost more because you will need more bricks to cover the same area.

Advantages: bricks blend well with most gardens, from the very modern to traditional cottage gardens. Mood can be reflected by the type of brick used: a hard, red, engineering brick will give one impression; a rougher, more 'rustic' brick with perhaps a mottled finish, will have a very different 'feel'. You may be able to match the house brick if you want to give an impression of unity between home and garden (though not all bricks used for building homes are suitable for the garden, so check first). You can also match bricks used for raised beds, free-standing walls and other garden features like a barbecue.

There is also the sheer variety of patterns that can be created.

Disadvantages: a big disadvantage is cost. Bricks are one of the most expensive forms of paving. Also because bricks are designed for mortar joints, you will either have to risk having a weedy path (though a modern herbicide will soon deal with weeds — see page 180), or there will be the job of mortaring between joints. Clay pavers (see below) do not have this disadvantage.

Clay pavers look similar to bricks when laid, but they are shallower and the other dimensions are also slightly different because they are intended to be laid without mortar joints. In other words they interlock without the spaces normally left when you use bricks.

Advantages: there are no mortar joints so they are very neat when laid, and are easier to lay if you have the right equipment (for a drive you really need to use a flat-plate vibrator, see pages 132-133). They are all suitable for paving, so you do not have to worry about choosing one that will withstand wetting and freezing.

Disadvantages: the range of colours and finishes is not as wide as with brick, and they are not so commonly stocked by builders' merchants. Because they are not as suitable for laying on edge, the pattern options are a little more restricted, and they are not as easily matched to other brickwork.

In-situ concrete is far from attractive, and there are almost certain to be better options for a path within the garden. For a drive, though, it has to be considered, especially if there is easy access for delivery of ready-mixed concrete to make the job simpler.

Advantages: it is strong if the site has been properly prepared, and is easy to lay to a curve if necessary.

Disadvantages: it is usually considered unattractive, though careful planting at the edges can help soften it. Laying it is hard work; ready-mixed will help, but you may need to move a large amount of concrete in a short time once it is delivered.

Gravel is a very 'sympathetic' material for the garden. Not everyone likes the crunchy feel underfoot, but it makes a good foil for many plants and is a quick and easy material to lay.

Unfortunately, gravel comes in many forms and, if you have set your heart on a particular type you have seen elsewhere, you may find it is not available locally. Some gravel is sea-dredged, some worked from inland gravel pits, and size, shape and colour can vary depending on source.

Weeds can sometimes be a problem, but are easily controlled with applications of a long lasting path weedkiller.

Advantages: gravel is easily laid to curved or irregular shapes. It is a good foil for plants, and is relatively inexpensive.

Disadvantages: it can be uncomfortable and noisy to walk on and it may be difficult to obtain a particular gravel that you like. Gravel will need more regular maintenance than many other paving materials, and some can be rather sharp and could be a hazard for children if they fall.

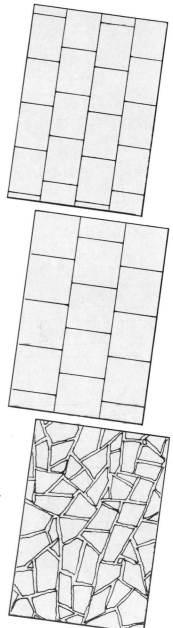

Top and middle: Two patterns for pre-cast concrete slabs.

Bottom: Crazy paving can look either very good or terrible, depending on the material and how well it is laid. It is easier to lay than natural stone.

Mixing materials, such as
the gravel and paving
slabs here, can produce
pleasing combinations.

Grass paths are not a good idea unless the area is wide and designed to link two other areas of lawn. A narrow grass path will receive too much wear. 'Stepping-stones' set into the grass will reduce the wear and make it more pleasant underfoot in wet weather.

Advantages: this is a natural choice to link other areas of grass.

Disadvantages: grass paths need intensive maintenance (mowing, edge trimming, possibly occasional patching), and are neither pleasant nor practical in wet weather.

Pre-cast concrete slabs have a great deal to recommend them. They are widely available, come in a wide range of colours, textures and finishes, and a multitude of shapes and sizes. They are also relatively inexpensive, though you should allow for the cost of foundations and mortar if you are laying them properly.

Advantages: a range of finishes is available. They are popular for patios, are useful where you want matching paths, and are widely and easily available.

Disadvantages: pre-cast slabs can look boring and unimaginative. They are not easily laid to curves unless used in conjuction with other materials such as gravel or cobbles.

Crazy paving is not everyone's idea of good taste, but this is probably because it is often made from broken pieces of coloured pre-cast slabs. A natural stone crazy paving path can be very attractive.

Advantages: it is relatively cheap — whether you buy broken, pre-cast slabs or broken natural stone, it will be cheaper than the complete slabs. Bear in mind, though, that you may use more mortar, and it will almost certainly take you longer to lay. Crazy paving is useful if you want plants growing between the stones — just leave out the mortar between some of the joints.

Disadvantages: it is difficult to lay well, and if joints are not mortared, weeds will be a problem (see page 179 for weed control in paths).

The chances are that you already have some kind of boundary hedge or fence. Even on new housing developments the builder will normally erect a closeboard fence or something similar. If finance for your garden is going to be a problem, it is probably best to leave this as it is while the rest of the garden is sorted out, then think about replacing hedges and fences when you have more time and money. Do not be in a hurry to rip up an existing fence if you are planning to replace it with a hedge. The hedge will take at least two or three years to start looking respectable, so it is worth retaining the fence if possible and planting the hedge against it at first. After about a year's growth remove the fence, but don't leave it much longer, or the hedge will begin to look bare on the fence side.

Boundaries need a lot of careful thought. They form an external skeleton that holds the garden together, are often a backdrop for other plants, and also provide privacy. Above all, they act as a psychological barrier to mark out your territory. A low, decorative hedge about 1 ft (300mm) high is not going to have much practical use, but it assumes a significance beyond its size.

Sometimes, though, a visible barrier is not a good thing. If you are lucky enough to have a panoramic view or a stunning focal point beyond the garden, it should not be obscured. If the garden is large enough to carry it off, you could cut the ground away vertically on the garden side to provide a barrier that does not block the view. A much simpler alternative, which is suitable even for a small garden, is a wooden post and rail fence, or even plastic coated wire mesh about 2 ft (600mm) high with compact shrubs planted against it. These provide a physical barrier yet blend in naturally without impinging on the view.

Although the choice of hedge or fence will probably be based mainly on aesthetic and financial factors, it is also worth considering *aspect*. A fairly dense hedge will be most useful on the side facing the prevailing wind. But you will not want a tall hedge on a side that will cast too much shade. If you live on a hillside, a good barrier on the high side will deflect some of the cold air coming down the hill, while at the lower end of the garden it is best to ensure that cold air can continue to flow downwards without forming a frost-pocket.

A white painted wall will often help to make a small garden look less oppressive, and can help to set off wall-trained plants. It has to be painted regularly, so it is an advantage to grow deciduous plants.

Windbreaks and shelters

A boundary can also provide shelter for the garden. This is especially important in cold or exposed areas, in which case hedges will almost certainly be preferable to walls or fences. A hedge is a permeable wind barrier, so it filters the air instead of creating the sort of turbulence caused when wind hits a solid barrier.

A hedge will provide some shelter for a distance of up to 30 times its height, and the effect decreases with distance. At a distance of 10 times the height of the hedge, the shelter is likely to be about a quarter of its original strength. The most benefit is likely to be felt at a distance of about three times the height.

As wind hits a fence or wall, it will create a turbulence for some distance on the other side (often worst at a distance of five times the height of the obstacle) and could damage the plants. Bear this in mind if you are making a walled garden: you should always restrict the width of the garden to reduce the risk of this type of damage. This effect is obviously less pronounced in built-up areas where the wind is already broken by buildings and other obstacles.

Coastal and very exposed areas create special problems, and a screen may be preferable to a hedge. A living screen can be made from many of the normal hedging plants, but they will need wider spacing and the height will be less restricted. Hedges and screens in coastal areas have to tolerate salt spray as well as the high winds and suitable plants are indicated on page 105.

Wall, hedge, or fence?

Walls can have real impact on a garden. Even a low wall can be useful as a maintenance-free boundary. It will not cast much shade, and, unlike a hedge, will not deplete the nutrients in the soil.

The disadvantages of a wall are the cost and effort involved. You must prepare proper foundations, and to the cost of the bricks or stones — which will be much higher than the cost of a hedge of equivalent height — you must add the price of hardcore, concrete, and mortar.

A screen block wall will be easier and quicker to erect, and also less expensive, but it will not be as private. Although a screen block wall can be very effective as a partition within the garden or to edge a patio, a large expanse could look overwhelming.

Concrete block walls, including imitation stone, are generally easier to build than brick. Concrete block is perfectly adequate for a low wall, and though high walls can look good, you will need to choose a suitable block very carefully.

Fences are generally cheaper than brick or concrete block walls. Like walls, they are also much more 'instant' than a hedge, but even a well-maintained fence will probably need replacing long before a wall or hedge. Otherwise, they tend to look tatty after a comparatively short time. But there are many different kinds of fence, made from materials as diverse as concrete and plastic, and some can add to the overall design.

Below: Conifers make effective evergreen screens, but they do not always have to be green. There are several 'blue'-foliaged hedging conifers, of which *Chamaecyparis lawsoniana* 'Pembury Blue' is one of the best.

Below right: These two drawings show how a solid barrier against wind creates eddies against and behind it. These can be devastating for vulnerable plants. A hedge, however, filters the wind without creating turbulence.

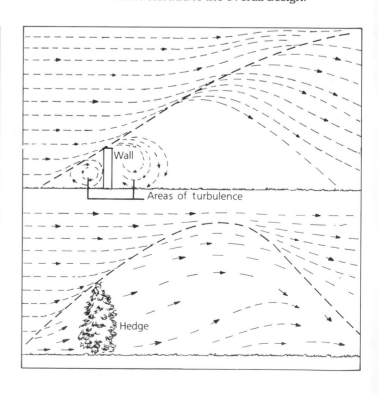

Wall

Areas of turbulence

Hedge

Hedges are difficult to match for sheer variety of shape, colour, and form, and not all of them need a great deal of trimming. Once a year is adequate for many types.

Hedges should be looked at creatively. They are useful within the garden as well as in their more usual role as boundary markers and barriers. There are low hedges of about 1 ft (300mm) as well as tall, thick, impenetrable barriers.

There are evergreens for year-round interest and cover, and deciduous hedges that will bring fresh delight each spring. There are also hedges which can be grown for flowers as well as for coloured foliage. Some of the suitable plants are listed on page 104.

Materials

The availability of walling materials and fencing panels varies considerably, and distribution is often regional, partly because it costs so much to transport them. The ideas given on these two pages reflect the types of materials you may find. Once you have decided which kind of wall or fence you prefer, it is best to send for as many catalogues and brochures as you can — then ask the manufacturer for the nearest stockist. Generally, though, bricks and concrete blocks are variations on a theme, and if you cannot find exactly what you want, you should be able to buy something similar locally.

Some of the materials sound unpromising — concrete and wire for instance — but they should not be dismissed; they have a use and some are

not as ugly as their names would suggest. I, for one, have been fooled into thinking that a concrete wall was brick!

Bricks are available in a bewildering choice, and even a builder's merchant may not know which are suitable for garden walls without checking

Above: Roses make a colourful hedge in summer, but can look far from attractive in winter when the leaves have fallen.

Do not be afraid to mix
The problem with looking at fencing materials in isolation is that you risk overlooking some good combinations which will provide the best of both worlds. For instance, a solid fence or trellis panel on a low brick wall looks attractive; a neat hedge behind a low brick or concrete block wall compensates for the sometimes bare base on a hedge; concrete screen blocks set into a brick wall add interest. There are many permutations, and it is worth looking critically at the boundary fences, walls, and hedges other people have used in your own area to see if any work particularly well.

with the manufacturer. House bricks may not be suitable for garden use, and if in doubt, ask. As a rough guide, try to scratch the brick with a coin; if the brick is soft enough to be marked it is probably best not to use it for the garden.

Choose your brick carefully to reflect the mood of the garden. A plain, smooth, fairly bright, red brick may be suitable for a modern, formal garden, but for a country cottage a more 'rustic' brick with muted colours and rougher texture will look better. Bricks that have a very rough surface, perhaps with pieces of embedded coke or aggregate exposed, can be dangerous where children are playing and are likely to fall.

Multi-coloured bricks in yellow and red shades can look very distinctive if you want to make a feature of the wall. Try to see as many different bricks as you can before choosing – and be prepared for a wide variation in price for different types.

Concrete blocks are available in solid or perforated forms, each very different in appearance and application. The solid concrete blocks are usually cast to look like natural stone. Pierced concrete blocks, also called screen walling blocks – though they do not provide any privacy – are however, usually much more suitable as an internal screen within the garden or around a patio than as a boundary. They can, however, make a very effective and striking boundary wall in the right setting, but even then, are usually best confined to one edge of the boundary.

There are several popular screen block patterns, and most of these are variations on the screen blocks illustrated below.

Some imitation stone blocks are so effective that from a distance they can be mistaken for real stone; but they can also be very crude. It is probably best either to choose one that is very realistic or one that makes no pretence at being anything other than a concrete block. Imitation stone that is not really credible will never be satifactory. Look at the catalogues and brochures, but also try to see the actual blocks before you order.

Natural stone is a very tempting choice, but an unwise one to set your heart on unless you have a local source of supply or can afford to pay a substantial carriage premium on top of an already expensive form of walling. Natural stone also needs the right setting: it can look fine in rural surroundings but incongruous in a town as a boundary, though you might be able to use it for an internal wall. Additionally, old-fashioned craftsmen who can build attractive stone walls can be very difficult to find.

The right type of walling for your requirements will probably depend on a combination of appearance and cost. Illustrated below are just a few of the many options.

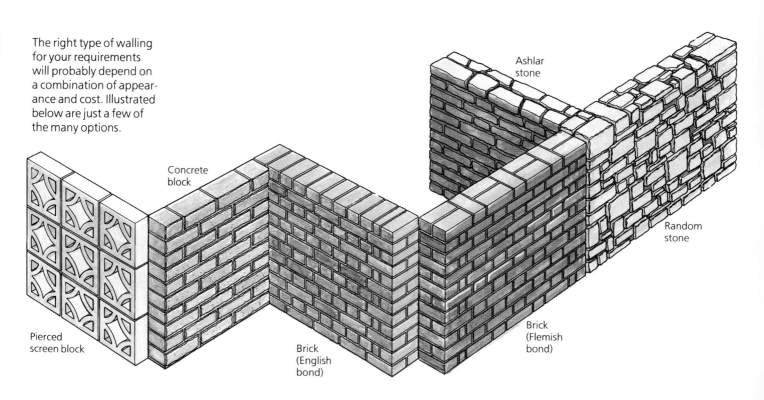

Pierced screen block

Concrete block

Brick (English bond)

Brick (Flemish bond)

Ashlar stone

Random stone

Wooden panel fences are erected as ready-made panels secured to wooden, concrete, or even steel posts (both concrete and steel posts have grooves into which you slide the panels). Some popular types of timber panels are illustrated below. If you want privacy, you will need to choose one of the closeboard fences, but some of the alternatives are more decorative.

Post and rail looks fine in a very large garden, but is probably best not used to enclose a small area, or your garden could resemble a paddock. It is, however, a useful fence where the garden looks out over open countryside, especially if softened with suitable shrubs.

Ranch-style fencing, known as baffle fencing in the United States, is generally more decorative than post and rail, especially if the broad horizontals are painted white. There are PVC versions as well as timber, and those with staggered bars that alternate on each side act as a reasonable screen and look attractive from both sides. This is well worth considering as a boundary between adjoining properties.

Picket or palisade fences give the garden a traditional cottage-garden or 'New England' look especially when painted white. Traditionally they are constructed of timber, but you can buy plastic versions. To look effective, a timber picket fence needs regular painting, otherwise it will soon begin to look shabby.

Trellis panels used alone are not particularly suitable for boundary walls, but you could use them in combination with other types of fence or wall (see below). However, as a way of dividing off a section of the garden — where privacy is not the aim — they can be ideal. They also provide an ideal opportunity to grow climbers. But a trellis must be substantial, so always use panels intended for fencing not panels intended merely as plant support.

Plastic coated chain link fencing can form a useful barrier to animals, and is not obtrusive if plants are set close to it. You could also grow climbers, like ivy or honeysuckle, along it to form a living fence or 'fedge'.

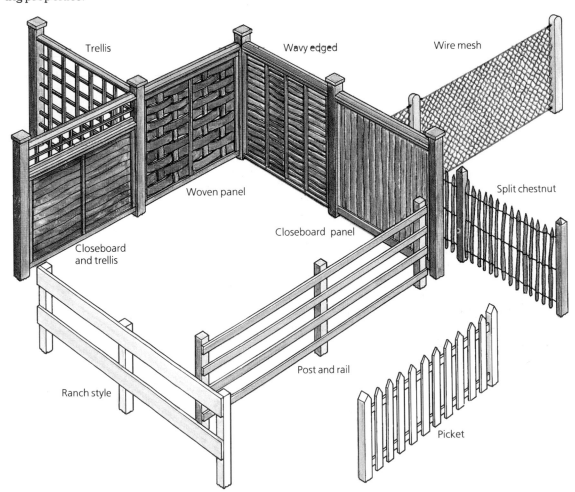

Trellis

Wavy edged

Wire mesh

Woven panel

Closeboard and trellis

Closeboard panel

Split chestnut

Post and rail

Ranch style

Picket

Fences can be mainly decorative, or merely boundary markers, or they can be practical animal-proof, peep-proof screens.

Patios are understandably popular, and they encourage the use of the garden as a place for living and relaxing as well as working in. In a very tiny garden, it might be worth treating the whole area as a patio. Two things need to be remembered if a patio is to be looked at creatively: the first is that a small area of paving does not, in itself, make a patio; the second is that although, traditionally, patios are sited against the house, they do not have to be.

Paved area or patio?

The original patios were actually courtyards, where a central well surrounded by the building became an outdoor room. Because patios were a feature of warm climates, the fact that they were often cool and shady places was not a problem. The modern patio of cooler climates is designed to catch the sun, though the concept of using it as an 'outdoor room' remains.

A patio should be conceived as a living area, not simply an area of paving. Putting a deck-chair, or a table and a couple of chairs, on a few square metres of paving slabs will not make it into a garden feature.

Pre-cast concrete paving slabs are perfectly acceptable, but quarry tiles or some similar material will give it a much better 'feel'. Brick too can give the patio a more integrated look, especially if the home, a built-in barbecue and perhaps seats, are constructed with the same brick.

Although a patio can merge into the garden, it will have a much stronger identity as an outdoor 'room' if it is bounded on at least three sides – the house usually forms one of them. Wooden beams are useful, providing some support cover for climbing plants, and also some useful shade in summer. They also help to give the impression of an outside room. Built-in 'furniture' such as a barbecue and perhaps a seat, will make it less bleak in the winter than a bare expanse of paving.

The side that opens to the garden should have a pleasant view, but some psychological boundary between the patio and the rest of the garden will generate a sense of entering and leaving. A small step up or down may be all that is needed or the patio could even be edged with a formal pool with stepping stones across which you enter the garden.

Getting the site right

It makes sense to have the patio adjoining the house if possible, especially if you can build it outside French windows or patio doors, so the dis-

Mixed paving materials provide visual interest, while the thoughtful use of containers will help to make the area interesting the year round.

tinction between house and garden really does become blurred when the weather is fine. But if that part of the house happens to face a sunless aspect, or it looks out over the least attractive part of the garden, having the patio there will be both disappointing and frustrating.

If there is not a suitable position by the house, consider other parts of the garden. There may be a suitable spot somewhere else, even looking back towards the house, where you can enjoy the sun and a pleasant view of the garden, or perhaps a distant view across fields if you happen to live in a rural area.

If you site the patio away from the house, make sure it is still integrated within the design (keep to a basic grid described on page 21), and link it with the home using suitable all-weather paving.

Keeping it in proportion

A small town garden could be paved completely without upsetting the sense of proportion, and a large country garden can almost always absorb a patio or terrace satisfactorily. Problems are more likely to be encountered with the kind of small garden found in many modern housing developments. In such gardens it can be difficult to maintain a sense of proportion. If the paved area is too large, the garden may look as though it is all concrete with not enough plants; if the paved area is too small it can look mean and pointless.

In a small area say 33ft × 33ft (10m × 10m) or less, it is probably best either to pave the whole area or to keep the paving to a minimum. If your patio takes up say a third or half of this area, it will draw attention to the smallness of the remaining garden. Being ambitious and treating the whole area as a patio, using plenty of beds and containers, can make the most of the limited space and will probably have much more impact.

The importance of variety

Just as an indoor room has furniture and ornaments, so should the outdoor room. The equivalents of pictures and other decorations indoors are hanging baskets, urns and other containers with a seasonal display of colourful flowers and a permanent framework of evergreen plants.

It is always worth having some permanent furniture too, though you can add temporary comfortable chairs when you are sitting outside. Built-in furniture has been mentioned, but an iron table and chairs, perhaps painted white, can help to give the patio, and the garden in general a much more planned appearance. The garden will look as though it is designed to be lived in and to be used, whatever the time of year.

Above: Brick is a material that merges well with the rest of the garden.

Below: Patios and paved areas close to the house will generally look much more interesting with a change of level.

Water in the garden never fails to have a restful, soothing effect. All the great peaceful gardens of the world incorporate at least a fountain, a waterfall, or a stream.

Somewhere suitable

Geometrically-shaped formal ponds, with no pretensions to attempting to imitate natural pools, are best in a formal layout, and look especially impressive in a paved area, perhaps as part of a patio. Set in a lawn they need to have their geometric outline echoed in the layout of formal beds.

Informal or 'natural' ponds are difficult to incorporate into a small garden. They are commonly given pride of place near the centre of a lawn, where they look pretty but not integrated – and certainly not 'natural'.

It is the search for a natural-looking setting that makes for partnership with a rock garden – though this too can pose positioning problems in a small, flat garden. Fortunately, both features are best in an open, sunny position, away from the shade of overhanging trees.

If a traditional pond simply will not work within the design, or the site is unsuitable, a formal pond, or one of the alternatives suggested below, is much more likely to be successful.

A sense of scale

Water can dominate a garden in the same way that a building can, so the design of a pond has to be good and in harmony with the scale of the garden. In a small garden it is probably best to use water in a formal or abstract way – in a circular, perhaps raised, pool or maybe a rectangular pond with a small fountain. Emphasize the geometric shape with a positive, well-defined edge (which should overlap the pool by 2 in (50mm).

A simple bubble fountain, or water cascading from an ornament on to stones covering the hidden reservoir, may be all that is required to contribute the sound, movement and reflective quality of water.

If you decide on an abstract water feature, perhaps in conjunction with a piece of sculpture or garden ornament, or maybe a formal pool with fountain but without fish or plants, the water can easily be kept sparkling clear with chemicals.

It will probably be difficult to keep the water clear in a *small* area of water that also has to support plants and fish, because it is easier to create a naturally balanced pool if the area is over, say, 40 sq ft (4 sq m).

In a large garden there is more scope for 'natural' pool shapes – sweeping curves, and streams and cascades. But there will still be scope for the small formal water feature, perhaps as a focal point at the end of a path, or as part of a patio.

With children in mind

If you are concerned for the safety of your children (and remember that very young children can drown in a few inches of water), when designing your garden it is still worth planning for a pond in the future. You could use the space as a sand-pit in the meantime, if the size and position are suitable, or as a flower bed for a few years.

Alternatively, an attractive, yet safe, feature could be introduced which depends on the flow of water over stones. The water could bubble up and

Plan for the power
Fountains and cascades need a power supply. Unless you have an ambitious project, a low-voltage submersible pump (with the transformer in the home) may be all that is required. If the pump has to move to a large volume of water, however, a mains-voltage pump, housed in a special chamber beside the pond, may be necessary.

Take this into account at the planning stage. If you have to lay a mains-voltage cable to a remote part of the garden – really a job for a professional electrician – it can be expensive. You also need to have all power supplies (for the greenhouse and outdoor lights as well as pumps) organized before you start laying paving and making beds. Careful planning at this stage will mean that you will not have to lay cables after you have laid your paving, or lawn, etc, which could prove to be disastrous.

run over large stones, to be re-circulated from a hidden reservoir below, or it could emerge from the centre of an old mill stone (or its modern artificial equivalent!), and cascade safely over the edge to be re-circulated again.

The traditional pond

The traditional pond is what most gardeners probably want as a water feature. There you can enjoy fish and waterside plants as well as the sight and sound of fountains and cascades if you want them — though cascades are exceedingly difficult to work into a typical suburban garden without them looking very contrived.

If you plan to buy a pre-formed glass-fibre or plastic pool, get catalogues and decide which one you are going to buy *before* you finish planning your garden. The size and shape of a pre-formed pond can influence many other aspects of design, such as paths and possibly associated features such as a rock garden. If you are going to use a flexible pool liner, you should be able to make a pool to fit whatever is called for in your initial design, though you should keep to gentle curves and not make the outline too fussy.

The choice will lie between a formal, regular shaped pool, such as a circle or rectangle, or an informal pool with gentle sweeps.

If the pool is large enough, it could be enhanced by intersecting it with stepping stones, but keep them to one end of the pool rather than letting them cut it in half visually.

Something different

A raised pool can be especially attractive because it raises the whole underwater world that much nearer to the eye. It will call for a little more skill to make than an ordinary pond, and you will also have the additional cost of bricks and associated materials in addition to the liner.

For something easier, you could make a tiny pond in an old wooden barrel (see illustration on page 11) or even a modern plastic planting tub, though you will find that this type of water feature can be difficult to maintain in good condition.

A 'stream' is another possibility. Most liners can be bought in long, narrow lengths as well as in the more conventional sizes, and you can use one of these to make a long, narrow watercourse. This can be far more unusual than a normal pond, and if you make a couple of streams you could link them by pumping water from the lower one to the upper one, which can then cascade back to the lower level.

A formal, rectangular pool enhanced by an island urn and a glorious display of summer blooms.

Even though the idea of a vegetable plot may seem to be somewhat unalluring, a herb garden is always an appealing prospect. This is partly because herbs have more romantic connotations than cabbages and potatoes, and also because they can be so much more attractive.

Some herbs are highly decorative, and even the less visually appealing herbs will not look amiss in a flower border.

If it is impossible to provide a proper herb bed, you can grow a few herbs in a window box or container near the back door, but this is a poor substitute for a proper herb garden.

An area 10 ft × 10 ft (3m × 3m) will provide plenty of scope for a wide range of herbs, and you can accommodate a surprising number of plants in a circular bed about 6 ft (1.8m) across. But some herbs can become very large plants – angelica will easily reach 6 ft (1.8m) and lovage can grow into an equally substantial plant. But as both of them are quite striking, if space is limited, consider putting these in the herbaceous border and keeping the more compact, slower growing plants for the herb garden proper.

No matter how you set out your herbs, it makes sense to have them near the house. One advantage of growing your own herbs, is the convenience of being able to pop out and collect a few fresh leaves when you need them.

Some ideas for herbs

There are many ways in which you can incorporate a herb garden, but the three suggested here generally work well. Do not follow them too closely, though, if they do not fit sensibly within the overall plan for the garden; you many be able to adapt the basic concepts so they work for you.

A herb wheel is a traditional, but still attractive way to make a feature out of your herbs. It is most effective used as a centrepiece where three or four paths join, or perhaps in the centre of a vegetable plot divided into four with paths, livening up this potentially dull part of the garden. As most herbs die down in winter, try incorporating a small statue or birdbath in the middle.

A typical herb wheel is illustrated below, showing some of the plants that could be used. An old cartwheel can look charming with plants growing between the spokes; the chances of being able to find a cartwheel are remote, but you may find a substitute that could be converted. If you use anything made of wood, be sure to treat the wood with a suitable preservative first, and support it on bricks or a concrete foundation so the wood is not in contact with the ground.

Brick can be used very effectively to form the outer curve and 'spokes'. It is an easy job that you can complete in a weekend. If you want to make even more of a feature of it, cover the soil between the spokes with gravel; or if you want a really striking design you could cover alternate spaces between the spokes with gravel of different colours. Gravel can actually help the plants by forming a mulch, but more important from a design viewpoint is that it makes the wheel look more interesting when there are not many plants to see, such as while they are becoming established and during the winter when some of them will have died down.

Herb 'wheels' are always admired yet they are very simple to construct from spare bricks. A centrepiece at the hub of the wheel will give it height and add interest in winter when most of the herbs have died down.

Above: Herb 'patch-works' are effective and practical, as even the rampant herbs are contained by the paving.

Herbs in a paved area can be very effective. Do not attempt to plant them in cracks between the paving, like plants in crazy-paving, but remove complete paving stones to make a bold, perhaps chequered, pattern. You may need to leave a group of several slabs out.

A herb garden of this kind should be positive: one or two slabs, or a small area of brick removed with a few herbs popped in, is not going to make the herb garden a strong element in the design. Either create a chess-board pattern with herbs and paving competing on equal terms and making a bold geometric design, or devote just a couple of large areas to herbs, with tall ones in the centre and dwarf, sprawling ones round the edge.

A rectangular bed devoted to herbs does not sound promising, especially near the house. To work well, it must be a positive feature – perhaps a raised bed, or a level bed with a bold edging. The success of this kind of herb garden depends on the planting. It needs plenty of shrubby perennials such as some of the variegated sages and thymes, lavender, and rosemary, to generate interest during the winter. And for summer there should also be some striking plants such as angelica (one plant may be sufficient), and herbs with pretty flowers, such as borage.

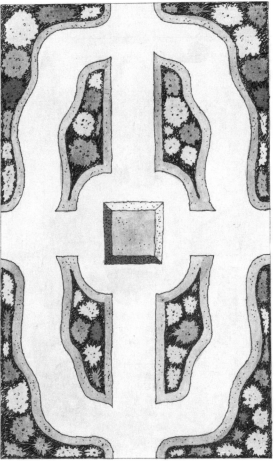

Left: To make a real feature out of a herb garden, you could plan one on classical lines, perhaps edging the beds with dwarf box and enclosing the areas with a box or yew hedge.

If you have a fairly large garden and a naturally sloping site, preferably in an open, sunny position, a rock garden will make an outstanding feature, especially if you can combine it with a stream and cascades.

Sadly, few town gardens provide ideal conditions and in a very small garden you cannot hope to create a natural-looking rock garden, so it is a mistake to try. It will be far better to grow your alpines in another way – perhaps in a scree or gravel bed, or in pots. This is not a second-rate way to grow alpines – many real enthusiasts grow their plants in pots. You can create a superb, eye-level display if you have them on benches in a greenhouse, preferably one used entirely for alpines, as they need particularly good ventilation.

Stone (or nowadays, imitation stone) sinks and troughs provide another way of growing choice alpines. And a surprising number can be grown in crevices in walls and between crazy-paving (some of the most suitable plants are listed on page 110).

Raised alpine beds, perhaps topped with gravel or stone chippings, can make a very attractive feature. You may be able to incorporate one or two small rocks into these, but they are not essential. The raised bed itself is the feature, and it has the bonus of bringing what are usually tiny flowers closer to eye level.

If you have a rock garden on your list of priorities, consider one of the alternatives if your garden is small, rather than compromise the design.

Be wary of attempting a rock garden on a flat site in a small area. Even if you form an artificial mound there is the danger of it looking terribly contrived, even if the rocks are well positioned. If you do try to incorporate a rock feature on a flat site, make the slope as gradual as you can – and this will require plenty of space.

It is, however, possible to have very convincing rock outcrops in a fairly large lawn even if the slope is only gentle, the extra height needed for the outcrop will not look amiss.

There are exceptions to most rules, and it is sometimes possible to create a stunning area on a small bank or on a larger flat site by bold and imaginative planting, as the illustration below shows. In this kind of rock garden there is no attempt to pretend the feature is a miniature replica of a natural rock scene; the rocks are used merely to act as a foil and a setting for plants of all kinds, not just alpines. If you have enough knowledge of plants to be able to carry this off, it can be very effective, but the emphasis should be on plenty of interest and colour from the plants; the rocks themselves are not the main feature in a bed of this type.

In a well-planned rock garden the plants will be more conspicuous than the rocks – at least for much of the year.

Choose the right rock

The principles of constructing a rock garden are described on page 140, but at the planning stage you should also consider the type of rock to be used – red sandstone, grey-white limestone, green slate etc. These and many others all have a distinctive appearance and can affect the tone and appearance of the garden. Generally it is best to keep to local stone, not only because it will generally fit in more easily with the landscape, but also because it is likely to be less expensive. (Transport is bound to be expensive with something as heavy as rock.) Bits of broken-up concrete, such as those left over from building works, never look right.

Left: If you do not have room for a proper rock garden, you can try planting alpines in an old sink.

Below: A rock garden like this will take several years to mature, and requires careful planning to start with.

Statues and garden ornaments should always be placed with care. In the right place, with the right setting, they can give a garden a sense of dignity and class that shows good taste, while adding a focal point or pocket of interest.

Garden gnomes apart (and some people like to add these for a bit of fun), statues, sculptures, and ornaments such as sundials and birdbaths, can act as a form of punctuation in the design. But if they are worth including, they deserve a prominent position so they either take the eye to a distant point or act as a centrepiece.

A white figure or bust, in marble if you can afford it, otherwise in reconstituted stone, will work wonders to liven up a dull, shady corner. A white ornament, perhaps on a plinth, will look especially good against a dark green yew hedge or some other evergreen. The greenery will frame and highlight the ornament, which will be shown off far more effectively than if it were in a lighter, more open situation.

A statue of a nude in the centre of a small front garden can look totally out of place, but the same statue set in a quiet corner, surrounded by dark evergreens, could look magnificent.

If you want an ornament or sculpture in an open position, perhaps the centre of a lawn or offset on a paved area, it needs to be simple, bold and possibly abstract.

Always look at the overall shape of statuary rather than at the detail, as its role in the garden is, initially, to catch the eye from a distance.

A garden that wanders aimlessly with no special points of interest, or focal points, is not going to have the desired impact. A sundial, a birdbath, a statue or an abstract piece of sculpture will give the eye something to rest on. The positioning should always be deliberate and have a purpose — a piece at the end of a walk, in a corner, at the end of a terrace, or in a recess is more likely to work well than one in the centre of a lawn.

Resist any temptation to overload the garden with ornaments, otherwise you will defeat the object of creating focal points.

There is an element of false snobbery which suggests that a reproduction or fake ornament will not serve the required purpose as well as a genuine antique, but from a design standpoint they should serve the same purpose. Modern ornaments are made from a variety of materials, from the classic marble and bronze, to glass-reinforced cement and glass-fibre (known as reinforced plastic in America), as well as reconstituted stone, not to mention more abstract designs in anything from scrap metal to brightly-coloured plastic.

Always choose materials suitable for the position. Bronze will mellow to a darker shade than it is when you buy it, so it needs a light background. Marble and stone mellow to some extent but still stand out beautifully against a dark green background.

Lead is not commonly used, but if you are fortunate enough to have an old lead ornament it will probably look best against an old brick wall or some material in keeping with its period.

Enhancing the plants

Plants can enhance a piece of statuary (the dark yew hedge as a background), but sometimes the plants can themselves be enhanced. The tone and atmosphere of a group of plants (especially foliage plants) can often be changed by a simple small ornament.

Above all, ornamentation should form an integrated part of the design, and not appear as though it has been bought and added as an afterthought.

Statues and ornaments should be seen in the context of the whole garden. These figures are appropriate because the garden has been designed to look Italian.

Above: Ornaments do not have to be big and expensive to be effective. These two small hens are on a low wall tucked among the plants.

Urns and troughs

Urns and troughs planted with flowers can perform many of the functions of a piece of sculpture, but generally they are suitable in different positions. They are especially useful for hard-surfaced areas, or for a geometrically planned garden.

Any container planted with flowers will have periods when there are very few blooms, so you should always bear in mind what the effect will be at various times of the year.

Sundials

Sundials need careful placing. They obviously have to have a sunny position, and if they are to be useful as well as ornamental, there has to be adequate access as you do not want to have to trample on the flowers to see the time!

A firm base

All ornaments should be on a firm base, and you may be able to buy a plinth that you can concrete into the ground. Remember that some shapes and textures are attractive enough for people, especially children, to want to touch, so they must be secure enough not to topple over.

Below: Do not be afraid to use ornaments to bring interest to a shrub or mixed border.

A pergola on the grand scale is only for the large garden, but something more modest can be a very useful device for diverting the eye to a particular area or for linking various parts of the garden. In a very small garden, though, it is best to avoid a pergola as it needs to be stout enough to support the weight of plants, and high enough to give adequate headroom below the inevitable cascading branches and leaves.

Such a large construction in a small area is bound to look out of proportion. If you want an overhead structure, up which you can grow plants, to add height and stature, it is best to build an overhead lattice work for the patio which uses the building itself as part of the support. You can buy special brackets to mortar into the brickwork to support the sawn-wood beams. 'Roofing' in the patio like this will help create the illusion of an outdoor room.

A pergola should always have a sense of purpose, and is often most effective over a substantial path that looks as though it leads somewhere.

Ideally, the pergola – which is, in effect, a covered walk – should lead to some focal point or into another outdoor 'room'. Above all, it needs a sense of purpose. There are, in addition, occasions when a pergola can be justified to overcome a particular problem of design.

It is a useful technique for overcoming the problem of an awkward corner in, say, a triangular plot or some other shape that has wedge-shaped corners. Here a pergola could lead to a prominent statue or ornament at the end; if the sides are well planted with shrubs the awkward funnel effect will be minimized. To make the journey more worthwhile, however, you could also try to accommodate a garden seat where you can relax on a hot summer's day and enjoy the smell of climbers such as honeysuckle, as well as fragrant shrubs planted all around.

A more versatile application, but worth considering where you want to create a cloistered effect, is a pergola that runs round three sides of your garden. This will give it a very enclosed feeling and can be useful if you want to concentrate the eye *within* the garden rather than to the view beyond. A garden with this amount of wooden construction has to be planned with great care, and particular attention must be paid to the plants. It will enable you to grow a wonderful collection of climbers, but to avoid bleakness during the winter months, it is very important to plant plenty of evergreens as well as the more popular deciduous climbers.

Pergolas

Most traditional pergolas are constructed from rustic poles (see page 168), but there are many other options, some of which may create a more integrated design. If you have a lot of brick paving, it may be best to construct the columns from matching brick, and use sawn wood for the beams. A garden with raised beds made from concrete or reconstituted stone blocks may look best if the pillars are made from the same material.

Generally, sawn wood will look better in a modern setting or as part of a patio; rustic wood tends to look best in a natural, less artificial garden.

Avoid placing a pergola over the lawn, because the grass will soon become worn and poor as a result of the shade and drips from the overhead beams and plants.

The proportions of the uprights and beams, and the height and width, must be right. If the verticals are disproportionately large the whole affair will look clumsy. If the beams are too thin they will warp and look mean; if they are too substantial, they will look heavy and ugly.

Arches

Even a simple arch can form a 'doorway' that will give a sense of purpose and direction to a vista.

If you are patient enough, you could grow a hedge either side of a path and train the plants over it to form a living arch. For quicker results, you can buy various metal, plastic, and rustic arches. These are all acceptable once clothed with plants, but they should always be positioned where there is a natural division to the garden. An arch sticking up in the air, which you feel you could easily walk *round,* will seldom be effective. If there is nothing more substantial to act as a divider, plant bushy shrubs at the sides.

If you want to have a classical feel, you could create a 'tunnel' of arches, over which you can train laburnum or wisteria, for example. For a few weeks during the year an established tunnel will look absolutely stunning, and for the rest of summer it should still look attractive when clothed with leaves. A tunnel of arches will call for a degree of expertise with pruning – it is not difficult to learn. You will also need to be patient for a few years, while the young plants grow.

An arch in a hedge will help to frame parts of the garden, and will certainly encourage one to explore.

Even if you have never had a greenhouse or conservatory, it is a good time to think about one while you are designing the garden. Although your finances may well not run to an elaborate conservatory, or even a greenhouse, at the moment, consider carefully whether one might improve or extend your enjoyment of the garden. If there is any possibilty of wanting to incorporate one later, work it into your design from an early stage. It will constitute such a dominant element that you should work out where you will eventually put it as you do your overall planning.

Greenhouses need careful siting, partly because the position must be chosen with the plants in mind, but also because an unsuitable size or shape, or unfortunate site, can impinge on the rest of the garden. Even if you have a kitchen garden that can act as home for it, the sheer height and size may dominate in a way that none of your vegetables could. And if your vegetable plot happens to be in a remote part of the garden it will be much more costly to lay on power and water supplies if you need them than it will be if you place it near the house.

Conservatory or greenhouse?

A proper conservatory will almost certainly enhance your property in a way that no greenhouse ever could. A well-designed conservatory will add a lot to your house (probably financially as well as visually), and it will almost certainly make the garden more attractive.

A conservatory that has doors which open both into the home and into the garden really will be a half-way house, and ideal link between the indoors and the garden.

The drawback is cost. The best conservatories are very expensive because they are modified to suit your own home, and they will almost certainly have to be constructed by specialist builders. It is not like buying a greenhouse in a kit that you can erect yourself.

Failing a proper traditional conservatory, you could consider one of the modern metal structures that are a compromise between a lean-to greenhouse and a traditional conservatory. These are normally glazed to the ground. Most, nowadays, have curved eaves to give a more elegant line; the aluminium is generally treated to give it a more acceptable colour.

Graceful though these are in line and appearance, they lack the elegance of a traditional conservatory and they are best used in a modern setting where they will fit in with the house.

A conservatory has a great advantage over most greenhouses in having all mains services on hand — water, electricity, maybe even a gas supply if you want to run a gas heater (natural gas is safe, but coal gas can affect plants). And the warmth of the house itself on one side will also make heating it less expensive.

Do not be tempted to run an extra radiator off the domestic system, though, unless you check with a heating engineer first to make sure that the boiler will support it. And you will really need a separate control for the conservatory anyway, because most central heating systems are turned down at night, which is just when the plants will need the most protection.

If all you want is somewhere to grow plants, and are not interested in making a feature of the actual structure, a lean-to greenhouse has many advantages. It benefits from the protection of the house wall, and it is not obtrusive if you can find a suitable wall — perhaps at one side of the house, provided the aspect is right for the plants (see below).

Free-standing greenhouses can be imaginatively designed too — they can be dome-shaped,

If the garden is small, it is sometimes possible to fit a lean-to along the side of the house (though if shade is a problem it will restrict your selection of plants).

octagonal, or with more conventional rectangular plans but with curved eaves to make them look more graceful.

The more imaginatively-designed greenhouses may have drawbacks — sometimes cost, sometimes the ineffective use of space within them or perhaps limited size. Often your choice of fixtures and fittings (benches for instance) is restricted because they need to be tailor made. If your greenhouse has to play a prominent role you may happily accept some or all of these drawbacks. If you have a small garden and your greenhouse has to go on the patio, for instance, then a small pinacle-shaped structure will look far more attractive than a traditional greenhouse. If it has to sit in an open position on a large lawn, then maybe you could make a feature out of a dome-shaped greenhouse.

From the point of view of growing, and from considerations of cost, there is nothing wrong with the conventional greenhouse shape. It is efficient, and if you are going to screen the greenhouse from view there is no point in buying anything more elaborate. It is best to spend your money on choosing the largest you can afford as a small greenhouse usually turns out to be frustratingly inadequate.

In attempting to screen the greenhouse, bear in mind the problem of a power supply and ready access so that you can keep an eye on it (plants in a greenhouse should never be forgotten, not even for a day in summer because of the possible adverse effects of overheating from rapid solar gain and too little watering).

The right site

Alongside the aesthetic considerations, and how the structure integrates with your design, go the practical ones. Unless you want to grow mainly ferns and plants which love the shade, the greenhouse should receive plenty of sun. Even though you will shade it in summer, good light is essential at other times of the year.

Avoid overhanging trees, and, if possible, do not choose a very open position exposed to strong winds from the north and east as winds can cause damaging draughts and rapid heat loss in winter.

Traditional alignment for a greenhouse is north to south, but much depends on the plants you want to grow (bedding plants need the best possible light in spring, for instance), and the whole question of orientation is much less important with aluminium-framed greenhouses because the glazing bars are so much thinner than the old wooden type. It is more important to choose a position that fits into the overall garden design.

By choosing a distinctive shape, the greenhouse can look quite at home on a patio.

Below: A conservatory that combines modern elegance with traditional style.

Although some superb garden designs do not have any lawn at all, for most gardeners a patch of green grass is what typifies a garden.

In a very small garden, think carefully before including a lawn, for the smaller the area, the more wear it is likely to receive and in some ways the more awkward it is to maintain. In a large garden, though, a lawn becomes almost essential as a means of covering a large area of ground and holding the design together.

In northern Europe, grass is a natural ground cover and lawn grasses grow easily. But this is not so in all parts of the world, and what is taken for granted in one country may have to be strived for in another. Either way, a lawn can involve a great deal of maintenance – on the one hand because it grows too rapidly and rampantly, on the other because it is difficult to persuade it to grow to the standard found in a typical, British 'putting-green' lawn.

A lawn can make a major contribution to a garden, but you must be clear about what you want from it, and what you can realistically hope to achieve. A really first-class lawn will be very labour-intensive: you will have to mow it twice a week; feed it regularly; use selective hormone weedkillers or lawnsand if necessary; probably use moss controls; spike or aerate it and then top-dress at the right time. For those alternating 'stripes' you will also have to use a mower with a roller to 'lay' the grass, and to finish it off properly it will be necessary to trim all the edges neatly too. If you started with the right kinds of grasses, after all

this work you should have a showpiece lawn.

Such lawns have their place, but not in an area of the garden that is going to be *used*. For a practical, hard-wearing lawn you will need stronger, coarser grasses that have the merit of standing up to wear much better. Mowing can usually be left for a once-a-week cut during the summer, though all lawns should be cut less in times of drought.

A formal, rectangular lawn, perhaps with geometric flower beds, will look much better with fine grasses and a short cut. Grass adjoining flower borders or a large rolling lawn, is usually best with less demanding, coarser species. The large, informal lawn will almost certainly have its fair share of weeds, but in this setting it should not matter. The scale is different and a more relaxed approach to the lawn should be reflected in less demanding maintenance. It is much easier to tolerate the weeds than to worry about them, and there are even times when the weeds may keep the grass looking green!

Types of lawn

The two most popular uses of grass have already been discussed. The formal, high-quality lawn, often in a fairly rigid framework, and the more natural 'flowing' or 'playing' lawn that acts as a ground cover, a broad informal path linking areas of the garden or as a recreation area.

It is worth thinking about more unusual types of lawn, too. It could be a setting for naturalized flowers, or you could use different cutting heights (which also means different cutting frequencies) to 'sculpture' areas of grass.

Bulbs are the easiest plants to naturalize in grass, and although spring-flowering bulbs come most readily to mind, there are summer and autumn-flowering types that can also be used. In a large garden where you can leave the grass long until the bulb foliage has had time to grow for a month or two after flowering, drifts of naturalized bulbs can make a pleasant feature. As an alternative to bulbs, you can let areas of grass become tall enough to allow wild flowers to grow and bloom. You may have to sow or plant the wild flowers to generate enough types to make it interesting and colourful, but this can be an exciting way to cover an area in a large garden (provided the thought of 'weeds' in your garden does not fill you with horror).

Where the area of the lawn is large enough, you could mow part of it weekly during the summer, and leave the rest long, cutting it either once a month or a couple of times a year if you want really tall growth to allow wild or naturalized flowers, such as bluebells and daisies, to bloom.

A classic British lawn, complete with stripes. Very attractive, but it needs a lot of dedication and effort to maintain it.

Left: A large area of lawn will also demand a lot of time, even if it uses quality turf. It is possible to reduce the area to be cut regularly by leaving some grass long. These areas can also be used for wild flowers and perhaps naturalized bulbs.

Below left: Most lawns fall between the high-quality lawn on the opposite page and the large, natural-looking grassed area above. This is a happy compromise where the grass provides a suitable setting for surrounding plants.

Non-grass lawns

Gardening books will often refer to 'alternative' lawns such as chamomile or thyme. Magazine advertisements sometimes even suggest plants like *Sedum acre*. If you want a small area to *look at* rather than to walk or play on, then these plants do have their uses – though it is hard to imagine anyone who has suffered from *Sedum acre* as a weed in the garden willingly introducing it, no matter how attractive the yellow flowers. All the alternatives suffer from drawbacks that make them no match for grass.

Chamomile is a substitute frequently mentioned, but it is not easy to establish over a large area and it will be expensive unless you propagate your own plants. If you do manage to establish a lawn, you may have second thoughts about the wisdom of it once you have to weed it all by hand, because you will not be able to use the selective hormone weedkillers used to control lawn weeds in grass.

A garden should be a place for relaxing as well as a place for work. There is not much point in gardening if you never have an opportunity to sit back to enjoy the results of your labours. You could always bring out a deck-chair or a fold-up picnic table and chairs, but these are poor substitutes for proper garden furniture.

It will always be necessary to move some of the garden furniture in and out of storage to take account of the weather – some of the luxurious garden relaxers and swinging seats with soft covers look nice but they need protection. They should supplement the type of furniture that is weatherproof and can be left out permanently.

There are good reasons for having as many pieces of furniture as possible as permanent fixtures. Every piece that you have to take indoors for protection demands storage space; and anything that you can leave outdoors will mean that the garden does not look too bare in bad weather; a patio that looks full of character with tables and chairs can look very uninviting once it is transformed into an area of bare paving.

It makes sense to have a mix of permanent and portable garden furniture. If metal, wooden, or even concrete seats do not appeal on the grounds of comfort or prettiness, you can bring out gaily coloured cushions that will transform them for the day, yet still leave something of interest when you take them in. A metal table that may appear cold and uninviting for a meal is quickly transformed by a suitable tablecloth.

The only proviso to make in recommending weatherproof garden furniture is that it should be well maintained. Metal furniture may need painting regularly (white for real impact), although plastic-coated metal needs less attention, and wooden seats should be cleaned and treated with a suitable preservative (or painted) at least at the beginning of each summer season.

Using furniture in design

The role of furniture can be contentious. There can be few who would deny the *need* for somewhere to sit, but whether seats and other furniture should blend inconspicuously into the surroundings or form a positive feature in their own right is a question of taste and what you want from your garden.

If you want a natural, flowing, garden with the accent on plants, garden furniture is likely to be incidental; if you have a garden with lots of hard paving materials and a very strong design with plants as a secondary feature, the furniture will take on more significance.

If you decide on metal or plastic tables and chairs for a paved area, beware of turning it into something like a pavement cafe. This is most likely to happen if you want lots of seats and have two or more groups of chairs; if you want plenty of seats, consider installing some built-in seating – a wooden bench can look very smart. Even a bench with concrete slabs to sit on can be transformed for the occasion with the help of cushions.

If all you need is somewhere to sit, consider the possibilities of building a seat around an existing feature, such as an old tree, or against a raised bed (though if it contains flowering plants, and stinging insects bother you, this may not be such a good idea!).

A tree seat almost always looks good, especially when painted white for emphasis. It is not difficult to make one if you are a reasonably practical person. If the tree is close to a boundary or some other inconvenient place, it will be possible to build the seat around only part of the trunk. Whenever you can though, let the seat encompass the whole trunk – you then have the opportunity to sit and enjoy the garden from many different angles, and the seat itself will be a linking theme as it will be seen from various parts of the garden.

A tree seat goes against all the general and sensible advice about not having seats beneath trees; the tree seat is a feature so much in its own right that it is worth putting up with the inconveniences that accompany a seat beneath a tree (drips from overhead branches can be annoying, and falling leaves may make the seat unpleasantly slimy at times).

If you want your seat in shade, let it be from a wall or something similar. A sense of privacy and seclusion, possibly with some shade, can be achieved by setting it in a bay of shrubs.

Plastic coated steel furniture is durable, lightweight and available in a variety of designs.

Stone and brick

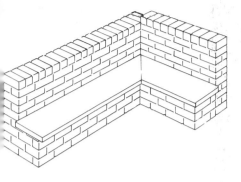

Seasoned timber

Wrought iron

Plastic

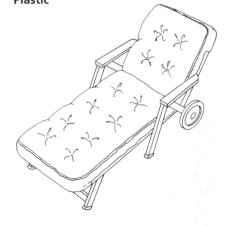

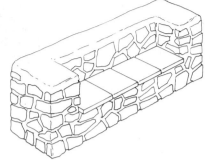

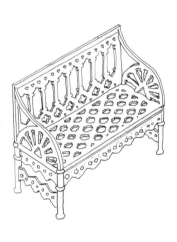

Barbecues

Barbecues are very popular, even among non-gardeners. They are a fun way to enjoy the open air, and if you cook and eat in your garden you really are using it to *live* and relax in.

Think very seriously about how much you will actually *use* a barbecue before opting for an elaborate built-in type that could dominate a small garden. In countries where the weather is dependably favourable, there is a much stronger case for incorporating a barbecue into the design than in a more unsettled climate. If you are planning to provide elaborate meals for a lot of people, you will need a large unit, and again this will need a garden of adequate proportions if it is not to remain a forlorn and dominating sight for the winter months.

You can still enjoy a family barbecue with many of the portable units that are available, and these may be the answer if you simply cannot accommodate anything more permanent. Have somewhere convenient set aside to store it out of season.

If you build a permanent barbecue, make sure there is a storage area for charcoal and cooking implements, and a worktop area on which you can rest plates and other utensils. And ensure that the cooking grill area is at least 3 ft × 1½ ft (about 1m × 0.5m) if you want to avoid some of your guests having to wait a long time for their food.

Positioning There are many practical considerations too. Do not have your barbecue underneath overhanging trees, especially evergreens, such as holly and conifers, which are highly flammable. Because of the potential fire hazard, keep the barbecue a reasonable distance from a wooden fence, and ideally have it sited conveniently near the kitchen.

Container gardening is an ugly expression, yet plants in containers of all kinds have a role in a garden of almost any size and shape. If your garden extends only to a balcony, or if you have just a tiny town garden, various types of containers will provide extra growing space, and the best of them will be features in their own right. In a large garden the containers may need to be bigger but the impact will be similar.

Grouping containers is almost always more effective that dotting them about the garden.

Where to use containers

Containers can make an important contribution to the overall impression of a garden and they can punctuate and accentuate a design.

A pair of tubs containing formally clipped shrubs either side of a doorway or opening in a hedge sets a particular tone before you even set foot in the garden. But both plants and containers can be used much less formally than this, and it is worth taking advantage of the mobility of smaller tubs and troughs and to move them about as much as you like, until you get the right effect.

Pots and containers can be thought of as the finishing touches to a garden. They will also relieve dull areas that lack colour or interest. If a particular part of the design has not worked out in practice as

well as it looked in theory on paper, a planted container can often retrieve the situation.

The very best use of pots and containers will, be planned, though. A suitable urn or large pot can provide a focal point in the same way as a statue or garden ornament (see page 40).

Containers often look best *grouped* rather than dotted about especially if they are all made of a natural looking material such as terracotta or reconstituted stone. To break up an expanse of lawn, you could form an oval of gravel on which to stand a collection of pots and suitable plants.

Pots grouped together for effect – to emphasize their different shapes and designs – should be suitably planted. There is not much point in filling attractive unusual pots with masses of bedding plants, including trailers, that will hide the beauty of form. Choose plants with positive outlines and interesting shapes – agaves, hostas, *Fatsia japonica* and phormiums, for instance. These will not mask the beauty and decoration of the container, and will themselves add shape and form.

You may want to hide plain isolated containers, which are not very interesting in appearance, by planting and suitable trailers. In this case it is the display of flowers or foliage that is important. Being clear about the role of the various types of container is important if you are to use them to their full advantage.

Materials

It is better to find containers in shapes and materials that fit a particular niche than to design your garden around the containers.

There are so many materials and designs that it is largely a matter of looking around to see what is available. You may think that a lead container would be too rare and expensive to contemplate, but there are firms that make imitation lead containers in glass-fibre (glass-reinforced plastic), and there are plastics that look like wood from a distance (though here the deception is not usually as effective as with the lead replicas).

Some reconstituted stone is very like the real thing, and can be recommended for a weighty urn or something similar that you are not likely to want to move about.

Glass-reinforced cement is not widely used, but can be particularly effective because the root area is generous in most designs, yet the wall section is not too thick. At first glance, it may be mistaken for asbestos cement, but in fact it contains none of this substance.

Asbestos cement is used for a number of containers of modern design – such as shallow, saucer-shaped dishes, but concern about the safety of asbestos may deter you from using these. In fact, the risk is probably negligible from garden containers *provided you take simple precautions,* such as not drilling additional drainage holes. The fibres are also safer if they are bonded with paint, and those with a white finish have probably been painted already by the manufacturer. If white does not appeal to you, it is a simple matter to paint the containers another colour: just use exterior quality emulsion paint.

The last two materials are heavy and you will find large containers very difficult to move once they have been filled with soil and planted. Glassfibre and plastic are both light. Plastic is by far the cheaper of the two, but is not usually as attractive as glass-fibre. If the containers are to be planted with a mass of flowers, though, it may be better to buy a number of plastic containers and have a really bold display than a single more tasteful, but expensive, one made from glass-fibre. In the garden, terracotta-coloured plastic containers look more natural than white ones, which compete with the plants for your attention.

Terracotta is beautiful in the right setting, and always looks right with plants, but the best and most interesting containers are expensive and they tend not to mix easily with other materials.

Wood is often dismissed nowadays because it combines expense with a tendency to rot – not an ideal combination. But treated with a suitable preservative (one that is non-toxic to plants), they can last for years. 'Versailles tubs', old cut-down beer barrels, or purpose-made round tubs, are all very effective if filled with plants of suitable stature and displayed prominently.

Window boxes

Windowboxes should always be chosen carefully to reflect the tone of the garden and the design of the house. A classical design can look out of keeping set against a modern house, for instance. If you choose a material such as asbestos cement or wood, consider painting the windowboxes to match the house – a red door with matching red windowboxes can look superb.

You could take a more abstract approach if the setting is right. If the plants are mainly silver-leaved, you could even paint the containers pink. Or to reflect a more flamboyant personality, you could have coloured stripes or even bold, contrasting circles (but do think of the neighbours!). All these ideas make the boxes more interesting for that part of the year when the flowers are not in full bloom.

Above: If you have a beautiful or interesting container, do not let the flowers hide it. The beauty of this container would have been lost if the flowers had been too dominant or if trailers had hidden its details.

Left: An old manger has been put to good use. You can be creative with your containers instead of conventional.

Unlike a dress or a suit, which you can make from a pattern, you cannot make a garden from someone else's plan. Each one has to be individually styled. Gardens are unique: they vary in size, shape, soil, aspect, and setting, as well as in established features such as mature trees and shrubs that you may wish to (or have to) incorporate. The size of your bank balance may also restrict what you can hope to achieve; some of the gardens illustrated in this section could cost you as much as a family car.

Taste, too, is individual, and one person's idea of good design may not be another's. To some people, a 'wild' garden is untidy; to others formal beds and lots of paving can be irritating and boring. There is no point in being dogmatic about design — some really charming gardens have just evolved with no conscious planning.

This is no excuse for not thinking carefully about the type of garden you want to achieve, and developing a style that encompasses both good design and individual preferences. The starting point is having an idea of the *type* of garden that appeals to you and then seeing whether you can adapt it to suit your garden and your skills.

Simply sitting with a blank sheet of paper and hoping for inspiration is a recipe for frustration. Looking at other people's gardens — in real life and in books — is far more productive. None of them will be just right, but they will probably give you ideas upon which you can build.

The designs that follow have been selected to reflect a diversity of taste and styles. Some are strictly formal, others reflect a more personal and informal approach to garden making.

We have used real gardens to illustrate the various styles, though sometimes the plans have been modified. In a few cases we have taken elements from more than one garden and incorporated them into a plan that demonstrates the solution to a particular design problem.

The symbols on pages 182-189 have been used for the plans, so if you like a particular feature, it should be relatively easy to copy it on to your own plan. Due to limitations of page size, we have had to use various scales. The scale is indicated beneath each plan. Those drawn to 1:50 can be traced off directly, because this is the scale used for the symbols in the back of the book.

Colouring in the symbols after you have traced them will help to bring the plan to life, especially with brickwork, where it is worth shading in raised walls in a different colour to bricks used for paving.

This view shows clearly how a long garden can be divided into a series of 'outdoor rooms'.

KEY
1. Gravel
2. Log rounds
3. Pergola with climber
4. Seat
5. Shrubs
6. Herbaceous plants
7. Paving slabs set in gravel
8. Dwarf golden hedge
9. Specimen tree
10. House

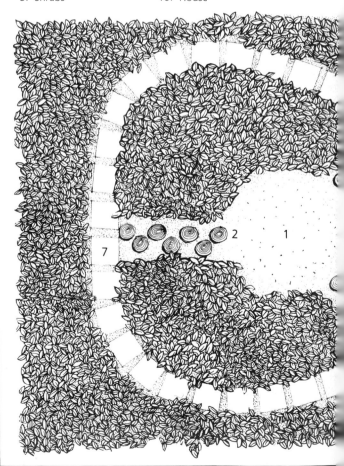

Here a long narrow site has been divided up into three distinct sections, each with a very different mood.

The rectangular area of paving, framed in a pergola, forms a sort of outdoor room, an extension of the house before you enter the garden proper.

The centrepiece of the garden is a the palm-like *Cordyline australis*. This is only hardy in favourable districts, but if you can grow a plant of this kind, it will give the garden a more exotic appearance than the normal range of broad-leaved trees or conifers.

The use of gravel for the circular area has the dual purpose of giving the garden a more unusual touch and of acting as a sympathetic link between the hard, synthetic paving and the plant-dominated end section of the garden. It is also very practical: there are no problems in mowing a circular lawn, and it will take any amount of wear at the access points.

By being densely planted, the shrub and tree area at the end of the garden stimulates exploration. The log rounds used for informal paths through the shrubs allow access to the plants and add interest.

Construction This is a very easy garden to construct. The patio is straightforward and the gravel is easy to lay. The paving slabs set in gravel and the log rounds set in earth through the 'wild' garden can be laid on a very modest base.

Other ideas An alternative to the cordyline as a centrepiece would be a Chusan or fan palm, *Trachycarpus fortunei*, which is perhaps a little hardier than the cordyline but still not suitable for cold regions. Alternatively, you could use an ornament or statue instead of a tree, and this could look particularly good if you wanted to have a lawn in place of the gravel.

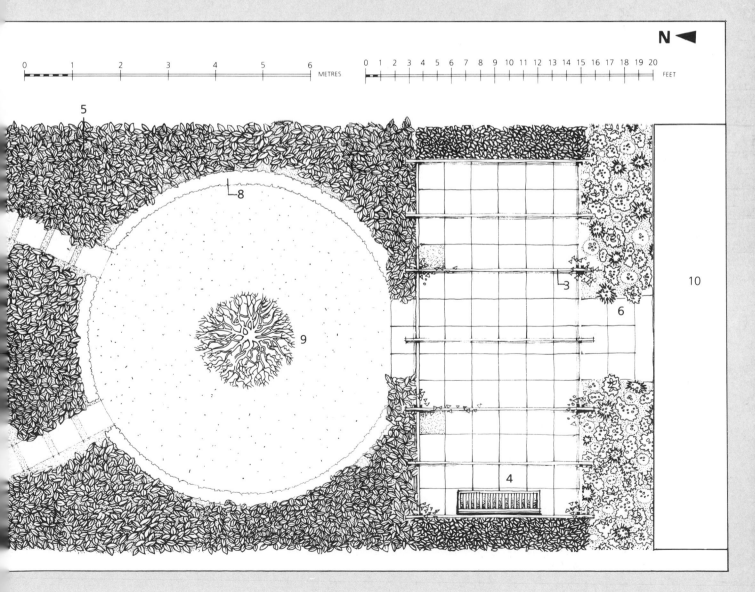

If you live in the countryside, it makes sense to try to merge your garden with the surroundings, so the view beyond can become an extension of the garden.

In this example a focal point has been created at the end of the garden to take the eye to the open fields beyond.

A garden of this size would also be expensive to construct on more formal lines. An informal, natural style makes it easier to create a garden that is relatively inexpensive for its size, and fairly easy to maintain.

There are no annuals, and the beds are planted with trees and shrubs that will demand very little maintenance once they have become properly established.

With any large garden there is a temptation to have a large lawn, but bear in mind the high maintenance required and the fact that an expanse of flat grass can look boring.

In this garden, interest has been created by 'wild' or 'meadow' areas of long grass, which also reduce the area that has to be mown regularly.

If you like a neat, formal type of garden, the idea of patches of long uncut grass full of 'weeds' may sound disastrous but, in an area surrounded by countryside, it looks perfectly natural, and these uncultivated areas are a major attraction for wildlife. In this garden the uncut areas contain wild orchids as well as a host of other colourful and pretty wild flowers that you never see in cut grass. These in turn bring a wide range of insects like butterflies, as well as birds and other animals.

If you are going to put the emphasis on a natural

Conifers and a seat have been used to form a focal point and take the eye to the countryside beyond.

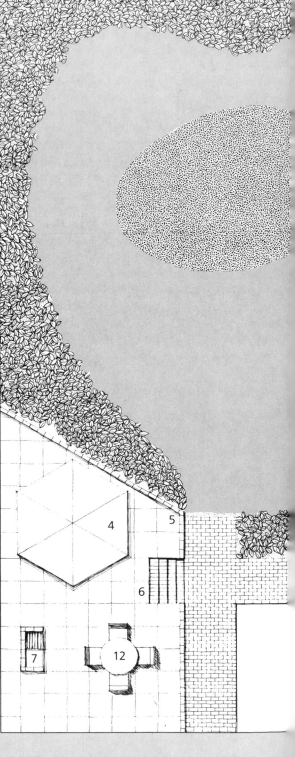

KEY

1. Long grass
2. Seat
3. Crazy paving
4. Hexagonal greenhouse
5. Low wall
6. Steps down to lower level
7. Barbecue
8. Natural stone paving interspaced with shrubs
9. Gravel edge

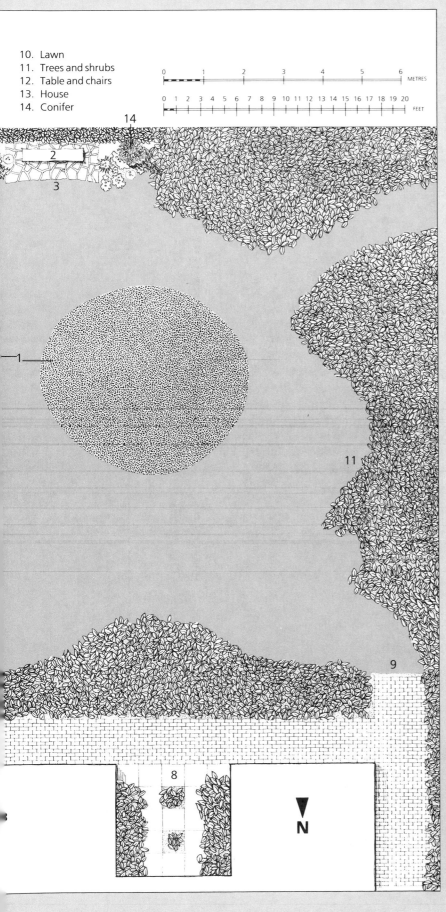

10. Lawn
11. Trees and shrubs
12. Table and chairs
13. House
14. Conifer

style of garden, try not to let paving, sitting-out areas and barbecues impinge on it. In this garden they have been placed to the side of the house.

Construction The main part of the garden is easy to construct. It could be reclaimed from a meadow by cutting out the shrub beds, then mowing, feeding, and perhaps using a selective weedkiller on the areas you want to cultivate as a close-cut lawn (though lawn weeds will not look amiss in this kind of grass).

In an established garden, the meadow areas can be created by sowing a mixture of grass seeds and native wild flowers. You should have no difficulty in obtaining wild flower seeds from seedsmen as an increasing number are now being offered in response to the widespread public interest in conservation.

The patio area will probably represent the biggest investment in time and money to construct, but tucked away at the side like this, it will not matter if you spread the job over several seasons.

Other ideas If you like the idea of water better than long grass, the large area of lawn could be broken up with one or more large, informal ponds, perhaps linked with a stream. This will also provide plenty of wildlife interest.

An area of long grass gives a 'natural' feel to a cultivated garden, as well as encouraging wildlife and wild flowers.

This plan is one solution to the problem of a small, L-shaped, corner plot. It is in effect two separate ornamental gardens, with a third section containing the vegetable plot and utilities at the side of the house. Arranging them like this makes the most of limited space by encompassing several styles in quite a small area. An internal hedge helps to provide the transition.

The pergola helps anchor the various areas together, and also provides height.

In small areas like this, which lack any natural focal point it is necessary to create them. Rocks and large boulders have been used in both the lawn and gravel gardens. And to give the grass walk beneath the pergola a sense of purpose, a piece of sculpture or ornament has been placed among a group of foliage plants at the end.

Even in a small garden such as this there can be a sense of discovery. If treated as one area of lawn, for instance, the whole garden could have been taken in at a glance. This design means that from the small patio you have to walk up a few steps and turn several corners before entering the next part through a gap in an internal dividing hedge. This principle can be as useful in a large garden as in a small one.

Using a slightly raised island bed in the gravel area gives height to the plants and again provides the stimulus for 'exploration'.

The area at the side of the house can be used for growing vegetables. By placing items like the clothes drier here, and maybe the greenhouse if you want one, the rest of the garden remains clear of these encumbrances.

Construction The most difficult part of this garden to construct would probably be the patio and steps.

Using rocks and boulders as focal points means choosing the right stones and positioning them carefully. You will almost certainly have to select the individual pieces yourself from a stone merchant or quarry.

Be particularly careful with any patio area close to the house that is lower than the surrounding ground. There must be an adequate fall to a drain or large soakaway to reduce the risk of flooding during heavy rain.

Other ideas If you do not like gravel, the lawn could be extended to cover this area. In this case you may not need a pergola to act as a link between the sections.

Using more interesting containers will add colour and interest to the small paved area, which is too small for a lot of elaborate garden furniture.

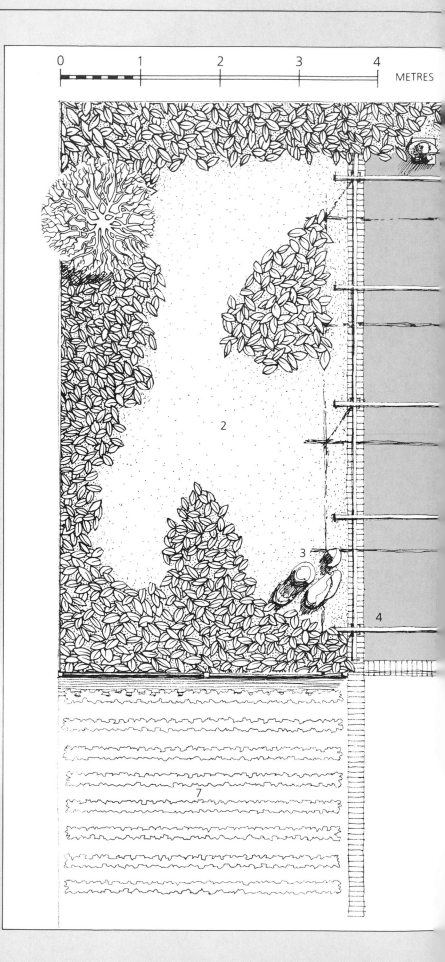

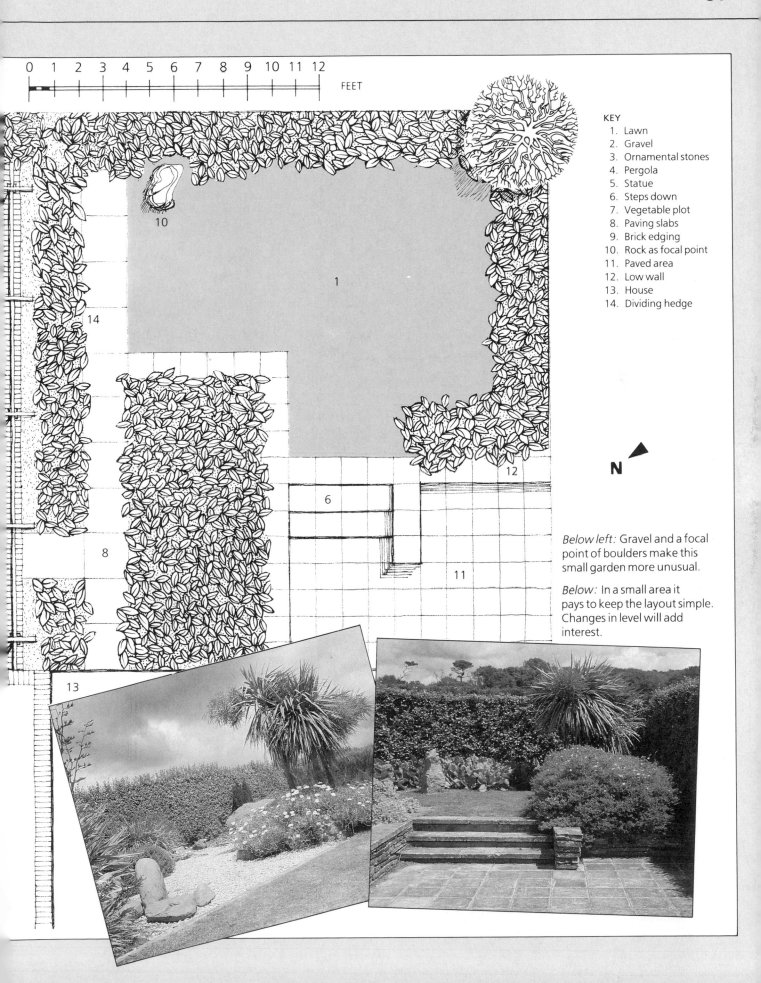

0 1 2 3 4 5 6 7 8 9 10 11 12   FEET

KEY
1. Lawn
2. Gravel
3. Ornamental stones
4. Pergola
5. Statue
6. Steps down
7. Vegetable plot
8. Paving slabs
9. Brick edging
10. Rock as focal point
11. Paved area
12. Low wall
13. House
14. Dividing hedge

N

Below left: Gravel and a focal point of boulders make this small garden more unusual.

Below: In a small area it pays to keep the layout simple. Changes in level will add interest.

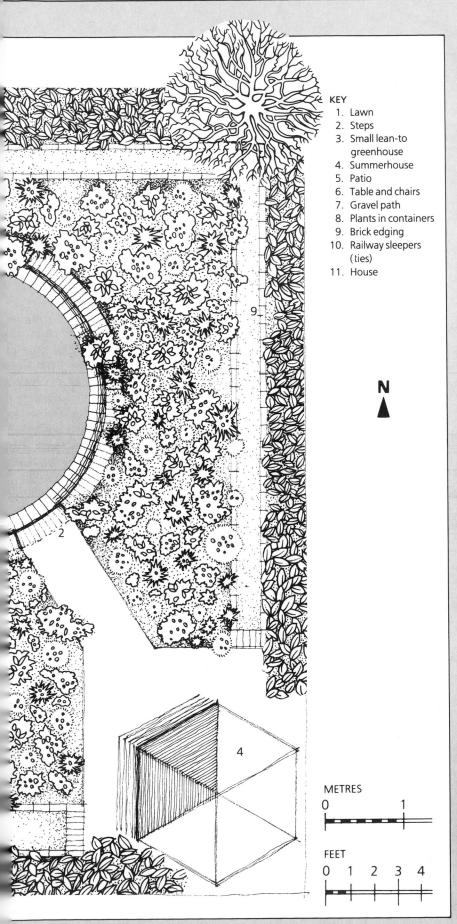

KEY
1. Lawn
2. Steps
3. Small lean-to greenhouse
4. Summerhouse
5. Patio
6. Table and chairs
7. Gravel path
8. Plants in containers
9. Brick edging
10. Railway sleepers (ties)
11. House

N

METRES
0   1

FEET
0   1   2   3   4

This small cottage garden has many drawbacks: it is tiny, a difficult shape, and surrounded on most sides by high boundary walls that could look oppressive in a confined space.

The problems have been overcome by treating the small area at the back of the house as a patio, and making a round, sunken lawn as a point of focus at the side.

While brick walls can be attractive in themselves, they could make the garden a dreary place to sit in this confined area at the back of the house. Simply painting the wall white has transformed the area, making it lighter and a more attractive setting for plants in containers.

Plenty of containers planted with colourful, seasonal bedding plants or bulbs help to brighten up the potentially rather dull patio area.

The pictures on the opposite page show the important role of the circular lawn as a centrepiece. These pictures were taken only months after the garden was planted, but already the surrounding beds are beginning to fill out. A garden of this sort can look mature in a relatively short time.

Plants have to be chosen carefully for a garden like this. For the central planting area, it is wise to stick to bushy, but fairly compact, shrubs, with herbaceous plants to provide a wider range of colour and interest. Too many large shrubs would make the garden appear smaller and the lawn insignificant.

Construction The only difficult construction job in this garden is the radius brickwork, but as the wall is not high it should be within the scope of a good DIY enthusiast.

The railway sleepers (ties) used to link the lawn with the main path may be difficult to obtain, but you can use bricks instead.

The lawn is best laid from quality turf as it could be difficult to establish a good lawn from seed over such a small area if it is likely to receive much wear.

Other ideas The grass path from the central lawn to the summerhouse could be fiddly to mow. This problem could be avoided by extending the other brick-edged, gravel paths to this area too.

The circular lawn could be replaced with bricks laid to a radius, possibly with a central ornament. It would lack the attraction of a bright green lawn, but would require no regular maintenance.

Opposite above: A coat of white paint can transform a dull wall. If painting only part of a wall, try to make the transition interesting and not too abrupt.

Opposite below: A sunken lawn makes the small garden much more distinctive than a flat one would.

The word 'disabled' tends to be used as a blanket term, but disabilities vary, and any garden for the disabled must take into account individual needs. The height and span of raised beds should reflect the height and reach of the person, and perhaps the dimensions of a wheelchair. The person who is going to use the garden is in the best position to know what is practical.

Rectangular raised beds, though feasible, can look boring and unimaginative. Here, a few simple circular beds provide scope for some wheel-

chair gardening without too much compromise in good design.

Although this garden has been designed with a disabled gardener in mind, it would also be suitable for anyone who wants a minimum-maintenance garden, or for a retired person.

Construction The paved area is straightforward, but unless you already have some bricklaying experience you should employ a contractor to lay the circular beds for you. Brickwork laid to a radius has

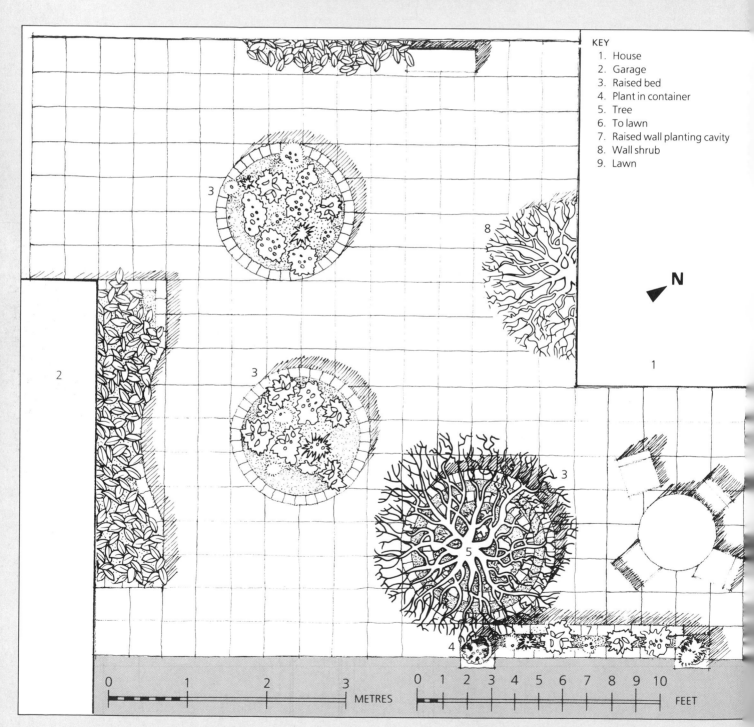

KEY
1. House
2. Garage
3. Raised bed
4. Plant in container
5. Tree
6. To lawn
7. Raised wall planting cavity
8. Wall shrub
9. Lawn

to be done well if it is not to look crude. In some of these beds there are also a lot of cut bricks, which will make it a tedious job unless you have equipment like an angle grinder to do the cutting quickly.

Other ideas The large bed around the tree has a pot-standing area. This would also be effective planted with suitable carpeting shrubs, or could even be made into a tree seat with a planting area in the centre.

If the chore of watering is not likely to be a problem, many more containers could be used to bring seasonal colour and interest, but bear in mind that plants in containers need frequent attention during the summer.

Left: The height of raised beds should be calculated carefully to suit the individual needs of the gardener.

Below: Although designed primarily for a disabled person, the circular raised beds are a pleasing feature for any patio.

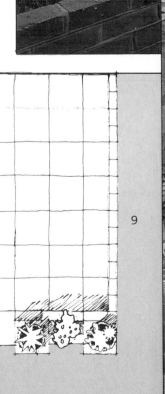

9

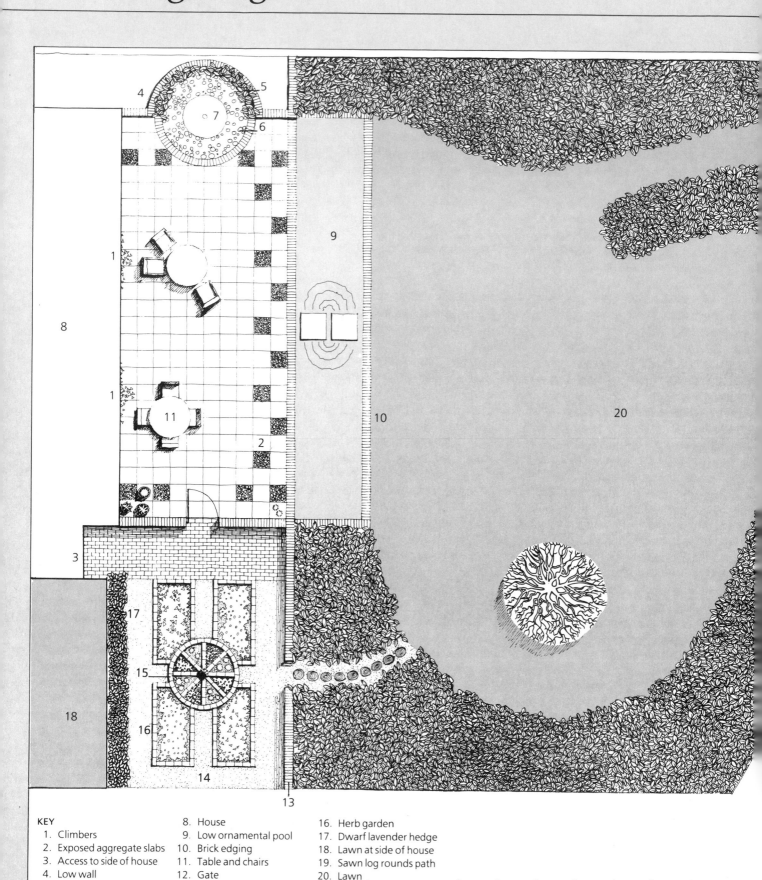

KEY

1. Climbers
2. Exposed aggregate slabs
3. Access to side of house
4. Low wall
5. Shrubs
6. Large pebbles
7. 'Mill stone' water feature
8. House
9. Low ornamental pool
10. Brick edging
11. Table and chairs
12. Gate
13. 6 ft (2m) wall
14. Gravel
15. Raised brick
16. Herb garden
17. Dwarf lavender hedge
18. Lawn at side of house
19. Sawn log rounds path
20. Lawn
21. Shrubs/mixed planting
22. Path to 'nowhere' as focal point

0   1   2   3   4   5   6   METRES

0 1 2 3 4 5 6 7 8 9 10 11 12 13 14 15 16 17 18 19 20   FEET

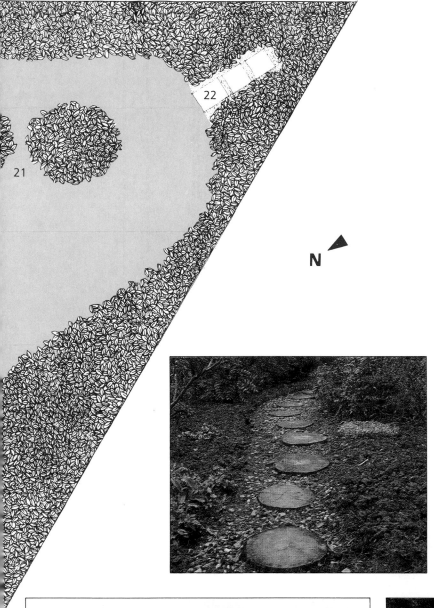

21

22

The main problem with a triangular garden, or any garden with difficult angles, is what to do with a pointed corner. In this plan the lawn has strong curves that hold the garden together so that these corners become less dominant.

A small path has been taken into the shrub border to provide access to plants further back and to create a focal point.

A large lawn like this one with an irregular shape will almost always benefit from a few specimen trees or shrubs and perhaps one or two island beds.

Tall walls have been used to separate the herb garden and play lawn at the side from the main part of the garden. This makes the garden more interesting by dividing it up into compartments.

Although stepping stones across water are always attractive, there should also be an alternative route like that provided here by a path between the shrubs to link the herb garden and lawn.

Construction A patio of this size, with linking formal pool and quite high walls to be built, is a taxing job for a beginner to tackle without some professional help, so you would have to employ a contractor unless you felt very confident about doing building work yourself.

Other ideas The short path at the end of the garden could lead to an ornament, perhaps backed by a hedge, to give it a sense of purpose.

Left: It is always worth trying to introduce a slight curve into a path of this kind, so the end is not immediately obvious.
Below : Island beds will relieve a large lawn.
Below left: One way to deal with an awkward corner.

This garden is suitable for anyone who enjoys gardening but is unable to tackle a great deal of routine work. If suitable tools are used to reach the beds from a wheelchair, it is also ideal for a disabled person.

Although paving predominates, the mixture of materials and patterns ensures that this garden is never boring. The beds are all low so that they are easy to work on.

The problem with any easy-maintenance garden is that it can look dull. This has been avoided here by using a variety of materials to edge the low raised beds, including bricks, log rounds, and blocks of sawn railway sleepers (ties). The many angles, bays and protrusions that would normally look fussy help to maintain interest.

With a garden of this kind, you can use plenty of annuals among the perennial plants in the beds, which will provide much visual interest. But if the time comes when you want to use less effort, simply plant minimum maintenance shrubs, in the containers as well as the beds, for a garden that is both enjoyable and easy to look after.

The beds here contain seasonal plants to add colour and interest, but they could easily be converted to minimum-maintenance by planting suitable dwarf shrubs.

Construction This has to be built for the disabled person by someone fit and good at paving.

Other ideas Although plants in attractive containers always look good, bear in mind that they need regular watering (a tiring, and often heavy job). If this becomes too much effort, you can always lift a few pavers and plant suitable dwarf shrubs direct into the ground.

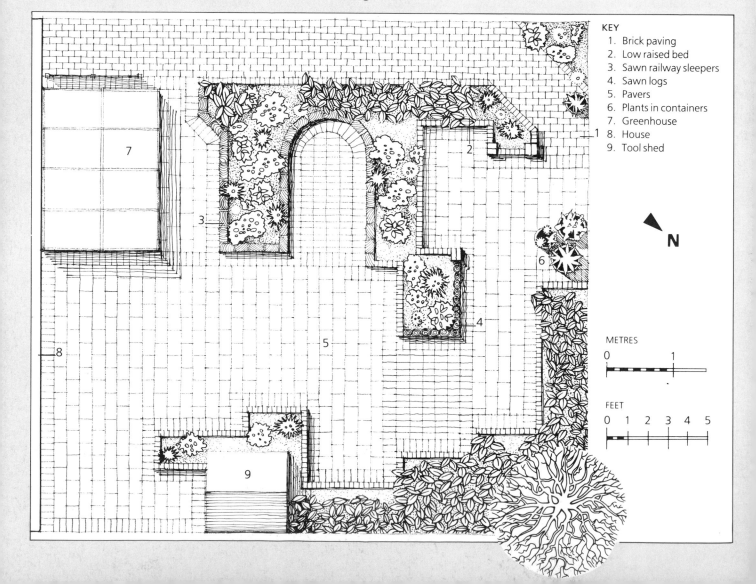

KEY
1. Brick paving
2. Low raised bed
3. Sawn railway sleepers
4. Sawn logs
5. Pavers
6. Plants in containers
7. Greenhouse
8. House
9. Tool shed

N

METRES
0   1

FEET
0   1   2   3   4   5

If you want a sitting out area in a very small garden it may be worth paving the whole area, rather than making a patio with mean proportions.

If you pave the whole garden, changes in level and height become even more important in order to add interest. In this garden, even the shallow step up from the paved area in front of the house provides the necessary break, and the raised pond gives the area much-needed height.

It is always worth considering a formal, raised pond where the design allows it, because it brings the underwater world nearer, making it more accessible.

Even in a paved garden like this plants are important. In a small area such as this, most plants have to be in narrow beds at the sides, but they will cascade over the edge of the paving and break up many of the harsh lines.

It is important to have some height within the garden too, provided in this case by a corkscrew or contorted willow, *Salix matsudana* 'Tortuosa'. Although ultimately rather large for a garden of this size, it has the merit of producing an interesting tracery of branches in winter.

Construction A garden like this is well within the scope of an average handyman. The paving is straightforward to lay, and the step shallow and simple.

Other ideas If you do not want a pond, it is worth considering a mini-greenhouse or a herb garden either raised or on the level, instead.

In a very small garden, it is sometimes best to dispense with a lawn and pave it instead.

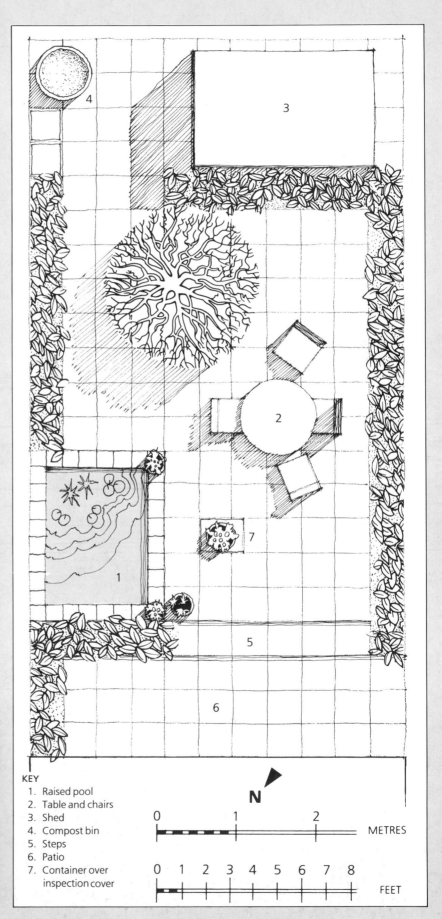

KEY
1. Raised pool
2. Table and chairs
3. Shed
4. Compost bin
5. Steps
6. Patio
7. Container over inspection cover

N

0   1   2   METRES

0 1 2 3 4 5 6 7 8   FEET

A combination of a small plot and a steep slope is an unpromising start for any keen gardener, but this plan shows what can be achieved by creating a series of terraces coupled with a careful choice of plants.

The style is very personal and reflects the owner's tastes and interest in plants. The central path in the middle terrace is made up of stones collected over a period of years, from various holidays, and gives the garden an individual touch as well as providing memories for the owner and a talking point for visitors.

Close planting helps give an enclosed, lush feel, even if you decide to sacrifice some plants later on.

Normally such a wide range of paving materials, including manufactured concrete slabs, slate, gravel and a miscellany of other stones, would lack harmony, but they work here because the terraces are well clothed and screened from each other by good planting.

Although this is a very individual garden, it follows the sound principle of dividing the area into sections that have to be explored in zig-zag fashion, so the whole garden is not taken in at a glance and it retains a sense of mystery.

Construction The hard work in this type of garden is in forming the terraces. Inevitably there has to be a great deal of earth-moving, and it may be worth hiring help with this if you want to make quick progress.

Retaining walls have to be constructed with particular care because of the pressures from soil and moisture. The lowest level must be laid with an adequate fall to a drain.

Other ideas If you don't want a greenhouse, the planting area for shrubs could be increased by taking another bed across the garden, perhaps planted with evergreens to ensure adequate winter cover and interest.

Top: Evergreens screen the bottom level from the middle terrace.

Centre: A Japanese lantern provides a focal point and brings to life what could be a dull corner.

Bottom: Close planting helps create a mature look quickly.

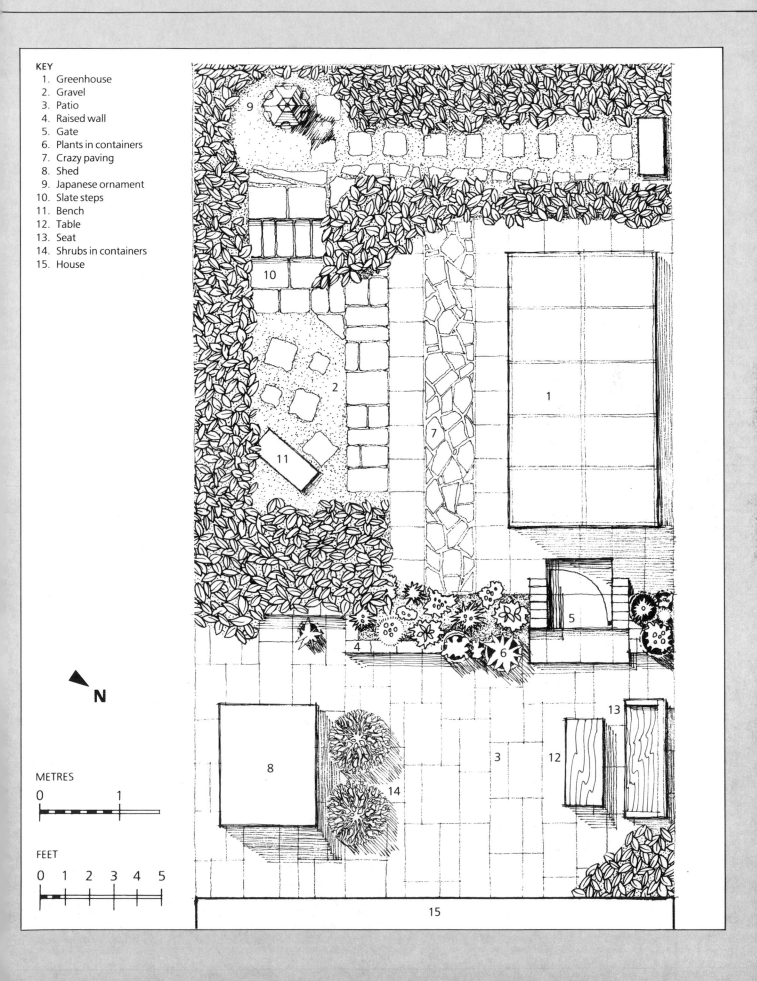

KEY
1. Greenhouse
2. Gravel
3. Patio
4. Raised wall
5. Gate
6. Plants in containers
7. Crazy paving
8. Shed
9. Japanese ornament
10. Slate steps
11. Bench
12. Table
13. Seat
14. Shrubs in containers
15. House

N

METRES
0   1

FEET
0   1   2   3   4   5

The basic ingredients for this garden are fairly typical of most gardens: a central lawn with shrub or flower borders round the edge. What gives it shape and character are the sweeping curves that bite right into the lawn, and generous, thoughtful planting.

For this approach to succeed, the curves must be big and bold, keeping to symmetrical ones whenever possible.

This garden also shows the importance and effectiveness of screening plants. The drive to the side of the garden, and the road at the end, have been well screened. Although it has taken several years for the trees and shrubs to grow to this size, the result is a garden that has a sense of privacy and seclusion as well as character.

Right: Never overlook the garden seat — after the work you want to be able to relax.

Below: A view down the garden from the house.

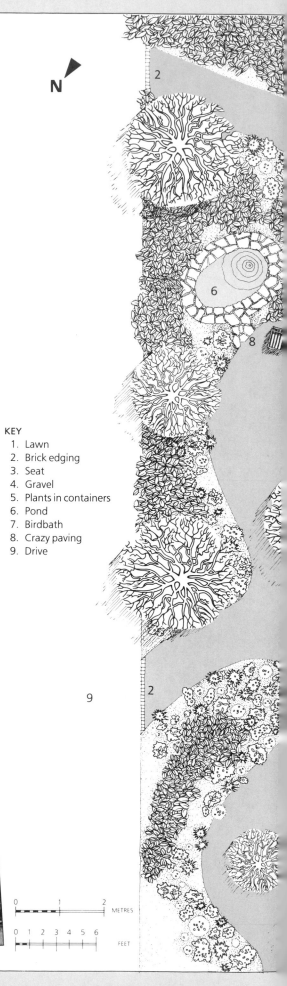

KEY
1. Lawn
2. Brick edging
3. Seat
4. Gravel
5. Plants in containers
6. Pond
7. Birdbath
8. Crazy paving
9. Drive

0 1 2 METRES

0 1 2 3 4 5 6 FEET

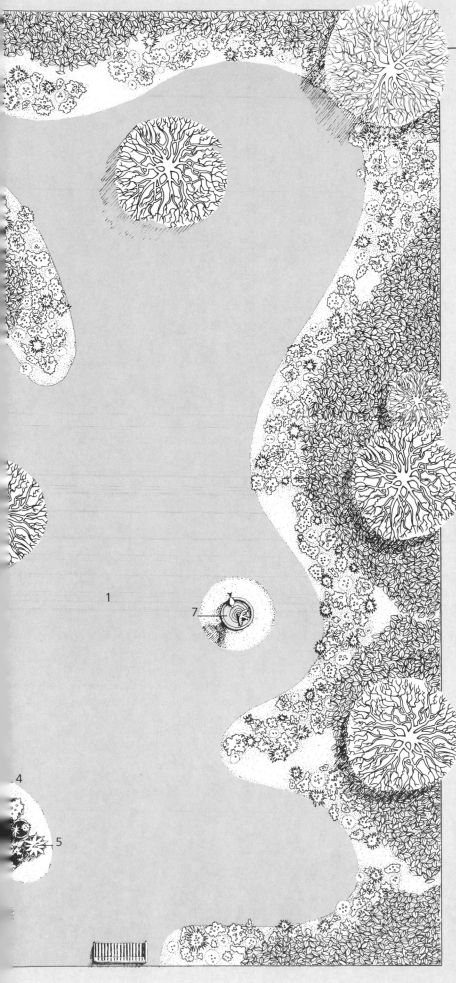

Where a lawn forms the major part of a garden, it is a good idea to make sure that there are 'punctuation points' to relieve it.

The birdbath in this garden makes an interesting feature in its own right, but it also acts as a focal point from almost any position in the garden. The gravel standing for a group of pots also breaks up the lawn and helps give the garden character as well as beauty.

Construction This is a very easy garden to construct. There is very little hard landscaping, and, apart from planting, the only major job is establishing a good lawn.

Other ideas In a garden where you are depending mainly on lawn and informal mixed borders, it is sometimes possible to introduce a few island beds.

Below: Gravel and terracotta make a happy combination against a lush green lawn.

Bottom: The entry from the drive.

If your garden is little more than about 30 ft × 30 ft (10m × 10m), and you have to accommodate a greenhouse, garden frame, clothes drier, and somewhere to grow a few vegetables as well, the problems for the design of your garden are considerable. Yet they are also very common difficulties today.

The solution here has been to divide the garden roughly into two, with a living screen formed by trellis that will be covered with climbers.

Although the ornamental area, which is the part viewed from the living-room, has been reduced to only half the size of a garden that is already small, it looks more pleasing than would a larger area that includes various unattractive elements.

Dividing even a small garden into sections means that you don't take in the whole garden at a glance: you have to move to several positions to see it in its entirety.

In this garden the gravel area is 1ft (30cm) below the previous soil level, which provides the opportunity to introduce a few steps, and also has the effect of making the fence 1ft (30cm) higher. This is enough to give an added sense of privacy and to obscure the view of an unattractive building nearby.

The fence is not particularly appealing to look at, but it has been retained while the evergreen shrubs in front grow and a screen of conifers planted behind it become established.

The gravel area has been curved at the end to help offset the rectangular shape of the site and to allow a greater depth of shrub planting at the top two corners.

The garden below had only been constructed for a few months when the photograph was taken, so the owner had planted plenty of annuals to fill out the gaps while the shrubs became established. Even selected houseplants have been used in the gravel area to provide interest for the summer while the permanent plants are filling out.

Construction Construction should present no problems.

Other ideas If you feel that every garden should have a lawn, the gravel area could be grassed. However, you would need a mowing edge, perhaps filled with gravel, so as not to have to mow right up to the edge of the walling.

Below: Although only newly planted, the effectiveness of gravel as a background for plants is already becoming evident.

KEY
1. Greenhouse
2. Garden frame
3. Plant standing area (gravel)
4. Gravel
5. Herbaceous border
6. Cobbles
7. Paving slabs
8. Concrete slab
9. Gravel (sunken 1 ft, 300mm)
10. Raised bed
11. Barbecue
12. Steps
13. House
14. Clothes drier

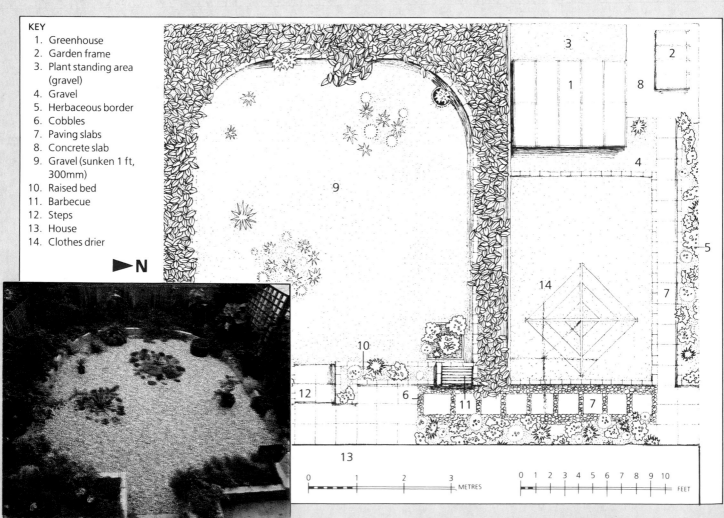

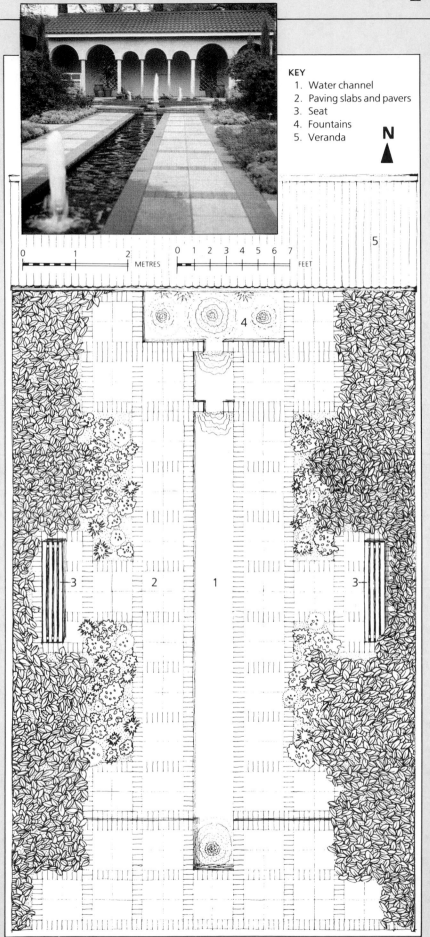

KEY
1. Water channel
2. Paving slabs and pavers
3. Seat
4. Fountains
5. Veranda

N

This garden, in complete contrast to the one on the previous page, is grand in conception and very formal in layout.

Although there are a great number of plants in the design, these are secondary to the architectural features. A plant enthusiast might find a garden like this unappealing, but where hard landscaping is a priority it would probably have tremendous appeal.

The garden demonstrates a Moorish influence, and the word 'paradise' was used to described gardens of many Eastern cultures where water, cool shade, and simple greenery gave relief from a harsh, arid climate. It would be equally refreshing in a modern city or a suburb.

If you are going to have a large area of paving, it is important that the design is interesting. Here a mixture of brown bricks and square, buff paving slabs with a textured finish have been used.

In a formal garden of this kind, symmetry is very important, and one half is basically a mirror image of the other as you look along the garden towards the veranda.

The symmetry helps give the impression of order and tranquillity, but there are few surprises, so without movement and activity of some kind it could soon become boring. The role of the fountains and shallow cascades is therefore crucial. As well as adding sound and movement, the fountains provide a high element where needed at the centre of the garden.

Most of the pumps sold in garden centres would be unable to produce a sufficient pressure of water to produce the geyser-like effect shown in the illustration, so if you want that effect you should consult a water garden specialist.

Unfortunately, this garden will be expensive to construct, especially as you will almost certainly need to employ a professional contractor. However, it will be very inexpensive to maintain, providing that you chose carefully when buying shrubs, and do not go for exotic varieties.

Construction This is a job that calls for professional help. The installation of the fountains needs specialist expertise, and the veranda certainly requires the advice of a builder, even if you help with the construction.

Other ideas Although the veranda gives this garden additional elegance, there may be many situations in which a design as grand as this would be too costly or unsuitable for other reasons. The garden would still look good with a stylish summerhouse at the end of the garden against a background of shrubs.

L-shaped gardens are often difficult to design in such a way that the whole garden is used and not just the part immediately in front of the house.

In this garden, the area at the side was seldom used. In order to remedy this, the focus of activity was shifted from the old paved area in front of the house to a new patio at the corner, which actually links the two legs of the L by setting it at an angle of 45 degrees to the house.

The paving itself, a mixture of brick and stone, reflects the angles of the building, and the tasteful mixture of paving materials gives the area a touch of distinction.

If a swimming pool is not to appear unsympathetic and dominate the rest of the garden, a great deal of thought needs to go into its shape and how it is integrated.

Radius paving has been used here to reflect the line of the pool and to integrate it with design so it is not in conflict with the patio and planted areas. By making this encompass a circular bed of low-growing plants the swimming pool is not divorced from the rest of the garden.

It is important to choose suitable plants to grow near a swimming pool — avoid deciduous trees and shrubs with leaves that are likely to drop into the water and be a nuisance. It is best to concentrate on small, compact evergreens and suitable herbaceous plants.

Construction The patio area is quite an ambitious project for a beginner, but quite within the bounds of a keen DIY enthusiast or anyone willing to take their time over it. Swimming pools are strictly for the professionals, unless you want to risk making some very expensive mistakes.

Always liaise with a swimming pool specialist at an early stage. There may be practical problems that rule out a particular design, and specialists will have expertise that can be invaluable. If you tell them what you are trying to achieve, they may be able to provide solutions.

It is also important to liaise closely on the actual construction, so you do not suddenly find that the swimming pool contractors need access across an area you have just constructed!

Other ideas On a smaller scale, or where a swimming pool is not feasible, the principle of radius paving and a circular bed could be adapted to link a formal pond in the same way.

Below and below right: If a swimming pool is to blend in with the garden, it too needs to be planned. Paving and plants can be used to integrate the pool with the rest of the garden.

3

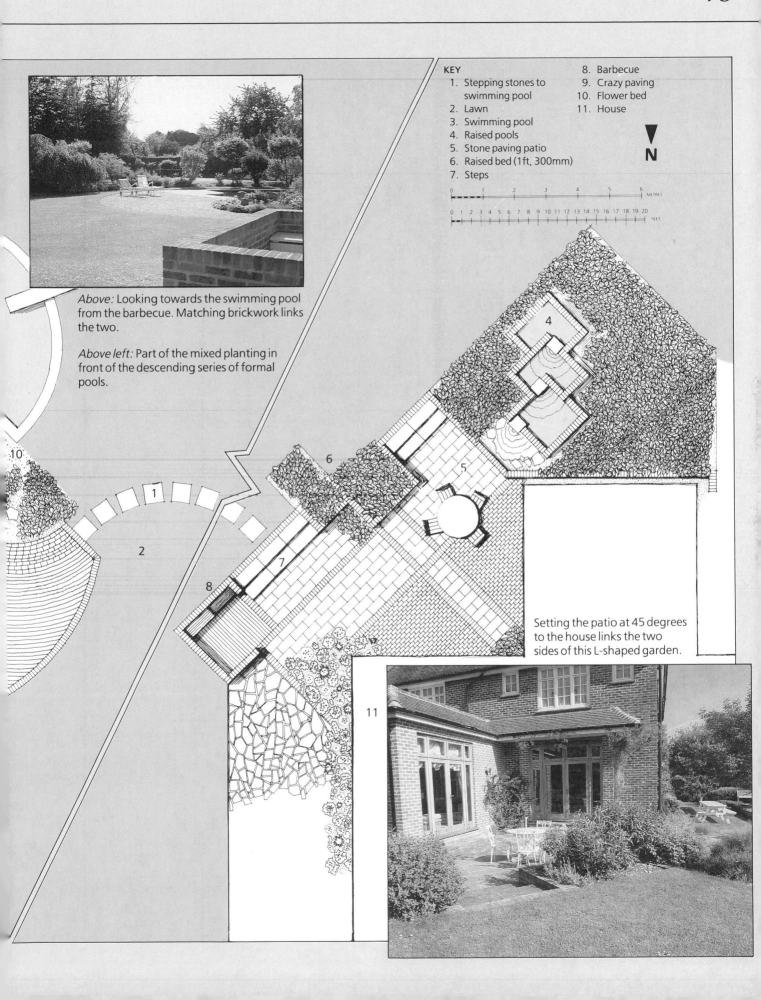

Above: Looking towards the swimming pool from the barbecue. Matching brickwork links the two.

Above left: Part of the mixed planting in front of the descending series of formal pools.

KEY

1. Stepping stones to swimming pool
2. Lawn
3. Swimming pool
4. Raised pools
5. Stone paving patio
6. Raised bed (1ft, 300mm)
7. Steps
8. Barbecue
9. Crazy paving
10. Flower bed
11. House

Setting the patio at 45 degrees to the house links the two sides of this L-shaped garden.

N

1

2

3

4

5

6

7

8

9

10

0   1   2   3   4   5   6
                                                    METRES

0 1 2 3 4 5 6 7 8 9 10 11 12 13 14 15 16 17 18 19 20
                                                    FEET

KEY
1. Swimming pool
2. Loungers
3. Gazebo
4. Urn
5. Steps
6. Table and chairs
7. Patio
8. Barbecue
9. Brick steps
10. Paving stepping stones

The view from the paved area in front of the house shows how the swimming pool has been planned to look inviting without overwhelming the rest of the garden.

View from the gazebo looking back to the house.

This garden is clearly a place to relax in. It is an extension of the home designed mainly for leisure and pleasure.

The borders are planted with trees and shrubs that need little regular maintenance, and the lawn though large, is relatively easy to keep short with a suitable powered mower. It is a garden in which you can spend most of the time relaxing rather than working.

The swimming pool plays a dominant role, yet because it has been designed along with the rest of the garden, does not look out of place. Often a swimming pool can spoil rather than enhance a garden unless either carefully integrated or well screened from the area around it.

The original garden sloped gradually from the house but, by extending the paved area in front of the house and making a positive change of level with retaining walls and steps, the fall of the garden has been made into a positive feature.

Setting the patio at an angle across the corner of the garden makes full use of what might otherwise be a neglected corner. Being let into the bank, it prevents the swimming pool from dominating the view from the sitting-out area.

Intersecting the stone paving with lines of bricks helps to emphasize the angles and makes the area visually more interesting than it would be if it were an expanse of grey paving.

Letting a patio into a bank increases the impression of an outdoor room by giving it firm boundaries or 'walls'. This area can be embellished with containers of all kinds on the patio, the steps and on the edge of the retaining walls.

The gazebo is both a practical feature, and a focal point, taking the eye across the swimming pool. From the lower level the gazebo brings to life an area that could be dull if there were only a swimming pool backed by shrubs.

Construction Swimming pools are clearly for professionals, although it is best if the constructor works to a plan agreed with the garden designer.

You could tackle the patio, retaining walls, and steps yourself, but on a sloping site it will save a lot of effort if a contractor does any initial levelling for you.

Other ideas If a swimming pool does not appeal to you, the lawn could be extended, and perhaps a few island shrub beds introduced into the lawn, provided these do not obscure the gazebo.

This stylish garden is relatively simple to construct, and is among the most 'instant' of the designs in this book. The gravel, paving, and water are effective immediately and, by using turf for the lawn, the garden can look mature from a very early stage, especially if you can make a feature of an established tree. If you are not fortunate enough to have such a tree in a convenient spot, planting a quick-growing type such as eucalyptus will bring results in very few years (though unfortunately a eucalyptus is unlikely to be hardy enough to be planted in very cold areas).

There are few shrubs and herbaceous plants in this design, and by buying good specimens these should look respectable in the second season. Meanwhile, since the garden depends heavily on textures and lines, it will still look good.

Close to the pool it is advisable to plant evergreen shrubs or herbaceous plants rather than deciduous bushes, so as to avoid leaves falling into it in winter.

When choosing a statue or ornament, make sure it will add enough height to the centre of the garden, and be sure that you can live with it!

Construction The formal pool will need the most care and work, but once this has been constructed, the rest will be straightforward.

Other ideas If you do not like the idea of loose gravel, the bricks could be extended over this area – but it will considerably increase the cost and the work involved.

KEY	
1. Formal pool	6. Shrubs
2. Plants in gravel	7. Brick edging
3. Statue	8. Lawn
4. Table and chairs	9. Paving slabs
5. Lounger	10. Gravel
	11. Gate to house

Below: A clean, simple, quick-maturing design for a small garden.

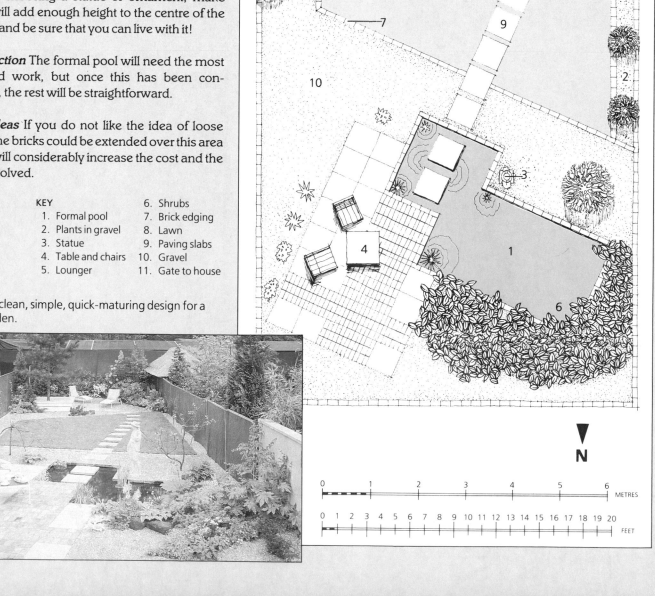

N

0 1 2 3 4 5 6 METRES

0 1 2 3 4 5 6 7 8 9 10 11 12 13 14 15 16 17 18 19 20 FEET

This very formal design has, as its centrepiece, a pool that runs most of the length of this compact and stylish garden and effectively divides it in two. To emphasize the symmetry and formality, matching rectangular pavilions have been placed in two corners.

To reinforce the formality, the paved and gravel areas are contained within a pattern of rectangles outlined by pavers.

While it is important to retain a degree of symmetry in a garden of this kind, a mirror image of one half in the other would be very boring, so the two halves have different features while retaining the same basic grid. The low wall on one side of the pool not only helps break up the garden visually, but also provides the opportunity to introduce a wall mask fountain.

It is important to introduce plenty of evergreen shrubs into a garden like this, otherwise it will look bleak once the herbaceous plants and deciduous shrubs have died down.

Construction You are likely to need professional help with major construction jobs like the pavilions, and it would be worth having the pool excavated to save this laborious task. Depth of water is not important in this kind of pool however, so if you keep it shallow, you will not have to do a great deal of excavating.

All the other jobs are comparatively easy.

Other ideas Instead of gravel, you could use bricks or clay pavers that contrast in colour or texture with the pavers already on the plan. However, gravel makes a particularly interesting texture that associates well with plants.

Gravel makes a superb background for many plants.

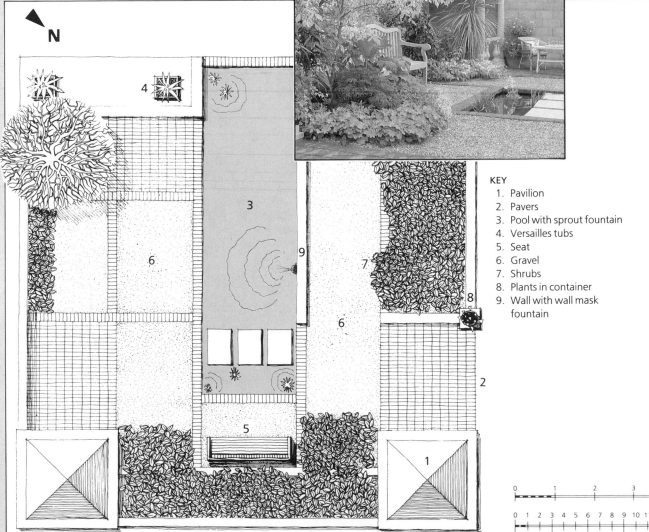

KEY
1. Pavilion
2. Pavers
3. Pool with sprout fountain
4. Versailles tubs
5. Seat
6. Gravel
7. Shrubs
8. Plants in container
9. Wall with wall mask fountain

0   1   2   3   4   METRES

0 1 2 3 4 5 6 7 8 9 10 11 12 13   FEET

Rather than making water an incidental feature you could design your garden around a large pond or stream. In this garden, water plays a dominant role, running out beneath the wooden decking to form a natural-looking 'lake' at the lower part of the garden.

It helps to have a naturally sloping site with a design like this, but if the slope is only very modest you could use the soil excavated from the pond to construct banks at the sides of the garden so as to make it look like a natural valley.

Rocks and water associate well, and here large rocks have been used within the grass and on the banks as well as at the water's edge to link the various areas. The exact positioning of rocks like this cannot be planned in advance - each one is different and you simply have to see which ones look best in a particular position when you have them in front of you.

A patio that incorporated paving would almost certainly look incongruous in this type of natural setting, and wooden decking has been used because being a natural material, it blends in more sympathetically.

If you are trying to create a natural looking garden, planting must also be done carefully. It will be better to have large drifts of a few plants in the borders, than many different types dotted about.

For a natural effect, plant in bold drifts of just one or two kinds of plants.

KEY
1. Decking
2. Rock
3. Plants in containers
4. Barbecue
5. Seat
6. Upper pool
7. Cascade to lower pool
8. Lower pool
9. Lower grassed bank
10. Upper bank with shrubs

N

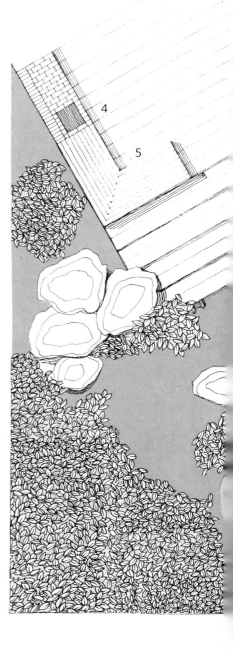

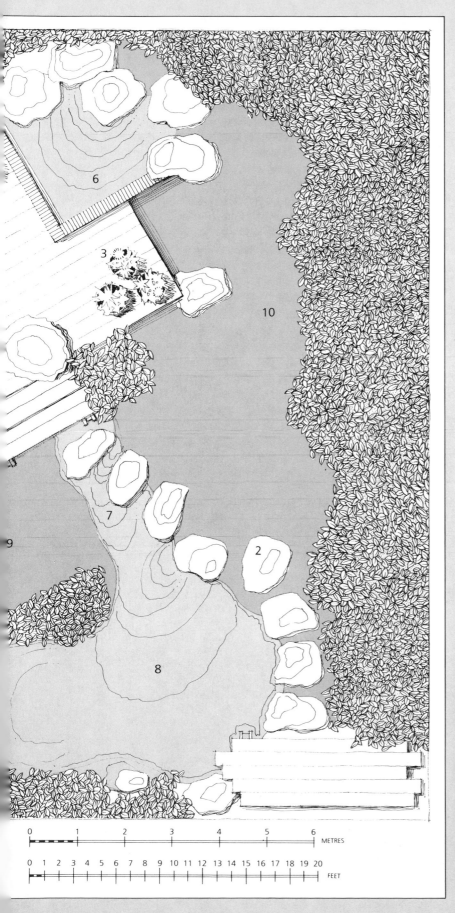

6

3

10

7

9

2

8

0		1		2		3		4		5		6	

METRES

0 1 2 3 4 5 6 7 8 9 10 11 12 13 14 15 16 17 18 19 20

FEET

Construction This is a very difficult garden to construct without professional help. You can excavate the pond and perhaps create the banks with a pickaxe, shovel and wheelbarrow, but it is hard work. The rocks, too, will take a lot of effort to handle and you will, at the very least, need help from a number of strong and willing friends.

Decking, too, requires careful construction, and if you plan to tackle it yourself it is worth reading a specialist book on the subject first.

If you like the idea of water tumbling along the stream, make sure that the watercourse is working properly before attempting the decking. You will find that most of the small pumps sold for garden pools do not provide a good flow of water through a stream of this size. Consult a water garden specialist over what is the best model for your needs.

Other ideas You could simplify this kind of design by adopting a less natural atmosphere and making it more clearly artificial. The water-course could be simplified by omitting the rocks and making it into a straightforward pond of similar shape then a brick or concrete paved patio would be much more acceptable. These steps would immediately make the garden much easier to construct without professional help.

If you have the determination and the skill, it is possible to create a very natural-looking garden, but you will probably need professional help to achieve this result.

To create an authentic Japanese garden in classic style requires research into the symbolic meaning of the various elements, but for most gardeners it is sufficient to re-create the mood and charm of a garden in Japanese style.

While the basic elements are the same as in a Western garden, stone, rocks, sand, earth and water will all be more visible than is normal. This garden will have only a few plants in it, but they have to be chosen for maximum impact. It is important to make a strong contrast between the structural lines of the garden's permanent elements and the shape and form of the plants.

A Japanese garden does not need a lot of space and could be the solution for a small plot. Alternatively it can make an interesting corner in a larger site.

It is easy to give a water garden a Japanese flavour, as this plan shows. A basic, shallow pond using plenty of natural stone and rocks, can be transformed by adding a few accessories.

The bridge immediately sets the tone. Careful placing of a Japanese lantern, and water trickling slowly through a large, hollowed-out, bamboo cane may be enough to give a Japanese flavour.

Construction Making the pond with a liner is easy. But choose a black liner as it will give even a shallow pool a feeling of stillness and depth, and will avoid the risk of the liner showing and spoiling the effect.

The bridge will probably have to be tailor-made — a job for winter evenings if you feel able to tackle it yourself; otherwise employ a carpenter.

Other ideas Instead of stone edging, try giving the sides of the pool a gradual slope and, using cobbles or large pebbles around the edge, taking them into the water and out into drifts around the edge.

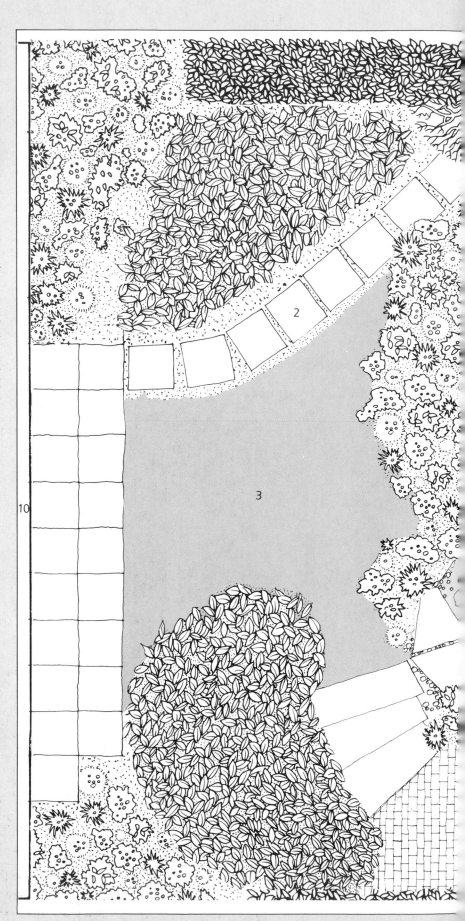

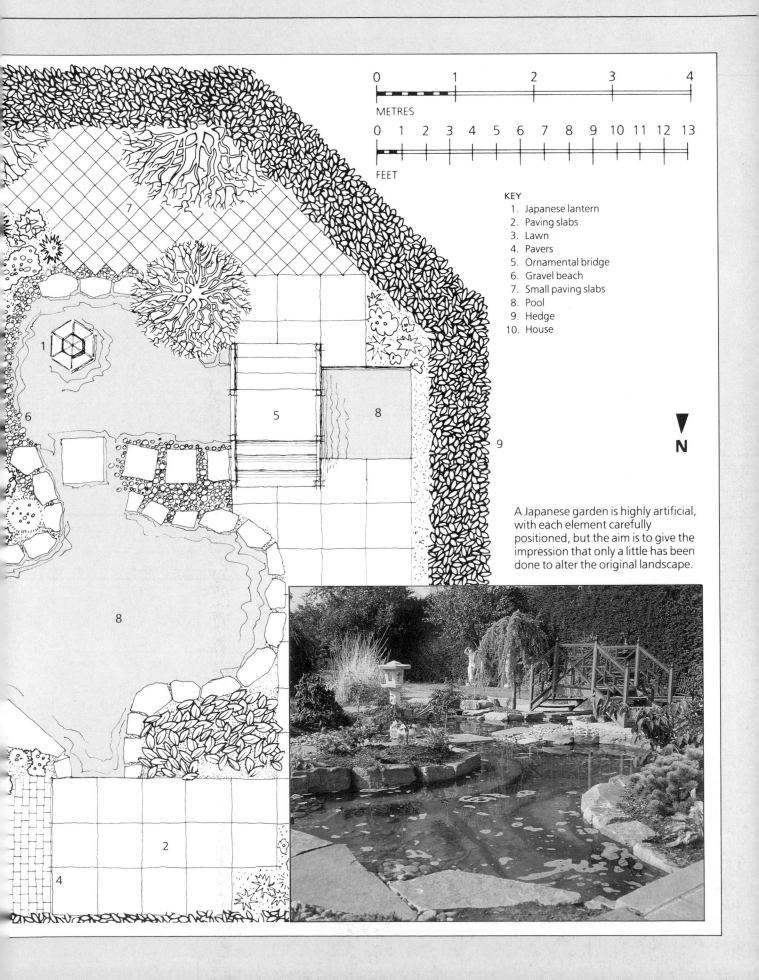

KEY
1. Japanese lantern
2. Paving slabs
3. Lawn
4. Pavers
5. Ornamental bridge
6. Gravel beach
7. Small paving slabs
8. Pool
9. Hedge
10. House

A Japanese garden is highly artificial, with each element carefully positioned, but the aim is to give the impression that only a little has been done to alter the original landscape.

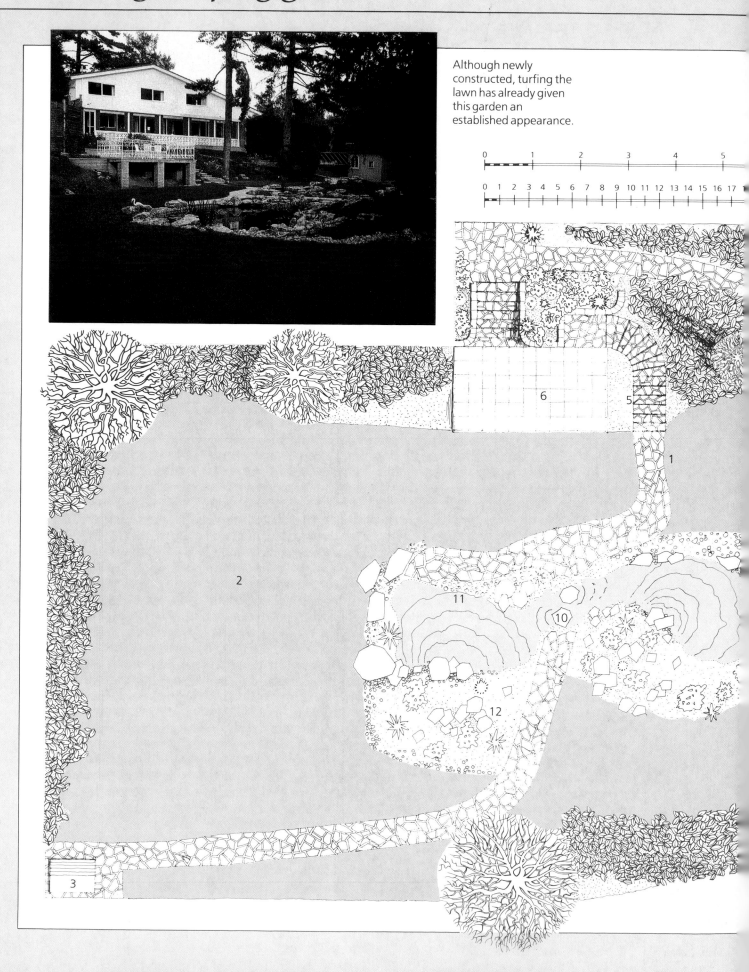

Although newly
constructed, turfing the
lawn has already given
this garden an
established appearance.

KEY

1. Crazy paving
2. Lawn
3. Shed
4. Sloping path
5. Steps
6. Elevated patio on piers
7. Steep slope planted with ground cover
8. Summerhouse
9. Pool
10. Stepping stones
11. Pebble beach
12. Rock garden

This garden is another example of what determination can do with an unpromising site. The house sits on the edge of what was originally a pit, and the garden fell away sharply into a rather overgrown area that could only be reached down steep paths.

The first decision was to raise the height of this area, and 297 truck loads of soil were tipped in to bring it to the level shown in these pictures!

The elevated house and patio were still divorced from the main part of the garden so the patio area was extended into a balcony, supported on piers, that projected into the lower area. This not only gives a good view of the main part of the garden but actually enables you to feel that you can walk into the garden without having to descend the steps or slope. The technique could work just as well in a garden that had smaller proportions than this one.

Ground cover or carpeting shrubs are needed on the steep banks leading up to the house to make cultivation and maintenance easier. Always avoid steep grass slopes if possible.

The main feature of this garden is the series of pools and rock banks, which form a focal point from all points of the plot. A generous amount of weather-worn limestone has been used, and isolated rocks extend beyond the rock beds into the lawn and shrub border as outcrops. This is an important principle that helps minimize the very artificial appearance that island rock beds usually create.

The garden has a Japanese tone, with extensive use of drifts of cobbles or pebbles extending from the water into the surrounding lawn or rock beds.

Construction If, like the owners of this garden, you have to do the filling and levelling, clearly you have to use contractors. Erecting a balcony on piers is also a specialist job. However, this kind of filling is unusual, and for most sloping gardens the work involved here is such that you could do it yourself.

Other ideas If you want to avoid water, perhaps because of the danger to young children, the rock garden could be extended over this area. If you want to keep maintenance to the minimum however, it may be best to go for island shrub beds.

The smaller the garden, the bigger the challenge to make something of it. This tiny, inner city garden is about 20 ft (6m) square, yet it encompasses a patio, lawn, and garden pool. Despite having many features, it does not take time to mature.

Interest is held mainly by the pool and patio which incorporate a small, but important, change of level, against a background of gravel and grass. Surprisingly few plants are needed in a garden like this, and the choice of a few bold herbaceous plants will bring acceptable results in the first year with an impressive show in the second. Wherever possible, any shrubs used should be evergreen to retain some leafy interest in winter.

A few bold foliage plants strategically placed will have more effect than flowering plants.

A built-in seat is particularly important in a patio like this; it economizes on space and can also look good painted white.

Construction Although a high proportion of the garden is paved and there is some retaining brickwork, the materials should not be prohibitively expensive, and all the jobs are within the ability of most DIY enthusiasts.

Other ideas Although the grass provides a welcome patch of green, which is as important in winter as in summer, you may prefer to dispense with a lawn and make it into a minimum maintenance garden. You could pave the grassed area with bricks, or clay or concrete pavers, but you would need to select a warm colour and leave planting spaces for shrubs. Otherwise use plenty of attractive containers, although these will increase the amount of maintenance required.

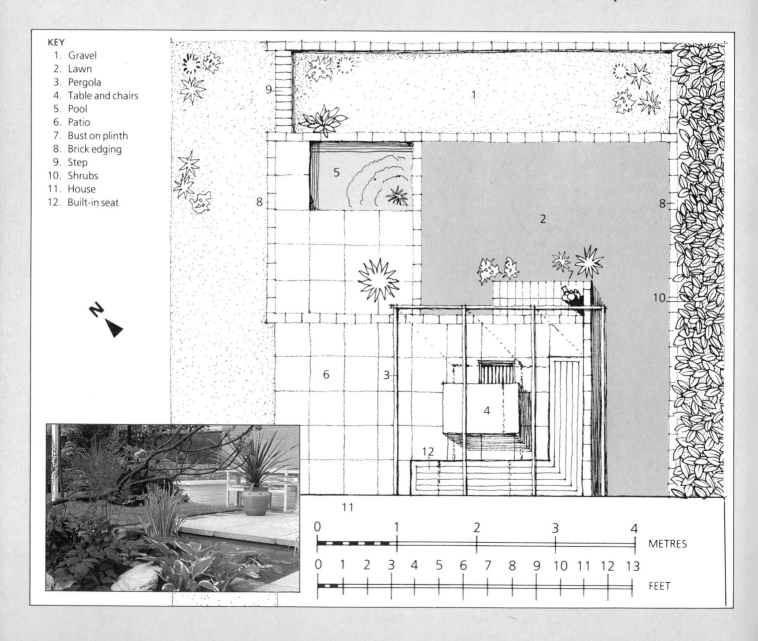

KEY
1. Gravel
2. Lawn
3. Pergola
4. Table and chairs
5. Pool
6. Patio
7. Bust on plinth
8. Brick edging
9. Step
10. Shrubs
11. House
12. Built-in seat

Sometimes town gardens are not only small but are awkward shapes too. A garden the shape of this one would be a challenge even on a larger scale, but when it is tiny the problems are yet more acute.

To make the most of this garden, the area at the side of the house has been integrated with the back by using paving that is gradually extended round the corner in irregular steps. Because the plants will soften the edges as they grow, the garden is taken round the corner with the minimum of harsh or awkward angles.

Strong ground planting also helps divert the eye from the shortcomings of the site. For this reason, evergreen shrubs, or ones that have a strong architectural shape, are needed.

Wall shrubs and climbers use vertical space when the area for horizontal planting is at a premium. They also help prevent the walls from looking oppressive. It is important to avoid a dark or claustrophobic effect, however, and the wall by the sitting-out area has been painted a pale colour

to reflect as much light as possible. The white-painted garden seat and table also help make this area brighter and more cheerful.

A patio overhead might seem to emphasize the shut-in feeling at first, but in fact it helps to link house and garden in a positive way, and the supporting poles give a much-needed vertical dimension in the centre of the garden. The beams have been painted white to match the garden furniture and to make them a more positive feature.

In such a limited space, where even a little paving plays an important role, quality slabs in a natural colour laid to an irregular or interesting pattern will help to set the right tone.

Construction A very easy do-it-yourself garden. A patio overhead is not difficult if you use joist-hangers to support the timbers. Painted scaffold poles can be used for the uprights.

Other ideas A barbecue could be substituted for one leg of the L-shaped seat.

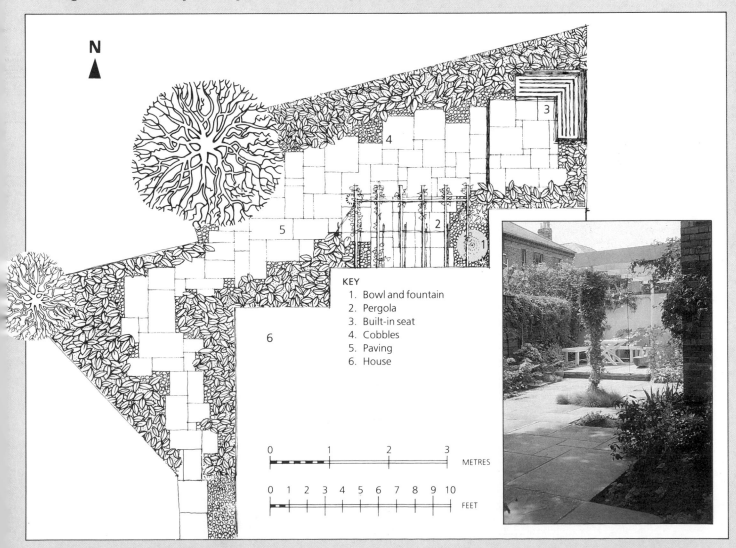

KEY
1. Bowl and fountain
2. Pergola
3. Built-in seat
4. Cobbles
5. Paving
6. House

N

0   1   2   3   METRES

0 1 2 3 4 5 6 7 8 9 10 FEET

We have included various designs for small gardens in this book, but for many people even these may seem comparatively large. Some homes with a reasonably generous area at the back may have a tiny front garden.

Because the area is tiny does not mean it has to be dull or uninteresting. There are many ways of making the most of even a minute garden.

The pictures on these two pages show some of the attractive and imaginative ways that other people have tackled the problem. They are all very different in approach, but demonstrate the point that it is worth giving even a very small garden quite a lot of thought.

Right: Where there is no wall or fence, it is a good idea to plant right up to the edge of the garden so the boundary is blurred. This is more effective than having a lawn right to the edge and a bed in the centre. Using climbing plants against the wall also helps to make the garden look larger and more interesting.

Right above: Fine grey stone chippings have been used here to provide a setting for just a few bold plants. Both phormiums (spiky leaves) and bergenias (rounded leaves) are useful evergreens to provide shape and form. A simple garden that is all the better for being uncluttered

Bold lines and black and red quarry tiles make this garden eye-catching despite its size. And because colour is provided by the tiles, and plenty of evergreen foliage plants have been used, the garden is interesting all the year round.

If a small, sloping, rectangular site sounds un-promising, this garden should dispel any doubts about the potential. The site is about 60 ft × 40 ft (20m × 10m) with a rise of over 6 ft (2m), yet the design has made a virtue of size and slope, giving the garden a sense of compactness and intimacy.

In a small area like this, built-in seats and a bar-becue not only make for a more integrated design but also save valuable space. Too much garden furniture could make the area look cluttered.

Where there are many different elements and changes of level, especially if the whole garden can be viewed at a glance, it is important not to have too many different building materials. By us-ing the same brick for all the main features, from barbecue to pool and garden building, the design looks busy without being fussy or confused.

Construction You will probably need help with the heavy jobs, such as moving and laying the natural stone slabs, and the radius brickwork is not a job to tackle without some previous experience. It may be worth hiring professional help for this.

Other ideas The lawn forms a key part of the de-sign and is conspicuous from most angles, so it has to be good. If you cannot tackle the work this involves, or if the lawn is likely to take excessive wear from a family with children, you could use gravel instead.

1. Lawn
2. Pool and bubble fountain
3. Raised bed
4. Summerhouse
5. York stone
6. Steps
7. Wall
8. Mixed planting
9. Planting at kerb level
10. Seat
11. Mowing edge
12. Tree
13. Step
14. Ground cover
15. Barbecue

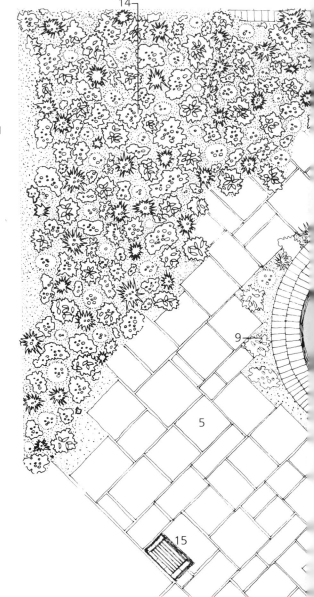

N

Plenty of curves have been used to overcome the main drawbacks of this site — a rectangular shape and sloping ground.

Below right
The pool with bubble fountain helps to focus attention within the garden.

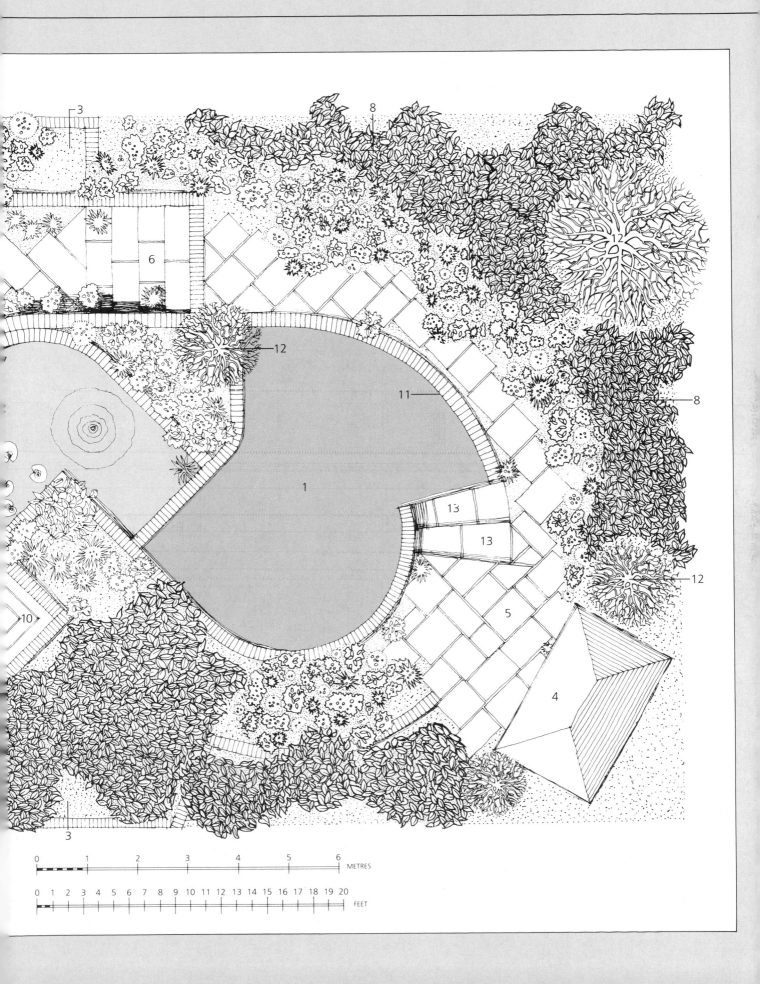

0 1 2 3 4 5 6 METRES

0 1 2 3 4 5 6 7 8 9 10 11 12 13 14 15 16 17 18 19 20 FEET

3. PLANTS

The garden plans in Section Two do not include detailed planting lists. This is because the problem of aspect and soil could make plants that are right for one garden quite inappropriate for another, apart from the fact that personal taste must inevitably play a part in any selection of plants.

What has worked in someone else's garden may not necessarily work in your own. Other gardens may have an acid soil, yours might be alkaline; other beds or walls might be in sun for much of the day, yours in shade. And the nutrient profile and other characteristics of the soil may make a plant grow to 6ft (1.8m) in their garden, while it reaches only 4ft (1.2m) in yours. Some plants may grow taller in a valley garden or in a mild district than they would in a garden on a mountainside or in a cold district.

Add to those variables the question of personal likes and dislikes, and the many thousands of plants that you *could* grow, and the magnitude of the problem is obvious.

But gardeners both old and young can benefit from suggestions and ideas and everyone can learn from the experience of others. A relative newcomer to gardening, bewildered by the huge choice of plants, would certainly be in need of some guidance.

This section of the book attempts to overcome some of these difficulties by shortlisting some good plants under *type* or *use*. If you want a climber there are suggestions on pages 92–95; if you want ground-cover plants there are suggestions on pages 98–101; plants for shade are on pages 108-109 and so on.

In each case there is a shortlist of recommended plants together with their requirements and a brief description. The Zone rating at the end of the description is the hardiness zone rating based on the hardiness map for North America produced by the Arnold Arboretum in the United States. This can be ignored by European readers, but for the benefit of anyone interested, most of the United Kingdom is equivalent to Zone 8, with some areas Zone 9. There is obviously a much wider range of zones over mainland Europe. All the plants listed should be hardy in the United Kingdom unless otherwise stated.

There are many more candidates than entries, and none of the lists included in this section can be exhaustive. But a large list can, in itself, be confusing, and there should be more than enough to choose from for all but the largest gardens.

To avoid repetition, and to allow more plants to be included within the confines of these pages, plants are only given a full entry once. Some plants that are particularly useful in more than one setting are cross-referenced to their main use.

Using the plants

This section is more than just a list of plants. It also sets out to suggest how they can be used within the garden design in association with one another. Try some of the ideas given here, but do not be afraid to experiment with mixing different plants together yourself.

Note: The following system has been used for plant names in this section of the book. Italic type has been used for Latin names with varieties in quotation marks. The common name appears in roman type and where the American name differs it is shown in parenthesis.

A dramatic contrast between a lawn and a well stocked border in full bloom.

The smaller the garden, the more important are climbers and wall shrubs. They use *vertical* space that may otherwise be wasted, and they will enhance a building whether it is a year old or built more than a century ago.

Types and uses

Self-clinging climbers such as ivy and *Parthenocissus* species need no extra support; they will cling to any surface they can get a grip on, such as a wall or tree. No form of trellis or other support should be necessary, which is as well because some of these reach a considerable height – they may even top the wall and grow over the roof of a modest house if not checked.

It is these vigorous, self-clinging climbers that tend to generate most concern about the safety of brickwork. If the mortar is old and crumbling, and the bricks are in serious need of repointing, it is possible that the roots may slightly exacerbate the existing damage. But if the brickwork and pointing are sound to start with these climbers should do no real harm.

Twining climbers, such as the Dutchman's pipe (*Aristolochia macrophylla*) and honeysuckle, need a suitable, though not necessarily elaborate, support. They can be very effective grown up 'wigwams' made of bamboo poles or against wires fixed at intervals to a wall.

Rambling climbers neither twine nor cling, but push their long branches in among other plants (or a trellis). Roses, for example, do this, and they can look very attractive growing up through other plants as well as against a wall or trellis. If trained against a wall, you will need to erect wires or other supports against which you can tie them.

Wall shrubs are sometimes difficult to define because they do not usually *need* a wall or fence for support, but can either benefit from the protection offered or will grow upright in a way that lends itself to training against a support. Some of the

Pillars are good supports for climbers such as roses if you want to create some height and colour, particularly at the back of a mixed border. Albertine is one of many roses which are suitable.

CLIMBERS AND WALL SHRUBS

Name	Description	Height	Position
Actinidia kolomikta	A 'talking point' climber. The large heart-shaped leaves open green but become splashed white and pink. Zone 5.	11 ft+ (3.4m+)	Needs a sunny wall for best variegation. Ordinary soil.
Aristolochia macrophylla (syn *A. durior*) Dutchman's pipe	Unusual saxaphone-shaped flowers, but the plant is grown mainly for its very large, heart-shaped leaves. Zone 5.	20ft+ (6m+)	Ordinary soil. Sun or partial shade. Any aspect.
Ceanothus 'Gloire de Versailles' (Delisle ceanothus)	Wall shrub with large clusters of powder-blue flowers in summer and autumn. Small, dark green leaves. Zones 7-8.	10 ft (3 m)	Full sun, good drainage. Avoid chalky soil.
Chaenomeles speciosa Flowering quince	Valuable wall shrub for early colour. Flowers usually red, pink, orange, or white. Edible fruit. Zone 6.	8 ft (2.4 m)	Ordinary soil, any aspect.
Clematis macropetala (big-petal clematis)	Semi-double, lavender-blue flowers in late spring. Silky seedheads. Zone 6.	10-13 ft (3-4 m)	Any soil, including chalky, if well drained
Clematis montana rubens (anemone clematis)	Magnificent show of pink flowers that cover the plant in late spring. *C. montana* itself is white. Zone 6.	26 ft (8 m)	Any soil, including chalky, if well drained.
Clematis tangutica (golden clematis)	Pendent, bright yellow, lantern-shaped flowers in autumn. Masses of silky seedheads. Zone 6.	13 ft (4m)	Any soil, including chalky, if well drained.
Clematis, large-flowered hybrids	Too well known to need description. By careful selection of varieties you can have them in flower most of summer. Zone 6.	6-12 ft (1.8-3.5m)	Any soil, including chalky, if well drained.
Hedera canariensis 'Gloire de Marengo' (syn 'Variegata') Canary Island ivy (Algerian ivy)	Large, olive-green leaves blotched grey and white. Not as tough as *H. colchica*; leaves may be damaged in harsh winter. Zones 7-8.	12 ft (3.5m)	Any soil, any aspect.
Hedera colchica 'Dentata Variegata' Persian ivy (colchis ivy)	A spectacular ivy in the right place. Large, bright green leaves with grey blotches and creamy-yellow margins. Zone 6.	12 ft+ (3.5m+)	Any soil, any aspect.
Hedera helix Ivy (English ivy)	Invaluable for covering ugly walls or for brightening dull ones. Many different leaf shapes and colours. Zone 6.	12 ft+ (3.5m+)	Any soil, any aspect.
Humulus lupulus 'Aureus' Hop	Not for winter cover as it is herbaceous, but a useful scrambler for summer. Soft yellow, lobed leaves. Zones 3-4.	12 ft (3.5m)	Ordinary soil, full sun.
Jasminum nudiflorum Winter jasmine	A popular winter-flowering wall shrub. Yellow flowers on naked green, late autumn to early spring. Can be untidy. Zone 6.	8 ft (2.4m)	Ordinary soil, full sun.
Jasminum officinale 'Affine' (syn *J. o.* 'Grandiflorum') Common jasmine (poet's jasmine)	A twiner with delicate-looking, divided leaves and sweetly-scented white flowers in summer. Zones 7-8.	15 ft (4.5m)	Ordinary soil, full sun.

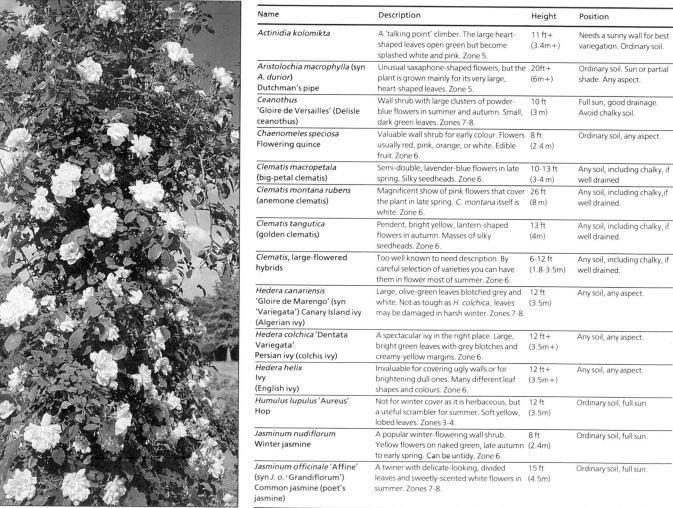

finest wall shrubs, the pyracanthas or firethorns, are tough plants that certainly do not need protection. They can also be grown as free-standing shrubs – but trained to grow upright against a wall they take on a stature and appeal far greater than if left to grow naturally. Properly pruned, pyracanthas can be persuaded to cover a garage wall, and provide a green screen from spring to autumn, a blanket of white flowers in early summer, and red or orange berries that will last from autumn until well into winter if the birds do not strip them first. (There are many varieties besides the one listed in the table below.)

Some shrubs are grown against a wall partly because they look effective there and partly because they can benefit from the additional shelter in areas where they are not dependably hardy as free-standing specimens.

Using climbers creatively

All climbers need careful positioning if they are to work properly. Rather than starting with a plant that you simply like the look of and then trying to find somewhere to plant it, start with the site and *then* select a suitable plant. There is a huge difference in the function of a large-flowered clematis and a rampant ivy, between a Russian vine (Bukhara fleece flower) *(Polygonum baldschuanicum)* and an actinidia.

Some solutions to design problems involving climbers are suggested below, but bear in mind that the rate of growth can be very variable and many climbers adapt to the height of their support. A clematis that will reach 30 ft (10m) in a tree, might sprawl happily over a 5ft (1.5m) fence; a climbing hydrangea that will eventually cover the roof of a small building or grow high into a tall tree, may take years before it begins to look out of place as a compact shrub beneath a window.

Hiding a wooden fence Timber fencing can look quite pleasing when it is still clean and new; but a year or two later you will probably want to camouflage it in some way. The most sensible

Although the quality of the variegation changes (not so good in poor light or as the season progresses), the leaves of *Actinidia kolomikta* are always interesting.

Name	Description	Height	Position
Lonicera japonica 'Aureoreticulata' Japanese honeysuckle	Semi-evergreen grown mainly for its variegated golden reticulation. Scented yellow flowers in early summer. Zone 5.	12 ft (3.5m)	Rich, moisture-retentive soil. *Roots* in shade.
Lonicera japonica 'Halliana' Japanese honeysuckle (Hall's Japanese honeysuckle)	Semi-evergreen. White flowers becoming yellow. Very fragrant. Flowers early summer; again in mid autumn. Zone 5.	12ft (3.5m)	Rich, moisture-retentive soil. *Roots* in shade.
Lonicera periclymenum Woodbine	Scented purple and yellow flowers. 'Belgica' flowers late spring and early summer. 'Serotina' from mid summer. Zone 5.	15 ft (4.5m)	Rich, moisture-retentive soil. *Roots* in shade.
Magnolia grandiflora (southern magnolia)	A magnificent evergreen wall shrub. Large, glossy green leaves and huge, creamy, goblet-like, fragrant flowers. Zones 7-8.	13 ft (4m+)	Best against sunny wall. Rich soil. Not totally hardy.
Parthenocissus henryana Chinese Virginia creeper (silver vein creeper)	Purplish leaves with silvery variegation, most conspicuously marked when grown in shade. Zone 8.	16 ft (5m)	Any soil. Colour best in shaded position.
Parthenocissus quinquefolia Virginia creeper	Dazzling autumn colour. Lobed leaves turn brilliant orange and scarlet in autumn. Zones 3-4.	25 ft (7.5m)	Any soil, any aspect.
Parthenocissus tricuspidata Boston ivy	Lobed leaves turning rich crimson and scarlet in autumn. Useful for summer cover for a large wall. Zone 5.	25 ft (7.5m)	Any soil, any aspect.
Passiflora caerulea Blue passion flower	Intriguing flowers. Creamy-white with a ring of purplish-blue, and prominent stamens. Orange, egg-shaped fruit. Zone 8.	20 ft (6m)	Sunny position against warm wall. Not fully hardy. Rich soil.
Polygonum baldschuanicum Russian vine (Bukhara fleece flower)	Good summer cover aided by rapid growth. Foaming white sprays of small flowers from mid summer to mid autumn. Zone 5.	20 ft+ (6m+)	Any soil, any aspect.
Pyracantha coccinea 'Lalandei' Firethorn	Popular evergreen wall shrub with bright orange-red berries in autumn. White flowers in early summer. Zones 6-7.	12 ft (3.5m)	Any soil. Sun or partial shade.
Rosa (climbing and rambling roses)	Roses need no introduction, and both ramblers and climbers have a role to play. Zone 6.	6-12 ft (1.8-3.5m)	Any soil, best in sun or partial shade.
Solanum crispum	A distinctive scrambling shrub with clusters of small but distinctive flowers – blue with yellow stamens. Zone 8.	15 ft (4.5m)	Needs a sunny wall and a mild district. Will tolerate chalk.
Vitis coignetiae Crimson glory vine	Huge leaves, impressive at any time but really spectacular when they turn crimson and scarlet in autumn.	30 ft (9m+)	Sun or partial shade. Any soil.
Wisteria floribunda Japanese wisteria	Long chains of fragrant, violet-blue flowers in late spring and early summer. Slow to establish. Zone 5.	13 ft+ (4m+)	Prefers moist, rich soil. Best against south or west wall.

approach is to plant plenty of shrubs so the fence becomes a mere boundary-marker and not an obtrusive feature. Sometimes, however, reasonably quick cover is needed for a length of fence.

It is not easy for plants to support themselves on a wooden fence, and you may need to provide canes or netting, at least until they reach the height of the fence. Then plants such as *Clematis montana* and *Polygonum baldschuanicum* will cascade down both sides and provide their own support as they extend along the fence. Both of these grow quickly, but for effective results in the first season the annual Japanese hop, *Humulus japonicus* will hide the fence effectively from seed sown in spring. There is a variegated variety that is particularly attractive. The hop in the table on page 92 (*Humulus lupulus* 'Aureus') is a perennial that can also be used for the same purpose—the leaves are soft yellow and very striking early in the season. Sadly, neither will provide winter cover, so they are best regarded as short-term solutions.

Plants to cover a brick or concrete wall There is plenty of scope for imaginative planting whether you want to hide a wall or draw attention to it. On the one hand there is a whole range of trained fruit trees (fans, espaliers and so on) that could be trained against the wall so that both wall and plant become a feature, and at the other extreme you could completely hide the wall with one of the evergreen ivies.

If you want to *hide* the wall, the self-clinging ivy is difficult to beat. Ivy need not be dull — there are many different leaf shapes and colours. For a small area it may be best to keep to one variety, perhaps a striking one such as the gold-splashed 'Gold Heart', but if the wall is large you could grow a collection of different varieties that would in itself make an interesting feature.

Sometimes it pays to be bold and plant and train wall shrubs such as pyracanthas, or go for something like the huge-leaved climber *Vitis coignetiae* (you will have to fix horizontal wires to the wall for support), which, in a sunny aspect, makes the most dazzling autumn display. For a shady wall, the self-clinging *Parthenocissus henryana* with its striking green, white and pink variegated leaves will be equally impressive.

Clothing the house needs careful thought. Roses look charming against an old cottage, but are less in keeping with a modern house which is, perhaps, tile-hung for the first floor. A vine such as *Parthenocissus quinquefolia* will cover a large expanse of wall wonderfully.

For a bungalow it is best to keep large-flowered clematis and similar flowers that can be provided with a trellis fixed to the wall. For a more natural effect you could use wall shrubs such as ceanothus, or semi-climbers such as *Euonymus fortunei radicans* which will break up an expanse of brickwork. Both of these are evergreen and provide year-round interest.

Roses round the door sound attractive, but you need the right kind of porch for this to work. They are most effective against the mellow brickwork of an old cottage, or against a white-painted wall.

Wall shrubs to frame the home Shrubs can be used to emphasize or enhance the structure of the house — perhaps leading the eye to the door by creating pillars of green either side, or forming an arch, or framing a window. Pyracanthas are particularly useful for this because they can easily be clipped to shape. Less widely used is the climbing hydrangea, *Hydrangea petiolaris*, which can be planted beneath a window and then climb up either side. This type of climber will need pruning to keep it in shape.

Flowering climbers for impact Although climbers are much used as 'cover-up' plants, some are worth using purely because of their floral beauty. The large-flowered clematis are always worth including, if not on a trellis against the home, then perhaps up 'wigwams' of stakes in the shrub or mixed border. Where the climate is favourable, *Solanum crispum* and the blue passion flower, *Passiflora caerulea*, are pretty and provide a conversation piece. If you are prepared to wait a year or two for an impressive display, it is always worth making room for that immensely popular queen of climbers - the wisteria.

Talking point climbers Among the plants to grow against a suitable wall, perhaps the house, are a couple of climbers that are real eye-catchers if you catch them at the right stage. *Actinidia kolomikta* is grown for its foliage, which, in a sunny position, has green heart-shaped leaves boldly splashed with white and pink — a very unusual sight. One of the evergreen magnolias, *M. grandiflora*, is a tall, but slow-growing, wall shrub that may take several years before it starts to flower. When it does bloom, however, the huge, fragrant, creamy-white cup-like flowers are stunning and the large, glossy leaves look good all the year round.

Cover-ups for eyesores Sometimes you want only camouflage from a climber. An old but useful shed that you want to retain but not see; an oil storage tank that you must have; a dead tree that you do not want to uproot – all need 'softening' if they are not to spoil the garden.

For an evergreen, one of the ivies is the best idea, but if you want a deciduous climber, then the Russian vine (Bukhara fleece flower), *Polygonum baldschuanicum*, will do the job admirably and quickly. It will also be attractive when covered with a foaming mass of small, creamy-white flowers from mid-summer to late autumn.

For deciduous, flowering climbers to cover a tree stump, roses and clematis are hard to beat.

Pergola or trellis A pergola or trellis does not have to be clothed, but it usually looks better if it is. Roses are always popular, but their thorny stems do not make them ideal for a pergola unless the proportions are generous. The various honeysuckles *(Loniceras)* are ideal because they are soft, pretty, and very fragrant. *Humulus lupulus* 'Aureus', the golden hop, can also be very successful trained over a pergola or trellis.

Left: One of the most magnificent foliage climbers is *Vitis coignetiae*. It is a wonderful sight in autumn when its leaves colour.

Below: Wisterias are surely the most splendid of the flowering climbers.

A garden will always look bare in winter without evergreens, even if there are plenty of winter-flowering plants.

Some of the shrubs in the recommended list on the opposite page are worth growing for their flowers alone, others have a shape and structure that makes them particularly valuable. Wherever possible, the position of evergreens should be decided with winter in mind. It is useful to place them so they provide pockets of interest at all times and do not become lost in winter among a mass of other plants. It is nice to be able to see them from the house, too.

Evergreen screens

Evergreen climbers are discussed on page 94, but sometimes a non-climbing screen is useful. Some of the bamboos will screen, say, a storage tank or a garage wall very effectively, and there are many bushy evergreens such as elaeagnus, griselinia, and *Viburnum tinus* that will hide a low but ugly fence or wall. For interest, though, it is best to plant a border of mixed evergreens rather than a row of plants that are all of the same species.

Evergreen hedges are discussed on page 104.

Focal point evergreens

A few plants combine year-round foliage with an interesting shape or habit. Strategically-placed, these will act as focal points in summer or winter, but will come into their own in those months when the garden lacks the 'clothed' look of summer.

Plants that fall into this category include *Fatsia japonica*, a super plant combining elegance with stature. It is an extremely tough, shade-tolerant shrub related to ivy, with attractive, ivy-like berries. A sun-loving shrub, looking rather like extra-large iris leaves, is *Phormium tenax* of which there are many beautifully variegated forms, ranging from small specimens to stately, imposing plants.

Hebe x *franciscana* 'Variegata' is a neat, compact evergreen that always looks bright and is also a good container plant.

Yucca filamentosa (Adam's needle) is another exotic-looking shrub with sword-like leaves. Very different in form, *Viburnum davidii* is also worth considering where you need a lower, more rounded, evergreen as a centrepiece; its beauty lies in its compact symmetry.

Evergreen trees

An evergreen, broad-leafed tree is lovely, if you have the room for one, and don't mind the year-round shade. For a small garden, try pruning one in a formal way. A bay tree or a variegated holly grown in a clipped tree form with a ball head as well as all forms of topiary look handsome whatever the season.

Conifers have a special role because they make good background plants. Coniferous hedges are discussed on page 103, but taller specimen trees can act as focal points in a broad expanse of lawn. The role of some of these in providing winter interest is mentioned on page 122.

Yuccas are bold in flower, but because of their distinctive shape and habit they need careful placing with other plants in a mixed or shrub border.

USEFUL EVERGREENS

Name	Description	Height	Position
Arundinaria murieliae Bamboo	A stately bamboo for a screen. Canes are bright green when young, turning yellow-green. Although large, not invasive.	6-8 ft (1.8-2.4m)	Ordinary, but ideally moist soil. Sun or shade.
Berberis darwinii Darwin's barberry	Small, dark green leaves make a neat bush at any time. In mid and late spring, a mass of orange-yellow flowers. Zones 7-8.	8 ft (2.4m)	Ordinary soil. Sun or partial shade.
Elaeagnus pungens 'Maculata' (thorny eleagnus)	One of the brightest foliage plants in winter sunshine. Green-edged leaves with central splash of yellow. Zones 7-8.	8 ft (2.4m)	Ordinary soil, tolerates chalk. Sun or partial shade.
Escallonia macrantha	An attractive combination of small, glossy foliage and pretty flowers, mainly shades of red or pink. Zone 8.	6-8 ft (1.8-2.4m)	Ordinary soil, tolerates lime. Sun, partial shade.
Euonymus fortunei (syn *E. radicans*) 'Silver Queen' (wintercreep)	Broad leaves, edged white. Will scramble up a wall, in which case it can reach 6 ft (1.8m) or more. Zone 6.	1-1½ ft (300-450mm)	Ordinary soil. Sun or partial shade.
Fatsia japonica False castor oil plant	Large, hand-like glossy green leaves. Of 'architectural' merit. White flower heads mid autumn. Needs mild district.	6 ft (1.8m)	Ordinary soil. Best in partial shade.
Griselinia littoralis (kupukatree)	Plain, apple-green leaves, but still a handsome evergreen. Neat, formal habit. Not dependably hardy in cold districts. Zone 9.	8-10 ft (2.4-3m)	Ordinary soil. Sun or shade. Not hardy in cold areas.
Hebe x franciscana 'Variegata'	A first-class shrub with neat, compact symmetrical shape. Cream margined leaves and mauve-blue flowers intermittently. Not generally grown in the United States.	2 ft (600mm)	Ordinary soil, tolerates lime. Not for cold areas.
Ilex aquifolium Holly (English holly)	Best grown in a variegated form – 'Golden Queen' for example. Plant female and male plants for berries. 'Golden Queen', a male, has no berries. Zones 6-7.	5-8 ft (1.5-2.4m)	Ordinary soil. Sun or shade.
Phormium tenax New Zealand flax (New Zealand fiber-lily)	Bold and large sword-shaped leaves. Clump-forming. Some have bronze or purplish leaves, some are variegated. Zone 9.	1-6 ft (300mm-2m)	Deep, moist soil. Full sun. Not for cold areas.
Pieris formosa	New leaves bright red at first, turning green later. Bunches of white flowers in mid and late spring. Zones 7-8.	7 ft (2.1m)	Moist, lime-free soil. Partial shade.
Rosmarinus officinalis Rosemary	Aromatic, narrow, grey-green leaves. Blue flowers along spikes in late spring. Zones 6-7.	6 ft (1.8m)	Well-drained soil. Sunny position.
Salvia officinalis Sage	Grey-green, felted leaves. 'Purpurascens' has stems and young leaves flushed purple. 'Icterina' is yellow and green. Zones 3-4.	2 ft (600mm)	Well-drained soil. Sunny position.
Senecio greyi	There is confusion over the nomenclature of the plant sold under this name*. Grey leaves, yellow flowers late summer.	4 ft (1.2m)	Ordinary soil. Sunny position.
Skimmia japonica	Glossy green leaves. Small cream flowers in late spring, followed by red berries (male and female plants are usually needed). Zones 7-8.	5 ft (1.5m)	Ordinary soil, best if lime-free. Sun or partial shade.
Viburnum davidii	A neat, symmetrical bush. Leathery, oval leaves. Berries, if formed, are a striking turquoise. Zones 7-8.	3 ft (1m)	Ordinary soil, ideally moist. Sun or shade.
Viburnum tinus Laurustinus	Invaluable for winter interest. White flowers (pink in some varieties) from late autumn to mid spring. Zones 7-8.	8 ft (2.4m)	Ordinary soil. Sun or shade.
Yucca filamentosa Adam's needle	Strap-shaped leaves forming a rosette-like clump. Spectacular spike of greenish-white bells on mature plant. Zone 5.	2½ft** (750mm)	Well-drained soil. Sunny position.

* The plant sold as *Senecio greyi* in Great Britain is sometimes *S. laxifolius* or more usually a hybrid between *S. greyi* and *S. compactus*. Increasingly sold as S. 'Sunshine'. In the United States, most plants are *S. compactus*. All are similar and attractive.

**Flower spike can add another 6 ft (1.8m).

The larger the garden, the more important the role of plants which effectively cover an area of ground and reduce the need to weed. Ground cover plants have an important place in a small garden too, of course, especially if you do not have much time for maintenance.

It is a mistake to look upon ground cover plants as second rate, lacking beauty or merit in their own right. Many are superb as isolated specimens, or grown as small groups in a border. Many gardeners grow heathers purely for their flower and foliage, and the weed-smothering effect of established plants is merely a bonus.

The early years
If ground cover plants are to be successful, they need nurturing during the first couple of years. Few worthwhile ground cover plants provide an instant effect. They need careful tending initially if weeds are not to become inextricably enmeshed and the whole effect lost.

Always start with weed-free ground (use weed-killers if necessary, see page 179), and be prepared to enrich the area with humus and a ba-lanced fertilizer to help the plants get off to a good start.

It is important to keep the ground weeded until the plants begin to meet, then the ground cover it-self will take over to keep weeds down.

A 2 in (50mm) mulch of compost, pulverized bark, or peat will suppress weeds and benefit the plants enormously, so this is well worth providing. Always apply a mulch to damp soil, and make sure the peat is moist before you use it.

Two factors affect how quickly ground cover will work: planting density and rate of growth. Close planting gives quicker cover, but increases the cost. And some plants are quicker growing than others. Your choice will depend on your taste, finances, and the area to be covered.

Once ground cover is achieved, you should have years of trouble-free growth with the minimum of maintenance apart from, perhaps, an annual cutting back where the plants are encroaching at the edge of the bed. Ultimately, though, the bed will probably benefit from a replant – dividing up the old plants and replanting the young pieces. This is not a major setback, because you will have plenty of material to replant and it will not be like starting from scratch. A few woody plants cannot be treated successfully like this, however, and you will need to propagate plants such as heathers from cuttings or layers a couple of years before you plan to replant. However, most plants can remain untouched for several years.

Types and uses
If ground cover is to be effective it is necessary to appreciate the different growth habits of the plants used, because they create a very different impression.

Clump-forming plants such as *Alchemilla mollis* and *Bergenia cordifolia* give the impression of a grouping of individual plants, until well established. They can look striking when planted as a large drift, but tend to look better as an area of ground cover in a bed or situated at the edge of a shrub border.

Mounding plants such as *Hebe pinguifolia* 'Pagei' tend to form a broad mound and will not spread in the same way as a creeping ground cover. This can make them quite expensive if you want them to cover a large area because they lack the natural ability to propagate and spread themselves and you have to take cuttings. For a small area which requires non-invasive ground cover, they can be superb.

Hebe pinguifolia 'Pagei', a low-growing grey-leaved shrub that makes an attractive ground cover.

Gaultheria procumbens, a creeping evergreen for a lime-free soil.

Acaena microphylla is a carpeting plant that is best grown in full sun and well-drained soil.

Spreading ground cover plants are by far the most common, and perhaps the best choice if you want to cover a large area easily, fairly quickly and cheaply. Examples are *Ajuga reptans* and *Lysimachia nummularia*. Generally, plants of this type can be expected to spread naturally, which will provide good cover, but they may spread further than you intended. Most of those in the list opposite are reasonably easy to control.

Ground cover for difficult sites

Ground cover is especially useful for a difficult area that is not easy to tend and cultivate — a steep slope for instance. *Hypericum calycinum* can be very effective and it has lovely yellow flowers in summer. *Cotoneaster dammeri* can be equally successful as a low-growing alternative. Its lack of height, can be compensated for by planting taller-growing shrubs nearby to provide additional interest. The shrubs should have an informal shape, like species roses, if they are to look natural among this type of ground cover.

Shade beneath trees and shrubs is particularly difficult to cope with. There are plants to clothe the ground, but they must be watered regularly until they become established. Ivy (see page 92) is useful in this situation, though one of the large-leaved variegated kinds such as *Hedera colchica* 'Dentata Variegata' will look more interesting than a plain small-leaved variety. For something more distinctive, *Pachysandra terminalis* 'Variegata' is worth considering.

GROUND COVER

Name	Description	Height	Position
Acaena microphylla New Zealand burr (redspine burr)	Forms an impenetrable, semi-evergreen carpet. Crimson burrs produced in autumn. Not a bold plant. Zone 7.	2 in (50mm)	Well-drained soil, full sun or partial shade.
Ajuga reptans Bugle	A rampant but attractive evergreen carpeter. Blue flowers in June. There are varieties with variegated foliage. Zones 3-4.	6 in (150mm)	Ordinary soil, but best if moist. Best in partial shade.
Alchemilla mollis Lady's mantle	A 'clumpy' spring-to-autumn cover, but handsome pale green leaves. Loose sprays of greenish-yellow flowers in summer. In the United States *A. vulgaris* is more popular. Zones 3-4.	1½ ft (450mm)	Moist but well-drained soil, sun or partial shade.
Bergenia cordifolia Elephant's ears (heartleaf bergenia)	Large, round, evergreen leaves. These tend to take a reddish hue in winter. Pink flowers in early spring. Zones 2-3.	1 ft (300mm)	Ordinary soil. Sun or partial shade. Tolerates lime.
Calluna vulgaris Heather	Useful evergreen. Colours mainly pinks or white. Some have gold foliage. Flowering late summer to mid autumn. Zone 5.	1-2 ft (300-600mm)	Needs acid, ideally peaty, soil. Sun or partial shade.
Cerastium tomentosum Snow-in-summer	Forms a dense, silvery-grey mat, with bold white flowers in early summer. Quick cover; can be rampant. Zones 2-3.	4 in (100mm)	Any soil, sun or partial shade.
Cornus canadensis (bunchberry)	A choice plant. Herbaceous with creeping roots. White flowers in early summer, set amid pale green leaves. Zone 2.	4-6 in (100-150mm)	Best in peaty, woodland soil. Shade or partial shade.
Cotoneaster dammeri (bearberry cotoneaster)	Evergreen carpeting shrub with small leaves that turn bronze in winter. Small white flower in spring; red berries. Zone 6.	3 in (80mm)	Ordinary soil. Sun or shade.
Epimedium pinnatum Barrenwort (Persian epimedium)	Dense, evergreen cover, but leaves can look poor by spring. Small yellow flowers in late spring. Zone 6.	1 ft (300mm)	Ordinary soil. Shade or partial shade.
Erica herbacea (syn *E. carnea*) Heath/heather (spring heather)	Invaluable for winter colour. Flowers between late autumn and mid spring. Pink, red, white. Some have coloured foliage. Zone 6.	6-12 in (150-300mm)	Best in acid soil, but can be grown if soil contains lime.
Euonymus fortunei 'Emerald 'n' Gold' (wintercreeper)	Spreading evergreen shrub. Gold and green leaves, showing pink and bronze in winter. Can be slow to establish. Zone 6.	1 ft (300mm)	Ordinary soil, sun or shade.
Gaultheria procumbens Partridge-berry (wintergreen)	Glossy evergreen leaves. Carpets from suckers. Tiny white or pink flowers mid and late summer. Red berries in the autumn. Zones 3-4.	6 in (150mm)	Needs moist, acid soil. Shade, but not under trees.
Glechoma hederacea (syn *Nepeta hederacea*) Ground ivy	Small, kidney-shaped, mid-green leaves. Lilac-blue flowers in spring and early summer. There is a variegated form. Zones 3-4. Highly invasive.	4 in (100mm)	Ordinary soil. Sun or partial shade.

Name	Description	Height	Position
Hebe pinguifolia 'Pagei'	Silvery-grey, evergreen leaves. Masses of small white flowers in late spring and early summer, often later too. Zone 9.	1 ft (300mm)	Ordinary soil. Sun or partial shade.
Hypericum calycinum Rose of Sharon (Aaron's beard)	A tough, invasive evergreen, but spectacular in flower. Large, golden cups with masses of conspicuous stamens. Zones 6-7.	1-1½ ft (300-450mm)	Ordinary soil. Tolerates chalk. Sun or shade.
Juniperus horizontalis	A prostrate, ground-hugging conifer. There are varieties in foliage colours such as grey-green and silvery-blue. Zone 2.	4 in (100mm)	Ordinary soil. Tolerates chalk. Sun or light shade.
Lamium maculatum Spotted dead-nettle	White-splashed or marbled leaves. Some have white flowers from mid spring to early summer, others pink-purple flowers. Zones 2-3.	6 in (150mm)	Ordinary, even dry, soil. Sun or shade.
Lysimachia nummularia Creeping Jenny	A tender-looking but vigorous evergreen. Yellow flowers in early and mid summer. The variety 'Aurea' has yellow leaves. Zones 3-4.	2 in (50mm)	Useful for a damp area. Sun or partial shade.
Pachysandra terminalis (Japanese spurge)	A glossy-leaved evergreen. White, rather insignificant, flowers in spring. 'Variegata' has white variegation. Zone 6.	8 in (200mm)	Ordinary soil. Shade or partial shade.
Polygonum affine (Himalayan fleece flower)	Forms a dense mat. Leaves turn russet-brown in autumn. Flower spikes pink in summer, darkening into autumn. Zones 3-4.	10 in (250mm)	Ordinary soil. Sun or partial shade.
Prunella x webbiana Self-heal	Mat-forming. Mid-green leaves and rose-purple flowers late spring and early summer. There are other shades. Zone 6.	10 in (250mm)	Ordinary or moist soil. Sun or partial shade.
Saxifraga umbrosa (S. urbium) London pride	Rosettes of dark green evergreen leaves. Sprays of pinkish flowers in late spring and early summer. Zones 7-8.	1 ft (300mm)	Ordinary soil. Sun or shade.
Stachys lanata (syn S. byzantina) Lamb's ears	White, woolly leaves resembling lamb's ears. Leaves remain through winter (though poor). Pink flowers on some. Zone 5.	1 ft (300mm)	Ordinary soil. Sunny position.
Tellima grandiflora (Alaska fringe-cup)	Clumps of hairy evergreen leaves. 'Purpurea' has bronzy purple foliage. Greenish-white flowers in early summer. Zone 5.	1½ ft (450mm)	Ordinary soil. Shade or partial shade.
Tiarella cordifolia Foam flower (Allegheny foam flower)	Semi-evergreen with heart-shaped leaves. Creamy-white feathery flower spikes in mid and late spring. Zones 3-4.	8 in (200mm)	Ordinary, ideally moist, soil. Shade.
Vinca major Greater periwinkle	Spreading evergreen. Glossy leaves, blotched creamy-white in 'Variegata'. Blue flowers mid and late spring. Zones 7-8.	1 ft (300mm)	Ordinary soil. Sun or shade.
Vinca minor Periwinkle (Trailing myrtle)	Smaller leaves and less vigorous than *V. major*, but otherwise similar. Zone 5.	6 in (150mm)	Ordinary soil. Sun or shade.

Invasive ground cover

Two of the plants in the list opposite can be rampant and invasive: *Cerastium tomentosum*, and *Hypericum calycinum*. These plants can be particularly useful if you have a large area to cover or want to plant them in a 'wild' area, but they are best avoided if you want more restrained plants.

A heather bed

Heathers are invaluable low-maintenance plants. Once established, they will suppress weeds, and the only attention they need is an annual trim with shears, usually after flowering. By choosing suitable species and varieties it is possible to have plants in bloom for most of the year, and some have gold or red-tinted foliage that will provide colour all year round.

The two most useful species are the winter-flowering *Erica herbacea* (syn *E. carnea*), and *Calluna vulgaris,* which flowers in late summer to mid autumn. But there are hundreds of varieties of these and other types of heaths and heathers, offering a wide range of choice. Some, however, need an acid soil, and few of them will tolerate a shallow chalk soil.

Because there are so many different heathers, it may be tempting to grow a mixture of varieties but a large drift of a single variety is almost always more successful visually.

Opposite page, left: Cornus canadensis is basically a ground cover for peaty or woodland soils.

Opposite page, right: For winter interest as a ground cover, many of the *Erica herbacea* are supreme. This variety is 'Springwood White'.

Far left: Although it can look tatty during the winter, *Stachys lanata* (the variety shown is 'Silver Carpet') gives an attractive grey-leaved carpeter.

Left: A rather rampant grower, *Cerastium tomentosum* is useful for providing quick cover.

Most people love to see a neatly-trimmed hedge, but few relish the prospect of hedge-cutting. Unfortunately a few widely-used, traditional hedges give the impression that all hedges are difficult to maintain, but in fact there are so many different types of hedge that it should not be difficult to find one you like, that will not involve too much maintenance. In the Table on page 104 the normal cutting frequency has been indicated and it will be seen from there that there are many hedge varieties which need clipping or pruning only once a year.

For ease of care, walls and fences certainly make the best garden boundary, but for sheer variety of form, shape, colour, and interest you cannot beat hedges. Hedges also have other uses apart from acting as boundaries; informal ones serve as features in large gardens, while dwarf ones make attractive surrounds to flower beds.

Making the framework
Hedges can define the shape of a garden and give it emphasis. As well as forming an external skeleton by marking out the boundary, 'internal' hedges are also useful to delineate areas — like the walls of a room — screening one part from the other and offering a degree of privacy. Some also help create an element of surprise by encouraging exploration, because with a tall hedge the whole garden can't be taken in at one glance.

Deciding what you want
Although hedges are sometimes grown for their beauty, usually they are also very practical.

Be clear about what you want from your hedge. Is it to be mainly decorative? A screen? A barrier to reduce roadside sound and dirt? Will it have to keep animals in or out? Is year-round cover more important than the beauty of the leaves or flowers? Do you want a neat, formal, tightly-clipped hedge, or a more informal wider hedge?

Boundary hedges
Most boundary hedges need to provide a clear

One of the most popular conifers for a tall hedge or a screen is x *Cupressocyparis leylandii*. But it is one of the fastest-growing conifers, and is not a good choice for a small garden.

barrier, but they can also be designed to blur the boundary and act as a link with the next garden or the surrounding countryside.

A hedge that borders a road ought to be evergreen, or at least retain its old dead leaves until new ones appear in spring, like beech and hornbeam. This way it will be a more efficient filter of noise and litter as well as a better windbreak.

Between properties you can often be more adventurous, and flowering hedges can sometimes be very successful. It is always worth discussing plans with your neighbour first — at any time as a matter of courtesy, but especially so with hedges grown for flower or berry because incorrect pruning can ruin the display.

It is also worth discussing the proposed *height* of any hedge between properties, because if you don't agree, a particular part of your design may not work, or could at worst lead to friction between you and your neighbour.

Poorly-considered boundary hedges can also cause other problems for you and your neighbour. Even a low hedge can take a lot of nourishment from the ground and make it difficult to grow other plants nearby. A tall hedge may cause substantial shade problems – and while it may be sunny on your side, it may well be shady on your neighbour's.

Internal hedges

Unless you have plenty of spare time, try to restrict internal hedges and partitions to those that will not need frequent clipping. Try to use informal hedges as these usually combine infrequent cutting with a good display of flowers or fruit, and the fact that most of them are deciduous will matter less *within* the garden than it would for a boundary.

Dwarf formal hedges

If you are feeling ambitious, and have a garden where the design will not look pretentious, you could use dwarf clipped hedges, such as box, to edge flower beds or to create geometric patterns on the lines of a traditional English knot garden or a French *parterre*.

Although there are few gardens in which this can really work successfully, even a small courtyard plot can be enhanced with small clipped box or yew hedges.

Coniferous hedges

Conifer hedges do not have to be dull, since they come in a variety of colours, including gold, blue-green, and grey-greens. One of the best is actually fragrant if you crush the foliage – the leaves of the *Thuja plicata* have a fruity smell.

Above: Beech *(Fagus sylvatia).*

Below: Thuja plicata grown as a hedge.

Top: Some conifers can make a neat, relatively low, clipped hedge such as this, *Thuja plicata.*

Centre: Buxus sempervirens 'Pyramidalis' is a box with an erect habit suitable for training as a hedge.

Bottom: The small-leaved *Lonicera nitida* shapes well, but needs frequent clipping.

Many conifers will make a nice hedge, or even a tall windbreak, if you allow wider spacing between the plants, and they generally make a tasteful backdrop to plants within the garden. Yew, though slow growing, is particularly beautiful.

Besides those listed on the Table below, some varieties of *Chamaecyparis lawsoniana* make an impressive tall screen or windbreak, even in an exposed position. But choose the variety carefully as some are dwarfs which are suitable for the rock garden and others become huge trees. 'Pembury Blue' is a good 'blue' variety, 'Allumii' a blue-grey, and 'Green Hedger' is a rich green.

For a really fast screen, *Cupressocyparis x leylandii* has to be considered. But it will grow tall,

so avoid it in a small garden or where it could cast too much shade.

For a neat, clipped hedge, the Western red cedar, *Thuja plicata* 'Atrovirens' is one of the best. Be careful which other varieties you use as some dwarf Thujas can take decades to reach a height of 4 ft (1.2m)!

Broad-leaved evergreens

Many broad-leaved evergreens are particularly useful for boundary hedges that adjoin a public road. The permanent covering of leaves will help to filter noise and wind, and will also provide a much more efficient visual screen than a deciduous hedge.

HEDGES

Name	Description	Height	Cuts/year
Berberis stenophylla (rosemary barberry)	Makes an informal hedge with arching sprays of yellow flowers in late spring and early summer. Evergreen. Zone 5.	7-8 ft (2.1-2.4m)	1, after flowering.
Berberis thunbergii 'Atropurpurea' (Japanese barberry)	Deciduous, but makes a fine formal hedge for summer. Small purple leaves make a bold feature. Zone 5.	4-6 ft (1.2-1.8m)	1, winter; lightly again in mid-summer for a formal hedge.
Berberis thunbergii 'Atropurpurea Nana' (Japanese barberry)	Similar to above, except for height. May be listed as 'Crimson Pygmy' in the United States. Zone 5..	1½-2 ft (450-600mm)	2, winter and mid summer.
Buxus sempervirens Box	Small-leaved evergreen, ideal for formal clipping. For a low hedge of about 1-1½ ft (450mm), choose 'Suffruticosa'. Zone 6.	3-4 ft (900-1200mm)	1, mid to late summer. Can also be trimmed in mid spring.
Carpinus betulus Hornbeam (European hornbeam)	Similar to beech. Deciduous, but dead leaves hang until spring. More suitable than beech for heavy, wet soil. Zone 6.	5-8 ft (1.5-2.4m)	1, late summer.
x *Cupressocyparis leylandii* Leyland cypress	Evergreen conifer that can grow 3 ft (1m) a year. Useful as a tall screen. Zone 6.	10-15 ft (3-4.5m)	1, late summer.
Crataegus monogyna Hawthorn	Makes a thick, dense, hedge, that can be clipped to a formal shape. Deciduous but impenetrable when established. Zone 5.	5-8 ft (1.5-2.4m)	1, summer. Can also be cut back hard in winter.
Euonymus japonicus	A good hedge for coastal areas. Medium-sized, glossy evergreen leaves. Tolerates city atmosphere and shade. Zones 7-8.	5-6 ft (1.5-1.8m)	1, spring.
Fagus sylvatica Beech (European beech)	Makes an excellent large hedge. Although deciduous, the dead leaves hang until spring. Zone 5.	5-8 ft (1.5-1.8m)	1, late summer.
Forsythia x intermedia 'Lynwood'	Spectacular when covered with yellow flowers in spring. Makes an informal hedge, perhaps behind a low edging wall. Zone 5.	4-6 ft (1.2-1.8m)	1, immediately after flowering.
Ilex aquifolium Holly (English holly)	A prickly barrier that also makes a useful hedge. For interest, plant some variegated varieties among the green. Zones 6-7.	5 ft (1.5m)	1, late summer.
Ligustrum ovalifolium 'Aureum' *Golden privet* (Californian privet)	The green version of this plant is often despised. The golden form makes a bright, semi-evergreen, formal hedge. Zone 6.	4-6 ft (1.2-1.8m)	Monthly, mid spring to late summer.
Lonicera nitida 'Fertilis' Shrubby honeysuckle (box honeysuckle)	A small-leaved evergreen for a formal hedge. Unfortunately needs frequent clipping. Zones 7-8.	2-4 ft (600-1200mm)	Monthly, mid spring to late summer.
Prunus x cistena Purple-leaf sand cherry	Rich crimson foliage, tipped bright red on young shoots. Bonus of small, white, single flowers in spring. Deciduous. Zone 2.	4-5 ft (1.2-1.5m)	1, after flowering.
Prunus laurocerasus Cherry laurel	A useful screen, with large, glossy, evergreen leaves. Needs to be pruned with secateurs to avoid unsightly leaves. Zones 6-7.	5-6 ft (1.5-1.8m)	1, mid or late summer.
Spiraea x arguta Bridal wreath (garland spiraea)	An informal flowering hedge, with arching sprays of white flowers in late spring. Not a good barrier. Zone 4.	4-5 ft (1.2-1.5m)	1, after flowering.
Taxus baccata Yew (English yew)	One of the finest formal hedges. Will grow on most soils, and tolerates chalk. Will grow in shade. Evergreen. Zone 6.	3-6 ft (900-1800mm)	1, late summer.
Thuja plicata 'Atrovirens' Western red cedar (giant arborvitae)	Conifer with bright green foliage. Bushy yet upright shape. Not all varieties of *T. plicata* are suitable. Zone 5.	5-8 ft (1.5-2.4m)	1, late summer.

Deciduous foliage hedges

Deciduous hedges have a freshness each spring that helps to compensate for the bareness of winter. If you are going to grow a deciduous foliage hedge, it is worth considering one with coloured leaves – perhaps purple – that you cannot find among the evergreens.

Flowering hedges

Most flowering hedges are decorative rather than practical barriers, and are most effectively used as an internal 'divider' within the garden, or as a boundary between adjoining properties. A dwarf flowering hedge like lavender can make a nice edging to an otherwise 'open-plan' garden.

Hedges in a coastal area

Salt-laden winds can wreak havoc with many garden plants, and if you live by the coast a hedge or shelter-belt of trees or shrubs will be the first line of defence in reducing their effect on the rest of the garden.

Many ordinary hedges will not do well in these conditions, but a few are able to tolerate the very adverse conditions. Worth considering are escallonia, *Euonymus japonicus*, *Griselinia littoralis*, and many of the hebes.

Sometimes hedging plants can be mixed effectively, but the growth rate and vigour need to be matched carefully. This holly and yew hedge is very fine, but is for the ambitious.

x *Cupressocyparis leylandii* is a fast-growing hedging plant useful for a tall screen. The variety illustrated is 'Haggerston Grey'.

This book is not specifically intended for anyone gardening in a hot, dry climate, and most of the plants mentioned are happier in, say, a typical British climate. But even in Britain and areas with similar climatic conditions, there are sites and soils that are unusually warm and dry. A sunny bank with sandy or free-draining soil can present special problems and opportunities, and for dependable results in a good summer you need to grow plants that are naturally adapted to these conditions, that will withstand drought and exposure to sun.

It is always worth watering any plant carefully until it has become established, but once plants for hot and dry sites are growing satisfactorily, they should thrive with little or no attention.

Because all the plants mentioned here will also succeed in a less hostile environment they are described in detail on other pages.

Shrubs
For flowers The buddleias are adaptable plants which will naturalize almost anywhere, even on old walls where there is very little in the way of nutrients or moisture. If cut back hard each year, they will produce lots of new growth on which the flowers appear, but old plants which are allowed to become woody will become very leggy. The brooms (*Cytisus*) are not long-lived plants, but are well worth including for their spring or early summer display even in the roughest conditions. The species are generally yellow, but *C. scoparius* hybrids contain reds and bicolours. Some are low, compact shrubs, but *C. scoparius* can become tall and leggy with age.

Hibiscus syriacus is one of the most beautiful late-flowering shrubs for a warm sunny site.

Much more impressive if you want a specimen shrub is *Hibiscus syriacus*, the tree hollyhock (rose of Sharon), which is especially useful because its flowers come out in late summer to mid-autumn. Blue, white, and pink are the usual flower colours, depending on variety.

For a reasonably large shrub that will produce a mass of flower earlier in the year, the beauty bush, *Kolkwitzia amabilis* 'Pink Cloud' is pleasing with its masses of small, foxglove-like, pink flowers in late spring and early summer.

To cover a hot, dry bank the hypericums are always a good choice as they produce vibrant yellow flowers for most of summer. Most will give good ground cover, and will even grow well on shallow chalk soils.

For foliage There are plenty of grey-leaved shrubs, such as lavenders (*Lavandula*), cotton lavender (*Santolina*), and *Senecio greyi* (or *S. laxifolius, S. compactus,* or *S.* 'Sunshine', all of which are confused in the trade). Some of the sages make superb foliage plants, *Salvia officinalis* 'Icterina' has yellow splashes on the grey-green leaves, and the stems and young foliage of 'Purpurascens' are suffused purple.

If purple-leaved shrubs appeal, *Berberis thunbergii* 'Atropurpurea' is also worth trying.

The sun or rock roses (*helianthemums*) are among the finest plants for a dry, sunny position, and there are many species and named varieties to choose from.

For striking appearance The *yuccas* are difficult to ignore, and are often particularly effective planted as a small group, where they will give the garden an exotic touch.

Herbaceous plants
There are plenty of herbaceous plants that will do well in hot, dry conditions, and a herbaceous border need not lack variety or interest.

If your whole garden is in an exposed, hot, site with dry, free-draining soil, it is best to consult a specialist book — the plants suggested here are only a small selection of possible candidates.

For flowers One of the finest early-summer flowers, the bearded iris, *Iris germanica*, will enjoy a sunny, dry position, but the spectacular display is fleeting. A whole bed of irises is particularly impressive, though, and this is a good way to fill an isolated bed.

Also spectacular as a massed display (though the beds can look bare in winter) are many of the oenotheras — the evening primrose (Ozark sun-

Above: Helianthemums are also known as sun roses, an indication of their suitability for a hot, dry site.

Below: The purple-leaved berberis are worth considering for a hot, dry site. Try contrasting them with a golden-leaved variety.

drops) – *Oenothera missouriensis* is typical but there are other good species and hybrids. Low-growing and spreading in habit, the yellow flowers appear in mid to late summer.

For contrast of colour, the blue catmint or catnip (Persian ground ivy), *Nepeta* x *faassennii,* and *N. mussinii,* produces a blue haze of flowers for most of the summer. Although it can be tricky to establish, catmint (Persian ground ivy) will make a superb edging to a border, or in combination with a plant such as the oenothera.

Sedums should be on any shortlist. There are many alpine species as well as several larger types suitable for the border. But if there is space for only one, it should be *Sedum spectabile* or its various garden forms. In early and mid autumn they stand out when most other flowers have finished, with large, flat heads in shades of pink or red. But these plants, with their large, succulent leaves and striking growth habits, are also attractive from spring until the frost sets in.

Where a large, distinctive plant is called for, the 6ft (1.8m) *Crambe cordifolia* might be suitable. It produced a cloud of small white flowers.

For foliage *Acanthus spinosus* is always eye-catching and has distinctive flowers too. As a carpeting plant *Stachys byzantina* (syn *S. lanata*), combines the beauty of its grey, woolly leaves, with a spreading, weed-suppressing habit.

Annual delights
Many of the most brilliant hardy and half-hardy annuals come from countries that are hot and dry, and they will generally flower well in a hot, sunny position. Although there is the trouble of sowing them each year, they are ideal for filling in gaps or clothing a newly created garden with colour for relatively little cost and effort.

Hardy annuals are ideal for bringing summer colour to a hot dry site.

Almost every gardener has to deal with shade. Even in an open area with no hedges, fences, walls or buildings, there will almost certainly be trees or shrubs to provide interest and shelter. In other words, if there is no shade to start with it is almost essential to provide some if you want a balanced and comfortable garden.

The idea that shade is bad news for the gardener stems from a lack of appreciation of the opportunities it offers.

A shady area is invaluable on a hot day, and the changing patterns and angles of the shadows will cast new perspectives. Shade provides a changing scene and can highlight one part of the garden and then another.

Always take shade into account when planning, and try to calculate where sunlight will fall at different times of the day. This is not only so you can choose the right plants, but also to ensure that the light patterns are used to best advantage. Maybe you want a garden ornament to be picked out in shafts of sunlight between darker areas of shadow; perhaps you want to create the impression of depth and mystery in a dark corner. Sometimes the sheer contrast between the same view in the morning and afternoon, shade and sun, may be all that you want.

In a hot climate, shade takes on a different significance. It is necessary for the comfort of both people and many plants.

Most plants will tolerate shade for part of the day, but any area that is permanently shady or receives shade for most of the day will require plants that are adapted to low light levels. Sun-lovers in

Hostas are among the most striking herbaceous foliage plants, and do well in shade. The species illustrated is *H. crispula*.

shade will become, drawn, straggly, and sickly; many will perish.

Do not expect a lot of brilliant colour in a shady area — most shade-tolerant plants have large green leaves to make the most of the available light (though there are exceptions), and flowers are often a secondary feature.

It is sensible to make your shady areas the place for a collection of interesting foliage plants. These

10 GOOD SHRUBS FOR SHADE

Name	Description	Height	Position
Aucuba japonica 'Variegata' Spotted laurel	Glossy green leaves mottled with yellow. Red berries if a male plant such as 'Crotonifolia' is nearby. Evergreen.	6-8 ft (1.8-2.4m)	Ordinary.
Camellia x *williamsii* 'Donation'	There are many excellent camellias, but this is a good all-rounder. Pink, semi-double flowers in spring.	6-8 ft (1.8-2.4m)	Acid, or ordinary soil well enriched with peat.
Choisya ternata Mexican orange flower	A plant of many merits. Evergreen, its white, fragrant flowers first appear in late spring and may continue for months.	5-6 ft (1.5-1.8m)	Ordinary. Best in partial or dappled shade.
Fatsia japonica	Large, glossy, hand-shaped evergreen leaves, on a large dominant plant. White ball-like flower heads in mid autumn.	6-8 ft (1.8-2.4m)	Ordinary. Avoid dense shade.
Garrya elliptica	Long, grey-white tassels (catkins) in February. The catkins are longest on male plants. Evergreen.	6-8 ft (1.8-2.4m)	Ordinary.
Mahonia aquifolium Oregon grape	Glossy evergreen leaves, which often take on red and purple tints in winter. Bright yellow flowers early/mid spring.	4 ft (1.2m)	Ordinary.
Osmanthus delavayi	Evergreen with small glossy, dark green leaves that set off fragrant white flowers in mid spring.	8-9 ft (2.4-2.7m)	Ordinary.
Prunus laurocerasus 'Otto Luyken' Cherry laurel	This is a dwarf variety of a popular evergreen. White flower spikes appear in mid spring. Large, glossy leaves.	3 ft (900mm)	Ordinary.
Rhododendron	There are hundreds of varieties, most with large, handsome flowers and glossy evergreen leaves. Most flower in spring.	3-10 ft (1-3m)	Acid or peaty.
Sarcococca humilis Christmas box	Small, narrow, evergreen leaves and rather insignificant creamy-white flowers in January — but fragrant.	1½ ft (450mm)	Ordinary.

will create a feeling of lushness that is often lacking in a sunnier position.

Matching plant to place

Quite apart from soil differences, there are two main types of shady environment – damp shade and dry shade. Damp shade offers much more scope for planting than a dry area. A plant beneath the dense overhead canopy of, say, a beech tree, or in the shady area between two buildings close enough to keep off most of the driving rain, has to contend with drought conditions as well as shade, so it has to be a very tough plant indeed.

A dry area beneath trees and shrubs is generally moist enough in spring, but dries out as the season progresses. Incorporating plenty of compost or other humus-forming material at planting time, and mulching while the ground is still moist, will help, as will watering.

Besides the plants described in detail elsewhere in the book (cross-references are shown in the box), there are a few other shade plants that are worth seeking out.

For moist shade

If you have a garden on the grand scale, one of the most imposing plants is *Gunnera manicata*, but as a single leaf of this giant rhubarb can be over 10ft (3m), it is not a plant for the small garden. Nor is it a plant for a cold climate. Much more modest in size, but with many of the same qualities, is *Rodgersia pinnata* 'Superba'.

Another fine foliage plant that associates well with water is *Peltiphyllum peltatum*. It has starry pink flowers in spring before the umbrella-like leaves appear.

The skunk cabbage (*Lysicitum americanum*) sounds unattractive, but is actually rather unusual, and the yellow, arum-shaped flowers appear in spring, followed by huge leaves. It is a bog plant and should only be considered for wet soil, but if you have a woodland stream it will create bold pockets of interest.

Most of the species mentioned so far are really waterside plants, but there are many others which make a good display in any shade with reasonable moisture at the roots. The astilbes are an example; their feathery plumes are superb when planted in bold drifts, and there are many varieties, mainly in shades of pink or red. The huge, buttercup flowers of trollius always make a bold splash of colour in spring, and there are several good varieties in shades of yellow and orange.

Ferns are sometimes overlooked, but they can create a restful feeling. There is a surprising variety of shapes and sizes, and they are interesting from the moment their fronds begin to unfurl.

For dry shade

Besides the plants listed below, it is worth considering lily-of-the-valley (*Convallaria majalis*), the male fern (*Dryopteris filix-mas*), *Euphorbia wulfenii*, Solomon's seal (*Polygonatum* x *hybridum*), and the butcher's broom (*Ruscus aculeatus*).

Ground cover in shade

For a large area of shade, the simplest solution may be to plant suitable ground cover. Carpeting plants that will do well in shade include epimediums, *Pachysandra terminalis* ('Variegata' looks particularly attractive), and ivies.

10 GOOD HERBACEOUS PERENNIALS FOR SHADE

Name	Description	Height	Position
Anemone x *hybrida* (also sold as *A. japonica*)	Flat open flowers, usually pink or white, especially valuable because they appear from late summer to mid autumn.	3 ft (900mm)	Ordinary soil; will tolerate full shade as well as dappled.
Dicentra spectabilis Bleeding heart	Feathery foliage, topped with arching sprays of pink, heart-shaped flowers in late spring and early summer.	2 ft (600mm)	Ordinary soil; best in only light or partial shade.
Euphorbia robbiae	Evergreen with upright stems and greenish-yellow flowers in mid and late spring.	2 ft (600mm)	Ordinary soil; will tolerate dry ground beneath trees.
Helleborus orientalis Lenten rose	An important plant for flowering in late winter and early spring. *H. niger*, similar but usually white, flowers earlier.	2 ft (600mm)	Ordinary soil; will grow beneath deciduous trees.
Hosta spp. Plantain lily	Although most flower in summer, hostas are grown for their handsome leaves (but they will need protecting from slugs).	2-3 ft (600-900mm)	Ordinary soil, but best in a moist position.
Omphalodes cappadocica	Intense blue, forget-me-not-like flowers in spring. Compact plants that are much more controllable than myosotis.	9 in (230mm)	Ordinary soil, but not too dry.
Polygonatum x *hybridum* (may be listed as *P. multiflorum*) Solomon's seal	A graceful plant in early summer when the long, arching stems are clothed with nodding white bells.	3 ft (900mm)	Ordinary soil.
Primula polyantha Polyanthus	Although there are many excellent primulas suitable for shade, the polyanthus is easy to grow and obtain.	9 in (230mm)	Ordinary soil.
Pulmonaria officinalis Lungwort	White-spotted leaves are attractive all summer; flowers tend to change from pink to blue and appear in mid and late spring.	1 ft (300mm)	Ordinary soil, but best in a moist position.
Rodgersia pinnata 'Superba'	A striking foliage plant with bronzy-purple 'fingered' leaves. Pink flower plumes in mid to late summer.	3 ft (900mm)	Ordinary soil, but best in a moist position.

Other plants to try
There are many other plants that could be used for a shady position. Some of them are included in other sections of the book:
Herbaceous perennials
Ajuga reptans (page 100)
Alchemilla mollis, or *A. vulgaris* (page 100)
Bergenia cordifolia (page 100)
Epimedium pinnatum (page 100)
Hemerocallis (page 117)
Lamium maculatum (page 101)
Tiarella cordifolia (page 101)

Shrubs
Euonymus fortunei radicans (page 97)
Hypericum calycinum (page 101)
Ilex aquifolium (page 97)
Pachysandra terminalis (page 101)
Skimmia japonica (page 97)
Viburnum davidii (page 97)
Vinca (page 101)

Nothing creates a feeling of maturity in a garden as successfully as plants growing among paving stones or in a stone wall. Even one season's growth can soften the raw appearance of a newly constructed crazy-paving path or a stone or pre-cast imitation stone wall.

It is always worth deciding at the outset whether plants are to be included among the stones, because it is much easier to incorporate planting pockets during construction.

Paths

Idyllic though plants in paving sound, they are not without problems. If there is exposed soil for the plants you choose, there is also, of course, a site for weeds to grow. And while normally you can use a weedkiller to keep paths looking well-maintained, in this case they will kill the desirable plants too. If you do decide to have plants, the weeds will have to be sprayed very selectively or pulled out by hand. Most effective is to remove all trace of weeds before constructing the path.

Avoid too many different plants in paving. A mass of a single type is often much more impressive than a collection of lots of different plants. Do not overplant either — there must be plenty of space to walk, and wherever possible keep the planting pockets towards the sides unless the path is wide and the slabs large.

Don't grow plants more than 6 in (150mm) high in paved areas for their sake as well as yours. In fact, the majority of plants in a paved area should be no more than an inch or two (25-50mm) high. Paved surfaces are especially suitable for growing plants with aromatic leaves, such as thyme. The aroma is released whenever you walk on the plants, and is intensified by the heat retained in the paving materials.

Walls

A retaining wall, particularly an old, stone one, is an obvious candidate for growing alpines and other suitable plants.

Raised beds with a planting area on the top and on both sides will provide plenty of scope for a wide range of plants, but it may look too contrived. Although very successful where you set out specifically to grow alpines in raised beds, this type of feature does not always integrate well with the rest of the garden.

Raised beds in a formal setting are generally left with the crisp outline of the building material, although plants cascading down from the top will almost always improve the appearance.

Brick boundary walls cannot be planted up, but if you do have stone walls, or live in a rural area where it is sensible to build one, then do plant in the crevices.

Sempervivums will grow in seemingly impossible places, even on an old roof if given the chance.

PLANTS FOR WALLS AND PAVING

Name	Description	Height	Position
Acaena microphylla (P/W) New Zealand burr (redspine sheepburr)	Mat-forming semi-evergreen; bronze foliage and crimson flowers. Burrs may stick to socks or stockings. Zone 7.	2 in (50mm)	Ordinary soil, sunny position.
Aethionema 'Warley Rose' (W) (Persian stonecress)	Low, bushy growth, glaucous foliage. Topped with deep rose flowers in mid and late spring. Zones 6-7.	6 in (150mm)	Ordinary soil, sunny position.
Alyssum saxatile (W) Gold dust (Basket of gold)	Greyish foliage. A mass of bright yellow flowers mid spring to early summer. Shade of yellow depends on variety. Zones 3-4.	6 in (150mm)	Ordinary soil, sunny position.
Arabis caucasica 'Rosabella' (W) Rock cress	Green hummocks covered with pink flowers in mid and late spring. There are also white-flowered and variegated forms. Zones 3-7 depending on species.	6 in (150mm)	Ordinary soil, sunny position.
Armeria maritima (P/W) Thrift	Neat, grass-like tufts of foliage, with white, pink, sometimes red, pompom flower heads in summer. A 'tidy' plant for paving. Zones 3-4.	6 in (150mm)	Ordinary soil, sunny position. Good coastal plant.
Aubrieta deltoidea (W) Purple rock cress	Spreading plant producing large sheets of colour in mid and late spring. Colours are mainly shades of blue and purple. Zone 5.	6 in (150mm)	Ordinary soil. Good on chalk. Sunny position.
Campanula garganica (P/W) (Adriatic bellflower)	Compact tufts of mid green leaves. A profusion of open-petalled, pale blue flowers from late spring to the end of summer. Zones 6-7.	3 in (75mm)	Ordinary soil, tolerates chalk. Sun/partial shade.
Campanula portenschlagiana (P/W) (Dalmatian bellflower)	Mid green, heart-shaped leaves, deep blue, bell-shaped flowers all summer and into autumn. Can be invasive. Zone 5.	3 in (75mm)	Ordinary soil, tolerates chalk. Sun/partial shade.
Corydalis lutea (W) Yellow corydalis	Feathery leaves and yellow flowers from mid spring to autumn. Self-sows and surplus seedlings may need weeding out. Zone 6.	6-8 in (150-200mm)	Ordinary soil. Sun or shade.
Dianthus deltoides (P/W) Maiden pink	Spreading tufts of narrow foliage topped by red, pink, or white flowers from early summer to autumn. Zones 2-3.	6 in (150mm)	Ordinary soil, tolerates chalk. Sunny position.

Name	Description	Height	Position
Erinus alpinus (P/W) (alpine liverbalsam)	Sprays of pink or white flowers over mounds of deeply toothed, mid green leaves. There is also a carmine variety. Zone 5.	4 in (100mm)	Ordinary soil, sunny position.
Iberis sempervirens (P) Evergreen candytuft	Compact evergreen shrublet. Forms an evergreen mat that is covered with white flowers from late spring to mid summer. Zones 3-4.	6-9 in (150-230mm)	Ordinary soil, sunny position.
Polygonum affine (W) (Himalayan fleece flower)	Green, lance-shaped leaves, above which small but striking pink 'pokers' flower all summer. Foliage turns reddish in autumn. Zones 3-4.	10 in (250mm)	Ordinary soil, sun or partial shade.
Raoulia australis (syn *R. hookeri*) (P) (silver mat raoulia)	Makes a silvery-grey mat. Flowers so tiny they will probably not be noticed. Will creep over paving, but avoid treading on the plant. Zone 8.	¼ in (6mm)	Ordinary soil, but well drained. Sunny position.
Saponaria ocymoides (W) Rock soapwort	A gay, bright trailer with bright pink flowers from late spring and early summer. An invaluable wall plant. Zone 2.	6 in (150mm)	Ordinary soil, sun or partial shade.
Saxifraga (mossy types) (P)	Moss-like hummocks covered with bright flowers in mid and late spring. Hybrids such as 'Peter Pan' are best for this use. Zone depends on species.	4-6 in (100-150mm)	Ordinary soil, tolerates chalk. Sun or shade.
Sedum (various) (P/W) Stonecrops	There are many suitable species (see text) with interesting, usually fleshy, leaves. Some also have attractive flowers. Zone depends on species.	2-6 in (50-150mm)	Ordinary, even dry, soil. Sun or partial shade.
Sempervivum spp (W) Houseleeks	Interestingly-shaped rosettes forming clusters, often tinged pink or red. Flowers usually pink, summer. Many types. Zone 6.	4-6 in (100-150mm)	Ordinary, even dry, soil. Sun or partial shade.
Thymus serpyllum (syn *T. drucei*) (P/W) Thyme (mother-of-thyme)	Creeping plant with aromatic leaves when crushed. Flowers usually pink or red, from early to late summer. Zones 3-4.	1-2 in (25-50mm)	Well-drained soil, tolerates chalk. Sun or partial shade.

KEY   P = Suitable for planting in paving   W = Suitable for planting in crevices in walls

Above left: Iberis sempervirens, a slowly spreading dwarf evergreen shrub that makes a dazzling splash of white in spring.

Above right: Acaena microphylla has lovely, spiky flowers.

Above: One of the 'musts' for a wall – *Alyssum saxatile.* It needs trimming back after flowering to prevent it becoming straggly, but is always eyecatching in spring.

Planting in a wall
Wherever possible, plant as you construct the wall as this way it is much easier to spread out the roots. If you are mortaring the joints, leave small areas free for planting.

It is always difficult to water a vertical surface, so if you plant after the wall has been constructed always try to do so during wet weather, and choose small plants that will be relatively easy to insert into small pockets of soil in the crevices.

Starting from seed is often easier. Roll two or three into a ball of soil, and press them well down into a suitable hole.

A garden without trees can be like a meal without salt – there will be an ingredient lacking that brings out the best in the other features, as well as contributing its own flavour. Large gardens usually present no problems; suitable positions and trees suggest themselves easily. It is with smaller gardens that choosing trees becomes difficult.

Some of the trees in the Table below will eventually be too large for a very small garden. Be guided by the estimated height (after about 15 years), but use these figures with caution. Much depends on the particular specimen, the soil and the environment. Two identical specimens planted in different gardens can show a huge variation in height after a few years.

If you only have space for one or two trees, give priority to 'multi-merit' ones: those with perhaps spring or summer flowers, attractive summer outline or foliage, and maybe autumn colour or attractive fruit. Do not overlook the importance of providing for winter interest, perhaps in the tracery of branches or attractive bark.

Conifers should be used with caution. Some will make fine specimen plants set in a lawn, or grouped together as a background. But they are much less successful when used individually and dotted around the garden or planted at the back of a border.

Position

Large trees should be kept a reasonable distance from buildings, although none of those listed in the Tables is likely to cause major problems to

Below: One of the most beautiful flowering trees, *Malus floribunda*, which flowers prolifically from an early age.

Bottom: This is one of the columnar conifers, *Chamaecyparis lawsoniana* 'Columnaris'. It makes an impressive focal point.

SMALL GARDEN TREES

Name	Description	Height	Position
Acer griseum Paperbark maple	A neat tree with dark green leaves that show good autumn colour, but main attraction is orange-brown peeling bark. Zone 6.	16 ft+ (5m+)	Ordinary soil. Sunny position.
Acer negundo 'Variegatum' Box elder	Palmate leaves strikingly variegated. Edges irregularly margined silvery-white. A very pretty tree. Zone 2.	20 ft+ (6m+)	Ordinary soil. Sunny position.
Amelanchier lamarckii Snowy mespilus (shadblow)	A foaming mass of white flowers in mid spring before the leaves have fully developed. *A. canadensis* is similar. Autumn colour. Zone 5.	20 ft+ (6m+)	Well-drained soil. Avoid chalk. Sunny position.
Betula pendula 'Youngii' Young's weeping birch	A dome-shaped weeping tree with branches cascading almost to the ground. Small leaves, yellowing in autumn. Zone 2.	10 ft+ (3m+)	Ordinary soil. Sunny position.
Catalpa bignonioides 'Aurea' (Southern catalpa)	A magnificent, large-leaved tree for a site that is not too exposed. Foxglove-like flowers and golden leaves. Zone 5.	16 ft+ (5m+)	Fertile soil. Sheltered, sunny position.
Cornus kousa (Japanese dogwood)	A profusion of flowers with conspicuous white bracts in early summer. Branches have attractive tiered appearance. Zone 6.	7 ft (2.1m)	Ordinary soil. Sunny position.
Corylus avellana 'Contorta' Harry Lauder's walking stick	Curiously twisted and contorted branches, providing interest even in winter. Catkins produced in late winter. Zones 3-4.	7 ft (2.1m)	Ordinary soil. Sunny position.
Crataegus oxyacantha (syn C. laevigata) 'Paul's Scarlet' Hawthorn	Small, double, red flowers produced in plenty in late spring and early summer. Crimson berries. Possibly as 'Paulii' in the United States. Zone 5.	8 ft (2.5m)	Ordinary soil. Sunny position.
Gleditsia triacanthos 'Sunburst' Honey locust	The pinnate leaves give this tree a feathery gracefulness, enhanced when the young leaves are bright yellow. Zone 5.	25 ft (7.5m)	Ordinary soil. Sunny position.
Laburnum x watereri 'Vossii' Golden chain tree	Cascading yellow tassels in early summer. Seeds poisonous, but few produced by this variety. Zone 6.	16 ft (5m)	Ordinary soil. Sunny position.
Malus floribunda Flowering crab	A mass of delicate pink flowers, fading to white, in mid spring. Small, cherry-like fruits follow. Zone 5.	16 ft (5m)	Fertile soil. Sunny position.
Malus 'Golden Hornet'	White flowers in mid-spring, later followed by clusters of yellow fruits that persist for months. Zone 6.	16 ft (5m)	Ordinary soil. Sunny position.
Prunus 'Amanogawa' Flowering cherry (Oriental cherry)	A narrow, upright tree covered with clusters of single or semi-double shell-pink flowers in mid and late spring. Zone 5.	16 ft (5m)	Ordinary soil. Sunny position.
Prunus 'Kanzan' Flowering cherry (Oriental cherry)	A distinctive flowering tree, which is smothered with double pink flowers in mid and late spring. Zone 6	13 ft (4m)	Ordinary soil. Sunny position.
Pyrus salicifolia 'Pendula' Weeping willow-leafed pear	A grey-leaved, weeping tree that makes a silvery mound of foliage. White flowers in mid spring. Zone 5.	20 ft (6m)	Ordinary soil. Sunny position.
Robinia pseudoacacia 'Frisia' Black locust	A tree that really stands out. Feathery, divided, golden yellow foliage is striking all summer. Zones 3-4.	16 ft (5m)	Fertile soil. Sunny position.

building foundations or drains. Poplars and willows, on the other hand, are notorious for their highly invasive and powerful roots, particularly when grown on clay soil.

An isolated, mature tree in a large garden can look magnificent, but a solitary specimen in a small garden is likely to be awkward looking. If there is room for only one, try to choose a 'bushy', perhaps multi-stemmed tree, such as the catalpa (though this needs a favourable climate), or the amelanchier which can be grown as a tree or shrub. Or choose one with spreading branches such as *Cornus kousa*. Generally, though, you will achieve a far more pleasing effect if you can group a few trees reasonably close together – provided that you can do this while leaving them with the room to grow and develop naturally.

Acer griseum is one of the more expensive trees to buy, and is not a particularly fast grower. But has a very attractive peeling bark, and makes an attractive shape and can provide lovely autumn leaf colour.

USEFUL CONIFERS

Name	Description	Height*	Position
Chamaecyparis lawsoniana 'Allumii' Lawson cypress	Soft, blue-grey foliage in large, flattened sprays. Spire-like habit. Combines nice shape and colour. Zone 6.	10 ft+ (3m+)	Ordinary soil. Sunny position.
Chamaecyparis lawsoniana 'Columnaris' Lawson cypress	A narrow, conical tree with densely-packed flattened sprays. 'Columnaris Glauca' has glaucous green-blue foliage. Zone 6.	11 ft+ (3.5m+)	Ordinary soil. Sunny position.
Chamaecyparis lawsoniana 'Lane' (syn 'Lanei') Lawson cypress	A columnar tree with feathery sprays of golden-yellow foliage. Seen best in combination with other colours. Zone 6.	7 ft+ (2.1m+)	Ordinary soil. Sunny position.
Cryptomeria japonica 'Elegans' Japanese cedar (plume cryptomeria)	Bushy habit for a conifer. Feathery foliage, browny-green in summer becoming red-bronze in autumn and winter. Zone 6.	10 ft+ (3m+)	Ordinary, ideally moist, soil. Sunny position.
Cupressus macrocarpa 'Goldcrest' Monterey cypress	Narrow, conical outline. Bright yellow feathery foliage throughout the year. Shows up well in winter. In US 'Golden Pillar' is an alternative. Zones 7-8.	10 ft+ (3m+)	Ordinary soil, tolerates chalk. Sunny position.
Ginkgo biloba Maidenhair tree	Fan-shaped leaves unlike those of normal conifers. Deciduous, the leaves turning an attractive yellow before they fall. Zone 5.	10 ft+ (3m+)	Ordinary soil. Sunny position.
Juniperus virginiana 'Skyrocket' (Eastern red cedar)	A very distinctive conifer, with a thin, pencil-shaped outline. Blue-grey foliage. Zone 2.	7 ft+ (2.1m+)	Ordinary soil, tolerates chalk. Sunny position.
Picea breweriana Brewer's spruce	A beautiful weeping tree. Broadly conical with spreading branches from which long, slender branchlets cascade. Zone 6.	10 ft+ (3m+)	Fertile, not alkaline, soil. Sunny position.
Picea pungens 'Koster' Colorado Spruce	Intense silvery-blue foliage. Narrowly conical with stiff, prickly needles. Cones not produced on young trees. Zone 2.	8 ft+ (2.4m+)	Fertile, not alkaline, soil. Sunny position.
Taxus baccata 'Fastigiata' Irish yew	An upright, columnar tree with deep green foliage. 'Fastigiata Aureomarginata' has leaves edged yellow. Zones 6-7.	8 ft+ (2.4m+)	Ordinary soil, including chalk. Sun or shade.

* Height is likely height after 10 years. Some will eventually grow much taller. Tree heights are greatly influenced by soil, site, and climate.

Far left: Laburnums are uninteresting out of flower, but are so spectacular in late spring that they are worth planting.

Too many green conifers can look dull. Introduce a few with golden foliage for contrast, such as *Cupressus macrocarpa* 'Gold Crest'. Although it tolerates sea winds well, this tree really does best in a mild area or a sheltered position.

A mature rock garden but something to aim for.

The choice of rock garden plants is huge, and the fact that most are small means you can plant a relatively large collection in a small area. The 20 selected plants listed in the Table below, and the other plants mentioned elsewhere in the book that can also be planted in a rock garden, are only a cross-section of the many desirable plants that are widely available. The Box below lists some of the plants described on other pages that are also suitable.

There are three particularly important groups of alpines that have so many good species that no attempt has been made to single out a particular one – primulas, saxifrages, and sedums. But a word of warning about *Sedum acre* – delightful though it is in flower, it will not confine itself to the rockery but will rapidly attempt to take over the garden. In this way it can become an annoying and highly invasive weed.

Arranging the plants

A large rock garden is relatively easy to plant. Upright-growing plants are best planted in small groups in large planting pockets to create bold patches; rock-hugging plants such as raoulia can be allowed to scramble or cascade down a rock face; and the rosette and tufted type of plants are best accommodated in rock pockets where they will be protected from the more invasive types of plants. In a small rockery, though, the rocks and

---

Plants on other pages

The plants in the Table on these pages are only a handful of the plants worth trying to grow in a rock garden. Among other suitable plants are:

Acaena microphylla (page 110)
Aethionema 'Warley Rose' (page 110)
Ajuga reptans (page 100)
Alyssum saxatile (page 110)
Arabis caucasica (page 110)
Armeria maritima (page 110)
Aubrieta deltoides (page 110)
Calluna vulgaris (page 100)
Campanula garganica (page 110)
Cerastium tomentosum (page 100)
Dianthus deltoides (page 110)
Erica herbacea (syn *E. carnea*) (page 100)
Erinus alpinus (page 111)
Iberis sempervirens (page 111)
Polygonum affine (page 101)
Raoulia australis (page 111)
Saponaria ocymoides (page 111)
Sempervivums (page 111)
Thymus serpyllum (syn *T. drucei*) (page 111)

ROCK GARDEN PLANTS

Name	Description	Height	Position
Achillea 'King Edward' Yarrow	Grey leaves, and pretty, flattish heads of primrose-yellow flowers during summer. Zone 6.	4 in (100mm)	Ordinary soil. Sunny position.
Androsace sarmentosa (syn *A. primuloides*)	Woolly rosettes that tend to form mats. Dome-shaped heads of rose-pink flowers from mid spring to early summer. Zones 2-3.	4 in (100mm)	Well-drained soil. Sunny position.
Campanula carpatica Carpathian bellflower	Large, open, outward-pointing, bell-shaped flowers throughout summer. Both blue and white varieties are available. Zones 3-4.	6 in (150mm)	Ordinary soil. Sun or partial shade.
Cheiranthus alpinus 'Moonlight'	May be listed as *Erysimum alpinum* 'Moonlight'. Primrose-yellow heads from mid spring to early summer.	6 in (150mm)	Ordinary soil, well drained. Sunny position.
Cotyledon simplicifolia (syn *Chiastophyllum oppositifolium*)	Rosettes of serrated, succulent leaves. Arching sprays of yellow flowers in early and mid summer.	6 in (150mm)	Ordinary soil. Sun or partial shade.
Dryas octopetala (Mt Washington dryad)	A mat-forming plant with white, saucer-shaped flowers in early and mid summer. Interesting fluffy seed heads in autumn. Zone 2.	3 in (80mm)	Well-drained soil. Sunny position.
Erodium chamaedryoides 'Roseum' (alpine geranium)	Neat plant with intense pink flowers that nestle above a compact mound of green leaves during summer. Zones 7-8.	2 in (50mm)	Ordinary soil. Tolerates chalk. Sunny position.
Gentiana acaulis Trumpet gentian (stemless gentian)	A mat-forming gentian with large, deep blue, upward-facing trumpets in late spring and early summer. Zones 3-4.	3 in (80mm)	Rich, leafy or peaty soil. Sunny position.
Gentiana sino-ornata Autumn gentian (Chinese gentian)	Clumps of narrow, mid green leaves, that come to life in autumn with cheerful, bright blue trumpet flowers. Zones 6-7.	6 in (150mm)	Leafy or peaty, acid soil. Sun or partial shade.
Geranium subcaulescens (syn *G. cinereum subcaulescens*)	Bright, crimson-magenta flowers with a dark eye, all summer. A neat and attractive plant. Zones 7-8.	5 in (130mm)	Ordinary soil. Sun or partial shade.

the pockets in between are generally smaller, and in a comparatively short time the plants will probably merge into a tangled, untidy mass.

The smaller the rock bed, the more carefully the plants should be selected and positioned.

There are no firm rules about the types of plants to include. If what you want is a bright, bold display, conspicuous from a distance, in spring and early summer, then plants such as *Alyssum saxatile*, *aubrieta*, *campanulas*, and *Cerastium tomentosum* are hard to beat. But these plants are best avoided if your interest lies more in the individual beauty of true alpines. A true alpine enthusiast would plant for individual pockets of interest, rather than overall impact within the garden. It has to be a matter of personal preference.

One of the criticisms often levelled against rock gardens is the predominance of spring-flowering plants. To avoid the rock garden becoming featureless later in the year, try to include some late-flowering species, and use dwarf evergreen shrubs and dwarf conifers so that there is always something of interest, even in winter.

Hardy annuals, sown in spring where they are to flower, can help to ensure pockets of colour throughout the summer. There are many suitable dwarf plants, but for a start consider plants such as *Alyssum maritimum* (syn *Lobularia maritima*), dwarf candytufts, *Ionopsidium acaule* and *Phacelia campanularia*.

Sedums are invaluable rock plants – this is *S.* 'Ruby Glow'.

Name	Description	Height	Position
Gypsophila repens (creeping gypsophila)	Trailing habit. Masses of tiny white to pink flowers during summer. Linear, grey-green leaves. Zones 3-4.	4 in (100mm)	Well-drained soil. Sunny position.
Hypericum polyphyllum 'Grandiflorum'	Low, shrubby mound of green, covered with conspicuous yellow flowers from mid summer to early autumn. Zones 6-7.	6 in (150mm)	Well-drained soil. Sunny position.
Lithospermum diffusum (syn *Lithodora diffusa*) 'Heavenly Blue'	Long-lasting, gentian-blue flowers from late spring to end of summer. Spreading, prostrate stems. Zone 7.	4 in (100mm)	Light soil, not alkaline. Sunny position.
Polygonum vacciniifolium (rose carpet knotweed)	A spreading evergreen. Erect, rose-red, 'poker' spikes late summer to mid autumn. Can be rampant. Zones 7-8.	6 in (150mm)	Ordinary soil. Sun or partial shade.
Primula spp	There are many primula species suitable for the rock garden, mostly flowering late spring to early autumn. Zone rating depends on species.	Various	Depends on species. Ordinary soil for most; moist for some.
Saxifraga spp Saxifrage	Too many good species to list. Most are excellent rock garden plants. Most flower in spring. Zone rating depends on species.	Various	Ordinary but well-drained soil, alkaline for most.
Sedum spp Stonecrops	Again, many excellent plants (see text). Particularly useful because most flower in summer (later than most rock plants). Zone rating depends on species.	Various	Ordinary, even dry, soil. Sunny position or partial shade.
Silene schafta (Schafta campion)	Low tufts of green leaves with magenta-pink flowers over a long period during summer. Zone 5.	5 in (130mm)	Ordinary soil. Sun or partial shade.
Thymus citriodorus 'Silver Queen' Lemon-scented thyme	Tiny, but pretty, variegated, evergreen leaves. A mass of delicate, pale pink flower heads in late spring/early summer. Zone 5.	8 in (200mm)	Ordinary, well-drained soil. Sunny position.
Veronica prostrata Harebell speedwell	Mat-forming, trailing habit. A carpet of deep blue flowers from late spring to mid summer. Zone 6.	6 in (150mm)	Ordinary, well-drained soil. Sunny position.

Aubrietas are widely planted because of their colourful spring display, but be careful about mixing them with other less robust and spreading rock plants.

Shrubs and herbaceous plants have been grouped together because it is more important to consider whether a particular plant will form a good association, or fulfil a particular function, than to be a purist about keeping a shrub border shrubby or an herbaceous border herbaceous. If annuals will help to fill a gap among the herbaceous plants, or bulbs will brighten a shrub border, then use them.

There are other advantages in mixing your plants initially, even if you have to sacrifice some of them later. Shrubs planted at the right spacing for their size in 10 to 15 years' time will look ridiculously sparse during the early years, and even the most patient of us like to see results reasonably quickly. One solution is to plant shrubs more closely than the normal recommended spacing, and gradually thin them out as they become over-crowded. There is, however, a less expensive solution to the problem.

Using ground cover plants (see pages 98-101) or drifts of bulbs is another way of covering bare soil – and they will get off to a better start than in an already densely planted border. A quick and easy solution is the use plenty of annuals and biennials to provide colour and height.

In Britain there is still a reluctance to plant shrub borders, partly because they conjure up images of Victorian shrubberies that may seem oppressive in many small, modern gardens. Mixed borders can be lighter and brighter, but you do not have to grow your shrubs in borders at all. Some of them will make superb isolated specimens in a lawn – though it will probably look more 'designed' if you group several shrubs in the same area, so they present a unified appearance.

Below: Although traditional herbaceous borders are to some extent out of fashion, they can be breathtakingly beautiful if you have the space to do them justice.

Herbaceous plants can be treated in a similar way by planting a bed of suitably imposing plants – such as acanthus, agapanthus, or kniphofias. Unfortunately, these always look rather sad in winter, so they should not be in a dominant area of the garden.

There are also herbaceous plants of such 'architectural' merit that they will stand alone – perhaps in the space of a paving slab, or planted in a gravel area. Some of the plants that can be used like this but are not included in the Table on the right are angelica (*Angelica archangelica*), and *Heracleum mantegazzianum*, which carries its huge cartwheel flower heads up to 10 ft (3m) above the ground.

Whether shrub, herbaceous perennial, annual, or biennial, it is always best to look at plants in terms of shapes and patterns so you can decide how each plant will make an individual contribution to the overall *melange* of plants. Even the arrangement of plants in this book is very artificial: the popular *ajugas*, for instance, will be equally at home in the front of an herbaceous border, as a carpeting ground cover on their own, placed among shrubs or in the rock garden. They will just as happily, and effectively, creep among paving, where some of the variegated varieties can look very striking. To put plants into watertight compartments is to miss many good opportunities. As many plants as possible have been cross-referenced within the book, to increase the number of options for a particular plant, but the possibilities are limited as much by your own imagination as by the visual and horticultural constraints imposed by the plants themselves.

Establishing a theme

There should always be a reason for a border. Long, narrow, single-sided borders might take the eye to a focal point at the end of the garden, or perhaps beyond; island beds might lead the eye away from a point ahead and take it to the sides; a border might break up an otherwise uninteresting expanse of lawn. Your choice of plants should be influenced by the purpose of the border. Straight herbaceous beds leading the eye towards converging points will still serve the purpose, even in winter, and may do so more effectively without the occasional shrub breaking up the outline. An island border placed to take the eye off the view ahead, or to break up an uninteresting area, will cease to fulfil its function if everything dies down to ground level in winter. For a bed like this, some shrubby plants, preferably evergreen, and possibly even a small tree, are needed to retain the shape and form of the garden even in winter.

HERBACEOUS PLANTS

Name	Description	Height	Position
Acanthus spinosus Bear's breeches	Bold spikes of white and mauve-purple flowers, mid summer to early autumn. Deeply cut, spiny foliage. Zone 8.	4 ft (1.2m)	Fertile soil. Sun or shade.
Agapanthus hybrids African lily (lily-of-the-Nile)	Strap-shaped leaves, usually blue flower heads mid and late summer. Needs a favourable area. Zone 9.	3 ft (900mm)	Fertile, well-drained soil. Sun. Not fully hardy.
Anaphalis triplinervis Pearly everlasting	Greyish, woolly leaves, topped with clusters of white, star-like 'everlasting' flowers in late summer. Zone 3.	1 ft (300mm)	Ordinary soil. Sun or partial shade.
Aquilegia 'McKana Hybrids' Columbine	Graceful plants with feathery foliage and spurred flowers in a wide range of colours in late spring and early summer. Zone 5.	2½ ft (750mm)	Fertile, moist soil. Sun or partial shade.
Aruncus sylvester (syn A. dioicus) Goat's beard	Broad, fern-like leaves and large ivory-white flower plumes in early and mid summer. An imposing plant. Zones 2-3.	5 ft (1.5m)	Deep, moist soil. Sun or shade.
Aster novi-belgii Dwarf Hybrids Michaelmas daisies (New York aster)	Compact, bushy plants with masses of daisy-like flowers in a wide range of colours in early autumn. Zones 2-3.	1-1½ ft (300-450mm)	Fertile soil. Sunny position.
Astrantia major Masterwort	Flattish heads of greenish-pink flowers on wiry stems in summer. Light green, divided leaves. Zone 6.	2 ft (600mm)	Ordinary soil. Sun or partial shade.
Campanula lactiflora (milky bellflower)	Light blue bells about 1 in (25mm) across, on tall, leafy stems. Summer. There are pink and violet-blue forms. Zone 6.	3-4 ft (900mm-1.2m)	Moist soil. Sun or partial shade.
Centaurea dealbata 'Steenbergii' (Persian centaurea)	Deep rose, thistle-like flowers in summer. Jagged leaves, grey-green above, silvery beneath. Zones 3-4.	2 ft (600mm)	Fertile and well-drained soil. Sunny position.
Chrysanthemum maximum Shasta daisy (daisy)	Single, white, daisy flowers, 3 in (75mm) across, with yellow centre, in summer. There is also a double form. Zone 5.	3 ft (900mm)	Ordinary soil. Sun or partial shade.
Cimicifuga racemosa Black snake-root (black cohosh)	Slender spikes of creamy-white flowers that tower above the foliage in late summer/ autumn. Zones 2-3.	4 ft (1.2m)	Fertile, moist soil. Sunny position.
Crambe cordifolia (colewort)	Broad, heart-shaped leaves on branching stems. A cloud-like display of white flowers on a big plant in early summer. Zone 7.	6 ft (1.8m)	Ordinary soil. Sunny position.
Echinacea purpurea Purple cone flower	Large, about 4 in (100mm), rayed flowers, with reflexed petals and dark centre. Mid summer to early autumn. Zones 3-4.	3 ft (900mm)	Fertile, well-drained soil. Sun or partial shade.
Echinops humilis 'Taplow Blue' Globe thistle	A substantial plant with grey-green leaves and steel blue thistle heads. Flowers through summer. Zones 3-4.	4 ft (1.2m)	Ordinary soil. Sunny position.
Eryngium x oliverianum (Oliver's eryngium)	Jagged-edged, blue-green leaves on stout stems, and small, 'thimble' flowers set in a 'collar'. Mid summer to autumn. Zone 6.	3 ft (900mm)	Well-drained soil. Sunny position.
Festuca glauca Blue fescue	A grass with blue-grey bristle-like leaves. Tuft-forming. Small, but useful for edging. Zone 5.	6-9 in (150-230mm)	Ordinary soil. Sun or partial shade.
Hemerocallis Day lily	Clusters of trumpet-shaped flowers, which are short-lived but constantly replaced. Mid summer to autumn. Zones 2-3.	2-3 ft (600-900mm)	Ordinary soil. Sun or partial shade.
Kniphofia (garden hybrids) Red hot poker (poker plant, torch lily)	Grass-like foliage and large, stiff poker-like spikes in red and yellow shades. Summer and into autumn. Zone 7.	3-6 ft (900mm-1.8m)	Ordinary soil. Sunny position. Can need protection.
Ligularia clivorum (syn L. dentata, Senecio clivorum) 'Desdemona'	Large, purplish, heart-shaped leaves. Large, vivid, orange heads of daisy-like flowers. Zone 6.	4 ft (1.2m)	Fertile, moist soil. Sun or partial shade.
Monarda didyma Bee-balm	Aromatic foliage. Heads of red, pink, violet, or white flowers in a whorl. Mid summer to early autumn. Zone 5.	3 ft (900mm)	Ordinary soil. Sun or partial shade.
Nepeta x faassenii (in UK often sold as *N. mussinii*) Catmint, catnip (Persian ground ivy)	Fragrant grey foliage forming an attractive background for the mauve-blue flowers. Late spring to early summer. Zones 3-4.	1 ft (300mm)	Well-drained soil. Sunny position.
Oenothera missouriensis Evening primrose (Ozark sundrops)	Prostrate growth habit. Bold, yellow flowers over bright green leaves. Flowers all summer. Zone 5.	10 in (250mm)	Well-drained soil. Sunny position.
Rudbeckia deamii (R. fulgida 'Deamii') Coneflower	Large, orange-yellow flowers with dark centres, mid summer to early autumn. Very free-flowering. Zone 6.	3 ft (900mm)	Ordinary soil. Sun or partial shade.
Salvia x superba (syn S. nemorosa)	Branching spikes of violet-purple flowers, mid summer to early autumn. Neat growth habit. Zone 6.	1½-2½ ft (450-750mm)	Well-drained. Sun or partial shade.
Sedum spectabile (showy sedum)	Fleshy leaves, shapely all summer. Becomes a mound of (usually) pink flowers, late summer to mid autumn.	1-2 ft (300-600mm)	Ordinary, even dry, soil. Sunny position.

Herbaceous borders on the grand scale are almost a thing of the past – they take up a lot of space, and are very time-consuming to maintain in good condition. Time and space are two things most gardeners lack today.

Nevertheless the plants themselves are as desirable as ever, so it is the method of displaying them that may have to be modified.

The 'island bed' is now a well-established garden feature but it is not without its drawbacks. An island herbaceous bed is generally designed to be viewed from all round, and a very good effect can be achieved in a small bed, especially if you are prepared to plant evergreen perennials in the centre. Though the bed itself can be relatively small, it needs space around it to look good. In a small garden, space may be used more economically with the conventional, single-sided border with tall plants at the back, tapering to low at the front.

A island bed should be at least 6ft (1.8m) across. The exact width will influence the height of the tallest plants for the centre. As an approximate guide, the tallest plants should be about half the width of the border.

A traditional, one-sided border will still benefit from a path about 18 in (450mm) wide at the back, to make staking and tying the tall back-row plants easier. If backed by a hedge, a path will also make trimming more comfortable.

A border of any size will contain many different plants and, no matter how carefully you group them according to anticipated height and spread, different species will react differently on a particular soil; some will grow vigorously, others will be more reluctant. Colours that seem right together on paper often fail to live up to expectations. Even good plant combinations that you are sure about can fail in some years because one blooms a little earlier or later in a particular season.

This should not deter you from careful planning – on the contrary, it is vital to plan a border on paper first.

The golden rules are to plan on paper first – graph paper makes the job easier – and remember to plant herbaceous perennials in *groups* of one kind. Consider three or five plants as the minimum, though the total size of the border will dictate how many plants you can accommodate in a single group.

If you include shrubby plants, they should normally be planted singly (page 120).

Finally, be prepared to keep an open mind, and to move a few plants next year if necessary. One of the joys of herbaceous plants is that most move easily when dormant, so you can correct any initial grouping mistakes.

Theme borders

There are some old-fashioned borders, based on plants of predominantly one colour – silver or

Below: To keep strictly to shrubs in shrub borders and herbaceous plants in herbaceous borders is to miss out on many excellent plant combinations. This picture shows how well they can harmonize together.

Below right: Acanthus; with its handsome leaves and flower spikes, can make a striking feature on its own or as part of a mixed border.

white, grey, or perhaps pink. This type of border can be very successful, and can include shrubs as well, because there are many with grey or silver foliage, or pink flowers. You will need to search the catalogues for more plants than can be mentioned in this book, which only suggests a shortlist of a wide range of easy-to-grow plants for different purposes.

A word of caution about theme borders. They need to be reasonably large to work well and are perhaps most effective in a garden big enough to be able to divide into 'rooms', perhaps by internal hedges or walls.

The silvers and pinks, particularly, look fabulous against a dark green background foliage. Themes also help emphasize the impression of moving from the style in one 'room' to an entirely different one in the next.

Planning for a long season
Some border plants have a breathtaking, but fleeting, display, which may be gone in a week — for the rest of the season you will have only foliage. Avoid the temptation, when planning on paper, for a mass of colour in, say, early summer, with little to follow from then until autumn.

The short list on page 117 includes some plants that will flower in late spring, like columbine, for instance, and others that will take you through until autumn (*Sedum spectabile*).

Over the season as a whole, foliage is likely to be as important as flowers. Attractive leaves are a real bonus on any plant. *Acanthus spinosus* is interesting in flower, but its foliage is attractive all through the season. Plants such as anaphalis and verbascums have silvery-grey foliage that is attractive in its own right and also acts as a foil for other plants, with, perhaps, brighter flowers.

Look for interesting shapes too — *kniphofia* is imposing because of its tall, spiky habit, *eryngium* for its jagged, blue-green leaves and unusual flower heads. Plants such as the *Ligularia clivorum* 'Desdemona' combine interesting leaves with stature, and with bold flowers — here the leaves are purplish and heart-shaped.

The smaller the border, the more important it is to include these 'multi-merit' plants.

It is always worth including some plants that are grown for their leaves alone. Among the most superb foliage plants, and ideal for planting alone in a damp, shady spot, as a border of mixed kinds alone, or even in containers, are the *hostas*. Many good species and varieties are available and it is worth trying to include several.

An herbaceous border in the grand style. You need plenty of space for this type of border. But you do not have to miss out on border plants if your garden is on a more modest scale — a small island bed similar to that shown on the opposite page will still provide plenty of scope.

SHRUBS

Name	Description	Height	Position
Berberis thunbergii 'Atropurpurea' (Japanese barberry)	Rich purple-red leaves throughout spring and summer. Brilliant autumn colour. Red berries. Zone 5.	5 ft (1.5m)	Ordinary soil. Sun or shade.
Buddleia alternifolia (fountain buddleia)	Graceful arching branches with long, narrow leaves. A cascade of lilac-purple flowers in early summer. Zone 6.	9 ft (2.7m)	Ordinary, even dry, soil. Tolerates lime. Sun.
Buddleia davidii butterfly bush (orange-eye butterfly bush)	Popular shrub. Best pruned hard in early spring to improve habit. Flowers mid and late summer. Various colours. Zone 6.	15 ft (4.5m)	Ordinary, even dry, soil. Tolerates lime. Sun.
Ceratostigma willmottianum (Willmott blue leadwort)	Rich blue flowers from mid summer and into mid autumn. Foliage turns red in autumn. Zone 8.	3 ft (900mm)	Light soil. Sunny position.
Chimonanthus praecox Wintersweet	Strongly scented, pale, waxy-yellow flowers in mid and late winter on bare stems. Does not flower on young wood. Zones 7-8.	9 ft (2.7m)	Fertile soil. Best near warm wall. Sunny position.
Cornus alba 'Sibirica' Siberian dogwood	Bright crimson stems, seen at their best in winter. Small white flowers appear in early summer. Zone 2.	5 ft (1.5m)	Ordinary, ideally moist, soil. Sun or shade.
Cornus stolonifera 'Flaviramea' Dogwood (golden-twig dogwood)	Young shoots are yellowish-green — a feature in winter sunshine. Green leaves turn yellow before falling. Zone 2.	6 ft (1.8m)	Ordinary, ideally moist, soil. Partial shade.
Cotinus coggygria Smoke tree	Smooth, rounded leaves — showing autumn colour. Fawn flower plumes create a 'haze' over the plant in summer. Zone 6.	8 ft (2.4m)	Ordinary or sandy soil. Sunny position.
Cotoneaster horizontalis Herringbone cotoneaster (rock spray)	Fan-like branches. Small leaves, vivid orange for short time before falling to leave the red berries. Zone 5.	2 ft (600mm)	Ordinary soil. Sun or shade.
Cytisus x praecox Warminster broom	Slender green shoots, covered with a tumbling mass of creamy-yellow flowers in late spring. Zone 6.	4 ft (1.2m)	Light soil. Sunny position.
Cytisus scoparius hybrids Broom (Scotch broom)	Sometimes short-lived shrubs, but pretty in late spring. Yellow is a common colour, but others are shades of red. Zone 6.	5 ft (1.5m)	Light soil. Sunny position.
Daphne mezereum Mezereon (February daphne)	An invaluable winter-flowering shrub. Very scented, purple-red flowers in late winter and early spring. Zone 5.	3 ft (900mm)	Ordinary soil, tolerates chalk. Sun or partial shade.
Deutzia 'Mont Rose'	Large, mauve-pink flowers borne prolifically in early and mid summer. Erect, arching stems. Zone 6.	6 ft (1.8m)	Ordinary soil. Sun or partial shade.
Fothergilla monticola (Alabama fothergilla)	White 'bottle-brush' flower heads in mid spring. Fragrant. Spectacular autumn leaf tints. Zone 6.	5 ft (1.5m)	Light, moist, lime-free, soil. Sun or partial shade.
Hamamelis mollis 'Pallida' Chinese witch-hazel	Shrub or small tree with scented yellow flowers in winter. Strap-like twisted petals. Zone 6.	8 ft (2.4m)	Light soil. Sunny position.
Hibiscus syriacus 'Blue Bird' (rose of Sharon)	Large, saucer-shaped, intense blue flowers, 3 in (75mm) across, from late summer to mid autumn.	6 ft (1.8m)	Fertile, moist, lime-free soil. Sun or partial shade.
Hypericum 'Hidcote'	A semi-evergreen. The leaves are almost hidden from mid summer to mid autumn, yellow saucer-shaped flowers. Zone 5.	6 ft (1.8m)	Fertile, well-drained soil. Sunny position.
Kolkwitzia amabilis 'Pink Cloud' Beauty bush	A mass of small, foxglove-shaped flowers in late spring and early summer. Pink, yellow throat. Zone 5.	5 ft (1.5m)	Ordinary soil. Tolerates chalk, dry soil. Sun or shade.
Paeonia lutea ludlowii Tree peony	A shrub of stature. Large bright green leaves and single, golden flowers in late spring, up to 4 in (100mm) across. Zones 6-7.	6 ft (1.8m)	Ordinary soil. Sunny position.
Philadelphus coronarius 'Aureus' Mock orange (sweet mock orange)	Leaves bright yellow spring/early summer, later greenish-yellow. Creamy-white, fragrant flowers early/mid summer. Zone 5.	6 ft (1.8m)	Fertile soil. Tolerates chalk. Sun or partial shade.
Potentilla fruticosa (bush cinquefoil)	Forms a dense bush with divided leaves. Yellow flowers from late spring to end of summer. There are several varieties. Zone 2.	3 ft (900mm)	Ordinary soil. Sun or partial shade.
Salix alba 'Chermesina' White willow (redstem willow)	Grown mainly for the winter impact of its bright orange-scarlet young shoots. Prune hard to encourage new shoots. Zone 2.	10 ft (3m)	Ordinary, ideally moist, soil. Sun or partial shade.
Sambucus racemosa 'Plumosa Aurea' (European red elder)	Deeply divided golden leaves. White flowers in mid spring, followed by dense clusters of red berries later. Zone 5.	7 ft (2.1m)	Ordinary soil. Partial shade.
Viburnum opulus 'Sterile' Snowball bush (European cranberry-bush)	Mid green leaves, turning yellow in autumn. Flowers form conspicuous creamy-white balls in late spring/early summer. Zones 3-4.	8 ft (2.4m)	Ordinary, ideally moist, soil. Sun or partial shade.
Weigela florida 'Variegata' (old-fashioned weigela)	Attractive, pale pink flowers in early summer. Creamy-yellow variegated foliage. Rather slow growth. Zone 6.	5 ft (1.5m)	Fertile, moist, soil. Partial shade.

Bulbs

Flowering bulbs (including rhizomes with corms and tubers) will grow in most gardens, beneath shady trees and rock gardens and naturalized in grass, as well as in the traditional herbaceous border. They are so diverse in their use that there is little point in trying to group them together except for the convenience of labelling and buying (most are sold by bulb merchants). It is much better to regard them as you would any other plant for a rock garden or herbaceous border: other plants are seldom included or excluded because they have, say, a fibrous root system or a tap root.

There are innumerable bulbs of all types to plant in borders, including the popular spring-flowering bulbs which create colour when there is usually little else in flower. Yet it is the summer- and autumn-flowering bulbs that can make the most valuable contribution to a traditional border.

Perhaps the most important group are the lilies. Bold clumps of Mid Century hybrids will compete with anything in the herbaceous border. Against a dark hedge as a background, the handsome *Lilium regale* and the magnificent golden-rayed lily (*L. auratum*), or the white Madonna lily (*L. candidum*) will look splendid. But there are many more, and many of which will do well among shrubs. Some lilies dislike an alkaline soil, though, so check that you plant species suitable for your soil.

Ornamental onions (*Alliums*) provide many good border plants, from the low-growing *A. karataviense* to imposing *A. giganteum*.

Fritillaria imperialis, the crown imperial, is another majestic plant, particularly useful as a clump in a mixed border because it will flower in April. Eye-catching from a distance, these bulbs will always attract attention.

No herbaceous border is complete without bearded irises (*Iris germanica* hybrids). There are now many forms of this plant, many with marvellous colouring. The bearded irises (which have rhizomes) flower in early summer, as do bulbous irises; useful though these are, however, the latter lack the stature of the bearded irises.

Other shrubs
The shrubs in the Table above are all deciduous (they lose their leaves for the winter). A selection of evergreen shrubs is suggested on page 97. In a mixed border or a shrub border, it is worth trying to mix evergreen and deciduous types to maintain interest all year round.

Some shrubs that do well in shade have been included on page 109. Many of these will also do well in other parts of the garden.

Gap fillers are invaluable for any newly created garden. Even quick-growing shrubs and trees can take several years before they become a respectable size, and in the meantime you will need to put something in the blank spaces of your garden.

Gap fillers are equally useful for the herbaceous border, because it will take at least a season to become established. Even in future years, there is always the chance of plants not surviving the winter, leaving a gap that needs to be filled while a replacement is establishing itself.

The best gap fillers are annuals and biennials (or perennials that can be treated as annuals), because these are the plants that grow and flower quickly. Some will grow to 6 ft (1.8m) or more during the summer, the sort of sheer cover-power that you could hardly expect from more permanent plants.

Which annuals?

All annuals can be used to fill in gaps between other plants, provided you give them the right conditions (shade or sun – they are seldom fussy about soil). But it is annuals that are bushy, and upright with bold flowers that are most useful for filling gaps in the border.

The choice is wide, but particularly useful are:
African marigold (Tagetes erecta) – many varieties, usually 2-3 ft (600 - 900mm) high; big, ball-shaped heads in yellow or orange. Strong, feathery foliage.
Foxglove (Digitalis) – best treated as a biennial, though some can be treated as an annual if raised under glass. Tall, about 5 ft (1.5m), and spiky, invaluable back-of-border or shade plants.
Cosmea (Cosmos) – large, single flowers and a mass of feathery foliage on a plant about 2-3 ft (600-900mm) high.
Mallow (Lavatera trimestris) – bushy plants about 2-2½ ft (600-750mm) tall, with broad-petalled flowers in pink shades or white.
Coneflower (Rudbeckia) – large rayed blooms produced freely over a long period. Shades of orange and yellow, usually with contrasting dark eyes. Heights mostly 2-3 ft (600-900mm)
Tobacco plant (nicotiana) – choose the tall varieties, usually about 2½ ft (750mm) high for a general gap filler, and a dwarf size for the front of the border. Flowers usually in red, pink, and white shades and magnificently scented.

Flowers for fragrance

It is worth including some annuals and biennials in the border at any time, for the contribution they make in terms of delicious scent. Some, such as night-scented stocks (*Matthiola bicornis*) look far from attractive during the day, but open to release their fragrance at night. Nicotianas, already mentioned, may close during the day, but modern varieties remain open.

Mignonette (*Reseda odorata*), sweet rocket (*Hesperis matronalis*), and sweet-williams (*Dianthus barbatus*) are also worth trying to include for their scent.

Covering a fence or wall

While the perennials are becoming established, do no overlook annual climbers. There are many with attractive flowers, but for sheer cover-power consider the canary creeper (*Tropaeolum canariensis*), and, of course, the ordinary *climbing nasturium* (*T. majus*), the Japanese hop (*Humulus japonicus*), or even *Cobaea scandens* (the cup-and-saucer vine) if you live in a mild area and start it off under glass.

African marigolds are bold border gap-fillers for a season.

It is relatively easy to devise a planting scheme that will be attractive from mid spring to mid autumn, but that leaves another six months during which colour and interest is especially useful.

It *is* possible to have year-round flowers and certainly plenty of interest in the form of coloured twigs or decorative bark, as well as, of course, the decorative foliage of variegated evergreens. Plan your planting to make the most of these, and if space is limited make sure you use lots of plants that are interesting in both summer and winter.

If the garden is large enough, you could have one section devoted to winter-interest plants, but it should be near the house so it can be appreciated. Even in a small garden it may be worth concentrating as many winter-interest plants as possible in a border near the door or by a path that you will use regularly.

Many of the winter-flowering trees and shrubs have small, scented flowers – two reasons for being able to admire them at close-quarters. The scent of some is not particularly strong, so you need to be able to get near them. This means that, particularly in winter, they should be alongside a firm path.

Trees grown for their attractive bark are usually better grown as isolated specimens, perhaps in a sunny part of the lawn, but in view of the window. Bark patterns and colours always look better in sunshine. Many shrubs grown for coloured bark, such as dogwood and willow, need regular pruning to encourage the young, most colourful wood.

Besides trees with flowers or attractive bark, some of which are listed opposite, the tracery of an interesting outline against the sky has its own fascination. Two trees worth considering for this are

Winter flowers are valuable, and bold drifts of heather can be especially effective. Some also have coloured foliage as an additional bonus.

SOME PLANTS FOR A WINTER GARDEN

Shrubs

Chimonanthus praecox 'Luteus'	Winter flowers. Scented.
Cornus alba 'Sibirica' (see page 120)	Red stems
Cornus stolonifera 'Flaviramea' (see page 120)	Yellowish-green stems.
Elaeagnus pungens 'Maculata' (see page 97)	Variegated evergreen.
Erica carnea	Winter flowers. Many varieties.
(syn *E. herbacea*)	Evergreen, some attractive foliage.
Erica darleyensis	Winter flowers. Several varieties. Evergreen.
Hamamelis mollis 'Pallida'	Winter flowers. Scented.
Ilex (see page 97)	Evergreen. Many variegated, Berries on females.
Jasminum nudiflorum	Winter flowers.
Lonicera x purpusii	Winter flowers. Scented.
Rhododendron dauricum	Winter flower.
Sarcococca hookeriana digyna	Winter flowers. Scented Evergreen
Viburnum farreri (syn *V. fragrans*)	Winter flowers. Scented.
Viburnum tinus (page 97)	Evergreen. Winter flowers.

Trees

Acer capillipes	Bark.
Acer griseum (see page 112)	Bark. Autumn colour.
Betula albo-sinensis septentrionalis	Bark.
Betula jaquemontii	Bark
Cornus mas	Winter flowers.
Prunus subhirtella 'Autumnalis'	Winter flowers.

Herbaceous plants

Helleborus orientalis (see page 108)	Winter flowers.
Iris unguicularis (syn *I. stylosa*)	Winter flowers.

Some early bulbs

Crocus (early-flowering species, such as *C. chrysanthus* and *C. tomasinianus*)
Eranthis hyemalis
Galanthus nivalis
Narcissus (early-flowering types that bloom in late winter)
Iris danfordiae
Iris histrioides

the contorted willow, *Salix matsudana* 'Tortuosa' and the more compact corkscrew hazel or Harry Lauder's walking stick, *Corylus avellana* 'Contorta'. Both of these are good 'talking point' plants. A third possibility is the unusual wire-netting bush, *Corokia cotoneaster*.

Background colour helps too. Conifers such as the blue-green *Chamaecyparis lawsoniana* 'Pembury Blue' and the gold '*C. l.* 'Lane' ('Lanei') are useful to provide a year-round background colour, as single plants or as groups or hedges.

Heathers and dwarf conifers

It is possible to have heathers in flower practically all the year round by choosing the right combination of species and varieties. The most valuable are probably the winter-flowering kinds and a winter heather-garden can be striking. There are many varieties to choose from, some of them having attractive gold or reddish foliage as a bonus.

Do not let the huge range of varieties tempt you into planting a few plants of lots of different kinds. The bigger the drift of one variety, the bolder and more effective it will be. Many different varieties with different flowering times and growth habits can look untidy rather than impressive.

Generally, heathers do not do well on alkaline soil, but the winter-flowering *Erica carnea* (syn *E. herbacea*) will tolerate some lime in the soil, though it will not do well on a shallow chalk soil.

Heathers look good planted as a carpet around a white-barked birch, or interplanted with the occasional dwarf conifer.

Late autumn

In your concern to include enough winter interest, it is easy to overlook late autumn — a somewhat depressing time when every lingering flower will help make winter seem shorter.

One of the finest sights of autumn is a large group of *Nerine bowdenii*, whose large, pink flower heads seem defiant facing shortening days. Unfortunately, they will need a warm position.

Some of the sternbergias (*S. clusiana* and *S. lutea*) will still be putting on a show of their yellow, crocus-like flowers towards the end of autumn. Some of the so-called autumn-flowering crocuses — colchicums — will continue to produce their huge flowers until late autumn, and there is a true autumn crocus, *C. speciosus* that will put on a late show, though being small they need mass planting to be effective.

Below: This clipped holly is a striking feature at any time of the year, but is especially effective in winter.

Because most of us want to cram as many shrubs as possible into the space available, shrub borders are the usual solution. Yet if a garden is to have character, some specimen plants strategically placed are almost essential. With so many plants in a garden it takes the impact of a distinctive, and conspicuously placed, shrub or tree to take the eye from the general to the particular. Shrubs to other plants are like punctuation to words – they bring the eye to rest for a moment and break up the components of the rest of the garden.

A well-chosen shrub, separated from its background, can emphasize a particular part of the garden. The horizontal stress of the layered branches of *Cornus kousa* (included under small trees – page 112) or the magnificent *Viburnum plicatum* 'Mariesii' or 'Lanarth', laden with white flowers in late spring and early summer, can divert the eye in much the same way as the sweeping line of a pagoda in an Oriental garden.

Quite commonplace plants can be made more intersting by treating them in a way that elevates

Far right: *Fatsia japonica* is one of the most useful shrubs for gardens of all sizes. Young specimens make good tub plants and older ones will grow into large specimen shrubs with year-round interest. Unfortunately, they are not suitable for very cold areas.

Right: *Rhus typhina*, a handsome large shrub or small tree, seen at its best as an isolated specimen.

them to the class of plant loosely termed 'architectural'. These are plants which add something to the line of the garden, just as a pillar or an arch might in a building. The overall shape contributes to the mood of the garden beyond the beauty of the flower and foliage. Clipped bay (*Laurus nobilis*) in a tub, box or yew as a topiary specimen, or a holly grown as a conical tree, or even clipped to an orb on a stem instead of shrub form, are examples. Even something like *Berberis darwinii*, normally a fairly straggly shrub, can be shaped to provide a glowing ball of gold when it is in flower, and the evergeen leaves are quite attractive during the rest of the year.

Fatsia japonica (though only suitable for reasonably mild areas) is an excellent example of what gives a shrub 'architectural' strength: the flowers are hardly beautiful or colourful, the leaves are generally plain green and, although divided like a hand, would not attract attention if they hung like those on a horse chestnut tree. It is the *stature* and outline of the plant that makes it so useful.

Among the other shrubs that fall into this category are *Rhus typhina* and the Japanese maples (*Acer palmatum* varieties), which are shrubby in stature and have striking leaves.

Sometimes trees with attractive leaves can be grown as a shrub by suitable and regular pruning. Eucalyptus are fast-growing trees, but if cut back regularly they will make bushy plants with a mass of the distinctive and aromatic eucalyptus foliage. *Catalpa bignonioides* 'Aurea' has large yellow leaves that hang to produce a blanket of colour. Try growing the plant as a large shrub – though be warned: this is not one for a cold or windy area. Paulownia, normally a substantial tree, can be 'stooled' (cut down regularly) to produce a bush with huge ornamental leaves.

Aralia elata normally makes a tall tree, but it can be kept shrubby by regular cutting back. The snag is having to cope with the suckers it will send up! The leaves can be up to 5ft (1.5m) long if treated this way.

Sometimes a neat shape and evergreen foliage might be enough to justify a shrub being grown as a specimen plant in a formal layout. The camellia qualifies on both points, with the bonus of a colourful display of wonderful flowers in late winter or early spring.

If the setting is right – perhaps a courtyard or a predominantly gravel area – a more exotic – looking shrub might be better. *Yuccas* and some of the *cordylines* (though needing a favourable area) have a spikiness that can be most effective when it is not lost among broad-leaved shrubs.

Acer palmatum 'Atropurpureum', one of the most popular Japanese maples.

Cornus kousa, always a distinctive large shrub.

Yucca filamentosa 'Variegata', an eye-catching specimen shrub. The distinctive shape of yuccas makes them more suitable for individual treatment rather than as part of a shrub border.

Although containers are, of course designed to have plants in them, if you have a beautiful one, perhaps an ornate terracotta or stone urn, you may wish to display it without plants. If you do, though, remember that it will then become a receptacle for fallen leaves, bugs and other garden debris.

The vast majority of pots, tubs, urns, troughs, and other containers, are nothing as garden features without plants in them. Some, in fact, are almost ugly, and need to be disguised with trailing evergreen plants.

The type of container and the material from which it is constructed may also influence your choice of plants. Evergreen shrubs with a strong outline, perhaps with a carpet of trailing ivies, can look perfectly acceptable in a large, pale concrete container: most annuals, on the other hand, tend to lack the stature and form needed to balance the material and, no matter how bright the display, the container will probably intrude.

Plain or mixed?

You may feel tempted to cram many different kinds of plant into the same container. In fact mixed planting *can* work, but it can also look a mess. One bold splash of uniform colour is usually far more impressive than a jumble of different colours, shapes, sizes, and heights.

There are however some exceptions to this general rule, in cases where trailers or other forms of 'ground cover' are required. This applies where the container is planted with trees and shrubs whose sheer size and height coupled with the large size of container needed will otherwise leave a conspicuous sparseness around the base. A concrete or glass-reinforced cement container, especially, can look better with ivies or other trailers cascading over the edge and most tubs containing deciduous trees or shrubs will be enhanced in spring by suitable early-flowering bulbs. A grey leaved carpeter such as *Stachys lanata* (syn *S. byzantina*) works well around the base of a tall plant, although the stachys will deteriorate during the winter.

Permanent or seasonal?

As containers form an integral part of the design,

Wide steps provide a wonderful opportunity to use plenty of containers.

you should consider how they will look throughout the year. Spring and summer planting is usually very colourful but planting will have to be done twice a year, every year, and there will be extended 'off' periods. Permanent planting can be interesting the year round but may have a less colourful and more subtle impact. A successful compromise is to use seasonal plants around more permanent subjects such as trees and shrubs.

If the tub or urn is to form a focal point, or is a key element in the overall design, then plant for permanency. Some of the most suitable plants will take several years to reach a respectable size, so the reward comes with time.

An alternative, if you can afford it, is to buy a large specimen plant. It will not matter if the plant's growth is checked, as all large plants in containers will inevitably be restricted.

If you are prepared to water the containers regularly, the range of appropriate summer bedding plants is vast. Almost all the spring flowering bulbs can be used too, though it is best to avoid those with tall flower stems unless you can provide a sheltered position, and these will generally require much less maintenance and attention than summer flowering plants.

If you want to concentrate on containers planted with trees or shrubs, the choice is enormous, and includes *conifers* and deciduous and evergreen *flowering shrubs*. Figs, peaches, nectarines, and even apples and pears, are all suitable fruits for growing in pots, but you need to choose the right varieties and rootstocks. The results can be well worthwhile, but to avoid disappointment a specialist book on fruit first.

As regards the positioning of permanently placed tubs and pots, there are no rules to follow and you have to obey your own visual sense.

Conifers

Many conifers, especially the dwarf and slow growing kinds, make ideal tub plants. By choosing suitable species and varieties it is possible to have many without them looking boring as there is such a variety of size, shape, colour, and 'texture'. You could even use two or three in one container, perhaps a globe-shaped variety of *Chamaecyparis obtusa*, an upright *Juniperus communis*, 'Hiber-

Hostas make attractive container plants, but only if you can ensure that the compost is never allowed to become dry.

Half baskets and other wall-mounted containers can often be as effective as a normal hanging basket.

nica' and a prostrate *Juniperus horizontalis*. Avoid varieties of *Chamaecyparis lawsoniana* if the containers are likely to dry out, because they are sensitive to drought.

The dwarf junipers and pines and dwarf varieties of *Chamaecyparis obtusa* and *Tsuga canadensis* will put up with dry soil if they have to, and will also tolerate the restricted root-run of a container. Tsuga does not need a lot of light and so is suitable for a shady position.

Other evergreens

The bay (*Laurus nobilis*) is the classic evergreen for a tub, and it is often clipped to shape. Unfortunately it is a rather slow-grower, which is a handicap in the early years so, if you can afford it, your best bet might be to buy a trained specimen rather than start with a cutting or young plant. The other drawback to bay is that it can suffer badly from a hard winter.

The other classic tub plant is box (*Buxus sempervirens*). It is best clipped, as natural bushes can look untidy. Choose a dwarf or variegated variety.

Aucuba japonica makes a useful shade tolerant tub plant. Choose one of the attractively variegated varieties.

Laurels may not suggest themselves as exciting container plants, but they are tough and evergreen, and their growth should be restricted within reasonable bounds in a container. You can use both the common laurel (*Prunus laurocerasus*) and the Portugal Laurel (*P. lusitanica*).

Holly, too, looks impressive when clipped, but choose one of the variegated varieties.

Finally, flowering evergreens such as the camellia look good in tubs. Camellias, however, may need careful pruning to create shapely bushes, and should be given a place where early morning sun will not thaw the frozen buds too rapidly.

Deciduous flowering shrubs

Although the best flowering tub plants are evergreen, there are many deciduous shrubs which can be grown successfully in containers. Hydrangeas and the early-flowering arching cytisus (such as *C. × beanii* and *C. praecox*) look striking when in flower, but they suffer from the disadvantage that they can often look dull when not in bloom.

The best rhododendrons for tubs are the compact varieties, preferably those with interesting leaves. The *R. yukushimanum* hybrids are particularly useful.

Special feature shrubs

There are a few plants that immediately give a garden an exotic touch, such as an *Agave americana* in a terracotta container, or a palm such as *Chamaerops humilis* or *Trachycarpus fortunei* in a *large* conventional clay pot.

Other spiky plants that look good in containers are cordylines, phormiums, and yuccas.

The agaves, palms and cordylines can all remain outdoors in very favourable areas, but where the winters are even moderately hard they should be taken in for the winter. That is one advantage of growing these plants in containers — you can move them into the home or a greenhouse with relative ease and back outside again when the weather improves.

Fatsia japonica also creates a special feature, and will withstand quite severe winters, but not very cold regions.

Windowboxes and hanging baskets

Windowboxes help to link the garden and the house.

Unfortunately they are usually very attractive during the summer but are left bare and uninteresting for winter. Spring flowering bulbs help to keep some interest going, but a 'permanent' planting is even better.

Two or three dwarf conifers, some ivies to cascade down the front, and *Euonymus fortunei* 'Emerald 'n' Gold' and 'Emerald Gaiety' are particularly suitable. But you could also plant hebes such as the green and cream variegated *Hebe × franciscana* 'Variegata' and the silver-grey leaved *H. pinguifolia* 'Pagei', or young aucubas with their variegated forms. Even shrubs that will grow quite large in the open ground will generally give several years of use with container restricted roots.

Hanging baskets are very demanding to maintain in good condition. They will need daily attention in the summer, and unless you can provide this degree of care your efforts will probably be better put into other kinds of containers.

HERBACEOUS PLANTS FOR TUBS

| Agapanthus | Nepeta x fassennii (*avoid if bees* |
| Hosta | *worry you*) |

Bedding plants		
Ageratum	Fuchsia	Petunia
Alyssum	Impatiens	Primula polyantha*
Begonia (*large-flowered tuberous-rooted*)	Lobelia	Tagetes (*marigolds*)
	Myosotis*	Tropaeolum majus
Begonia semperflorens	Nemesia	Verbena
Bellis perennis*	Nicotiana alata	Viola (*including pansy*)**
Cheiranthus*	Pelargonium	

* for spring bedding   ** for spring and summer bedding

4. TECHNIQUES

No matter how simple or how grand the design on paper, there comes a point at which it has to be transformed into reality. This is where the hard work really begins, and where design ability and DIY skills are put to the test. It is also the point at which the prospect of actually carrying out the plan seems very daunting. The cheques have to be written, the soil excavated, and the hard physical work undertaken, and, at first, progress always seems slow.

It is worth making a timetable to give yourself realistic targets. You will probably have to modify them as you go along because jobs usually take longer than you expect, and a couple of wet weekends can upset the best-laid plans, but at least you will have a list of priorities and an idea of whether the work will take six weeks or six months.

A team of experts with all the right equipment, including mechanical excavators, can take a couple of weeks to build a small garden. Doing the same job on your own with tools that you are likely to have or hire, could take you months.

Because few gardeners have the same range of specialist equipment or the physical fitness as a professional, progress is bound to be slow and the effort sometimes considerable. Provided you realize this, and do not expect to achieve too much too quickly, there is no reason why the whole job should not be thoroughly enjoyable. If your expectations of quick results are too high though, disappointment will set in and the labour will become a chore.

You could, of course, hire a contractor to do the whole job for you; but this book assumes that you will want to do at least some of the work yourself. There is nothing to be ashamed of in using outside help for those tasks that are too difficult to tackle yourself. If you have a large area of soil to excavate it might take you weeks of back-aching work, and you will still have the problem of disposing of it. Hiring someone with a mechanical excavator will probably mean the job will be done in less than a day, and the same firm will usually take the soil away. A good operator will excavate or build up soil with great skill, and you can have the topsoil put on one side to be returned after the sub-soil has been dealt with, so the garden is left in a fertile condition. A decision such as this will cost you money, but will save considerable physical effort. It could also speed the job up by several weeks.

There are other tasks for which you could hire, say, a bricklayer or a carpenter or, if you just want an extra pair of hands, a local jobbing gardener should be able to help. It is far better to hire a little help at the right time than to let the job take so long that you begin to lose interest – and perhaps a season's growth.

The other time- and labour-saving option is to hire specialist tools. A concrete mixer, post-hole borer, a rotary cultivator, perhaps a chainsaw, block splitter and so on are well worth considering. Some very specialized equipment, such as a flate-plate vibrator for laying flexible paving, is necessary if you want good results.

Be prepared to buy some tools if necessary – a good bricklayer's spirit-level, club hammer and bolster are always worth having anyway. Do not under-estimate the importance of having the right tools as they will make the job both easier and quicker (see pages 132 and 133).

The photograph on the left shows the garden before it was reconstructed. Note that the new layout was plotted out on site before work began.

1. A complex garden construction project underway. Although this job, in London's Chelsea, is being handled by professionals working within a very tight schedule, with careful planning and plenty of time the practical amateur can achieve similar results and save considerable expense.
2. A brick patio being laid on compacted sand.
3. Laying clay pavers.
4. Pegs and a spirit-level being used to level ground.
5. Laying paving slabs.
6. Cutting a paving slab to shape.
7. Building a brick wall.
8. Checking a brick path with a spirit-level.
9. Setting pebbles in concrete.

1

2   3

4

5

6

7

8

9

Basic gardening tools
The chances are that you have most usual gardening tools already; but if you are starting from
scratch, perhaps in a first home, you may have to
buy basic necessities such as a spade and a fork.

If you do not have even the basics then it is particularly important to choose a few quality tools
wisely, and to buy only the important ones at first.
With all the other expenses of creating a garden it
makes sense to spend your money on quality
tools that you will need now, and buy the less important, or less immediately necessary, ones later. The lawn-mower can wait until you have a
lawn to mow; a dibber until you have seedlings to
plant (and even then many gardeners go through
life without one). But a spade and a wheelbarrow
are going to be essential if you are to make an impression on a new garden.

The tools you really do need to buy are:
Spade The choice is still vast, even though many of the
regional variations, especially in handle size and shape,
are almost a thing of the past. If you want to indulge
yourself, buy a stainless steel spade, especially if you
have heavy clay soil. But you can buy a strong, quality
spade that will last for many years at far less cost. Most
people prefer a spade with a 'tread' (a small lip where
you press your foot), but the overall balance of the
spade is just as important. This is for you to judge, so
handle as many different makes as possible in the
shop. Some wooden shafts can be weak, but the best
are as strong as plastic-covered metal **4**.

Fork You need a fork with prongs that are not going to
bend if you hit a large stone. Forks are often abused by
using them to lever up tree roots or paving slabs,
although they should not be used for this.

A plastic-covered metal handle will probably
withstand the weather better than a wooden handle if
you forget to put it away after use **5**.

When buying either a spade or a fork, check that the
joints between the socket and shaft are flush, with no
sharp edges. And make sure that the grip is wide
enough for your hand, bearing in mind that you might
be wearing gloves.

Rake Once the garden is established, a hoe will be
used much more frequently than a rake. But a rake is
essential for gathering leaves. Look for a light handle
and a head with about a dozen teeth. The better rakes
tend to have flattened, angular teeth **3**.

Wheelbarrow Although a light barrow is adequate
for normal garden use – carrying lawn clippings or
garden refuse for example – you need a *strong* barrow
for construction work. One with a pneumatic tyre is

Essential gardening tools

Nobody wants to buy tools unnecessarily, but there are some that you cannot do without. Tools that are either expensive or that you are unlikely to use often once construction is complete are best hired (see below). Those shown on the opposite page are ones that you will almost certainly find it worthwhile to buy if you don't already have them. These are draw hoe **2**, rake **3**, spade **4**, fork **5**, garden trowel **13**, hand fork **14**, – though you will be able to do without this, it is useful.

Construction tools

Among the tools that you might need specifically for construction jobs are: spirit-level **1**, shovel **6**, bricklayer's trowel **8**, club hammer **9**, bricklayer's hammer **10**, cold chisel **11**, waterproof protective gloves **12**, wheelbarrow **15**.

Tools to hire

There are certain tools that it makes sense to hire, either because of cost or because you are unlikely to have a long-term use for them once you have built your garden: angle grinder **16**, builder's pick **17**, sledge hammer **18**, crowbar **19**, rammer **20**, post-hole borer **21**, cement mixer **22**.

good for heavy loads, and you could hire one. Ball-type wheels make the going relatively easy over soft ground **15**.

Gloves may sound trivial, but they are inexpensive and well worth using. For construction work, choose those made of vinyl-impregnated fabric or vinyl-coated fabric. The latter are especially useful for wet or dirty jobs **12**.

Construction tools

Those tools that are unlikely to be needed for other household jobs, or are expensive to buy, have been included in the illustration. Tools that you might have to buy are:

For mixing concrete, moving earth Do not be tempted to make do with a spade as the job will be harder, take longer, and the spade will suffer. Use a *shovel* **6**. If you are not likely to use it often, a cheap one will probably be suitable.

A *bucket* will be useful for measuring materials. A plastic bucket of 2 gallon (10 litres) capacity is ideal.

For laying slabs or bricks A good *spirit-level* **1**, at least 2 ft (600 mm) long, with a pair of easy-to-see vials to indicate both horizontal and vertical planes, is indispensable for laying paving or brickwork correctly.

For bricklaying a *trowel* is essential, but ideally you should have two: a large one of about 10 in (250mm) and a smaller *pointing trowel* **8**.

For vertical brickwork you will need a *line and line pins*. You can manage by improvising with a piece of string, but will find this unsatisfactory if you are doing a lot of bricklaying.

To cut bricks or paving slabs you will need a *bolster chisel* **7** and *club hammer* **9**. A bricklayer's hammer is

also useful for cutting stone and brick, but this requires more skill to use, and is not necessary unless you do a lot of bricklaying. You could hire an *angle grinder* **16** to cut through them and this is especially useful if you have to cut bricks at an angle rather than straight across.

For making post holes There are special spades for digging holes, for fence posts for example, but these are only worth considering if you are going to have a regular use for them. It will not cost much to hire a *post-hole borer* **21**.

Hiring tools

Concrete mixer This is well worth considering if you have a lot of concreting to do **22**.

Plate vibrator This is an invaluable tool for laying clay or concrete pavers in sand (see page 165). Doing the job by hand is tedious and not as satisfactory.

Chain-saw This is well worth considering if you have several small trees to remove or fallen trees to cut up for firewood, but large trees call for real expertise and you should consult a qualified tree surgeon.

Angle grinder This makes easy work of cutting through stone or brick but is noisy and dusty to use **16**. Explain what you want to do, and ask how to use it.

Builder's pick Cheap to hire and easy to carry home, this can be invaluable on hard ground **17**.

Sledge hammer This is useful for breaking up hardcore and for knocking in fencing posts **18**.

Post-hole borer Simple to use and inexpensive to hire, this makes relatively short work of holes for posts **21**.

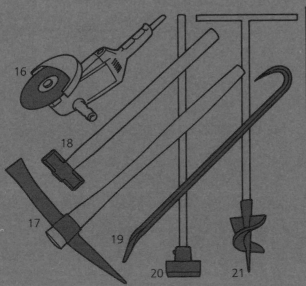

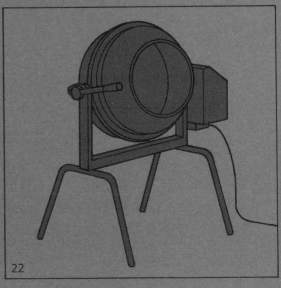

If you have a lawn it will almost certainly be a dominant feature, so it is worth making a good job of it. Even if it is only to be a play lawn for the children, it ought to be level enough to mow without having to encounter hollows and bumps; and to avoid bare patches later you need to choose the right grass for the job.

Turf or seed?

There are two major considerations that will influence your decision to use turf or seed: cost and timescale.

Even if you use expensive seed, it will be cheaper to sow a lawn than to use turf, and you can choose the grass mixture yourself. On the debit side, a lawn from seed takes much more effort and time to establish.

Turf produces instant results, and although it is more expensive than seed, you are buying a year or two of growth. A possible drawback is the variable quality. Unless turf comes from a good source, you could simply be bringing a lot of weeds and meadow grass rather than top quality lawn grass into your garden. You are also unlikely to know which grass mixture it contains, although this might not matter if you are concerned mainly with a play area. On the other hand, it is possible to buy quality turf that will equal anything that you can sow – at a price.

Preparing the ground

This is the most important aspect of making a lawn, and the part most gardeners skimp on. If the ground is not well dug first, the grasses may not grow well. If it is not carefully consolidated and levelled, there will be bumps and hollows which look ugly and make mowing difficult. And if it is not thoroughly weeded before the grass is planted the weeds will dominate before it can become established.

Modern selective weedkillers can control most weeds satisfactorily once the lawn is established, but there is little point in starting off at a disadvantage.

Ground preparation is less important for turf, but it still has to be consolidated and level.

Sowing from seed

If the ground tends to become waterlogged, lay land drains first. This is one of the less pleasant construction jobs, and will add to the expense, so it is only really worthwhile where there is a genuine drainage problem. If not done when necessary, moss is likely to become a problem.

Check your plan to make sure that electricity cables or water pipes or hoses will not run across the lawn. If they do, lay them first, even if you are not proposing to connect them for some time to come. Taking out a trench on an established lawn almost always leaves a mark afterwards.

Fork over the area to loosen the soil and remove as many perennial weed roots as possible. Pay special attention to coarse grasses because these cannot be removed by selective weedkillers later.

Level the ground methodically. If the area is already reasonably level, or if the lawn is to slope anyway, you might be able to do this by eye. Otherwise use a spirit-level on a straight-edge between pegs.

Insert small, flat-topped wooden pegs about 6 ft (1.8m) apart, and use the spirit-level on a straight-edge (piece of straight timber/lumber) between each peg in turn. When all the pegs are at the same height, use a rake to level the soil between them.

If the ground is very uneven, make a mark about 2 in (50mm) below the top of each peg, and level to this, otherwise the tops of some pegs may be below soil level.

Tread the ground to consolidate it by shuffling over it with feet close together, or use a garden roller. This is a job for dry weather when the soil will not cling. Then rake again to maintain levels.

A week before sowing or laying, sprinkle on an autumn lawn fertilizer (a summer one contains too much nitrogen), following the manufacturer's instructions. You do not need to rake it in yet.

If the ground is poor, or the soil very light and likely to dry out quickly, work plenty of damp peat into the top 3 in (75mm) of soil. This should not be necessary for turf.

Leave the ground for a couple of weeks, then hoe off weed seedlings that have germinated before sowing or turfing.

Sowing seed

Rake the soil level again if necessary, then mark out the ground into yard or metre strips or squares using string

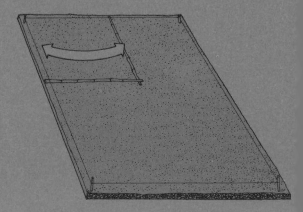

or canes. For a large area strips will be easier – you can simply calculate the amount of seed per strip

Sow the seed at *half* the recommended rate first, working methodically along the rows, then apply the remaining half working in strips in the opposite direction. This should ensure an even distribution of seed.

Scatter the seed with a swirling motion, not too close to the ground, so that it does not fall too thickly.

Rake the seed in *lightly*. If you bury it deeply, germination will be affected. Do not rake deeper than about ¼ in (6mm).

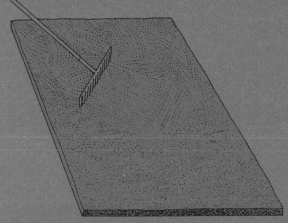

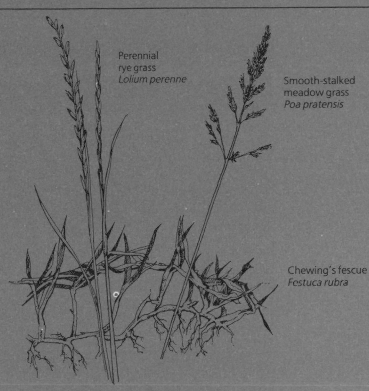

Perennial rye grass
Lolium perenne

Smooth-stalked meadow grass
Poa pratensis

Chewing's fescue
Festuca rubra

Even if the seed has been treated to make it unattractive to birds, it is worth using bird scarers or deterrents because birds will be attracted by the sight of the seeds and can also be a nuisance dust-bathing in the finely raked soil. Because bird scarers lose their effectiveness after a few days, use several types and keep changing their positions. Black cotton thread stretched across the soil may be enough to discourage them from taking dust baths.

Water thoroughly if the ground is dry, using a sprinkler, and keep it irrigated until the grass is growing satisfactorily. Do not cut the grass until it is at least 3 in (75mm) high, and do not cut it low the first few times.

Choosing the right seed
Seedsmen usually give their grass mixtures fancy names that may or may not indicate the sort of lawn to expect. There is only one way to be sure of the quality of lawn you are sowing: look at the constituent grasses in the mixture.

In Britain, mixtures containing *Agrostis tenuis*, and fescues such as *Festuca rubra* varieties, will produce the very finest lawns, while for a coarser but hardwearing lawn perennial rye grass (*Lolium perenne*) and smooth-stalked meadow grass (*Poa pratensis*) are likely to be included. Some of the new 'amenity' as opposed to agricultural varieties of perennial rye grass will produce a very respectable

lawn. Sometimes wood meadow grass (*Poa nemoralis*) is included in mixtures for a shady area, but this does not make an ideal lawn grass as it does not respond well to cutting.

Different grasses may be used in different countries. In North America, for example, smooth-stalked meadow grass is commonly used for fine lawns north of a line between Quebec to Winnipeg, because most of the bents (*Agrostis* species) are vulnerable to various diseases. South of a line from Washington to Kansas City the summers are too hot for the bents to succeed, yet the winters are too cold for Bermuda grass (*Cynodon dactylon)*, which is a popular choice for the warmer, southern states.

Follow the seedman's instructions for the *rate of application*. Do not asssume that more seed will produce a better lawn. Some seeds are very much smaller than others, so weight-for-weight you may have more potential plants in a given area in one mixture than you would in another. Sowing rates normally allow for some losses to birds, and you should still be left with enough to grow and knit together to provide adequate turf.

Worry about beds and curves later
Whether using turf or sowing seed, leave curved edges and any flower beds until later. Put the whole area down to grass first, or at least overlap the final edges. Once the grass is growing well, the beds and any curved edges can be cut out and, because the roots will bind the soil together, any edges will be stronger and more robust than if they were taken out before or when the lawn was laid.

Pre-seeded rolls

There is another way to lay a lawn to seed: pre-seeded rolls with the seeds embedded in a biodegradable base may be available, although they are much less widely used than loose seed. You simply unroll it and cut to size and shape with scissors. This method is obviously more expensive than sowing loose seeds, and there will be less choice of mixtures, but you do get an even cover and there is the great advantage that birds are unlikely to get at the seeds. Also, they generally suppress weeds during the vital early stages of growth of the lawn.

Prepare the ground normally, and unroll the pre-soaked strip, cutting it to size. Leave cutting intricate shapes until the grass has become established.

Cover each strip with a fine layer of sifted soil. Water with a fine sprinkler and keep moist until the seeds have germinated and started to grow properly.

When to sow seed

The best time to sow a lawn is in spring or early autumn, when the soil is warm and damp. You can sow throughout the summer, but watering in dry spells will be very important.

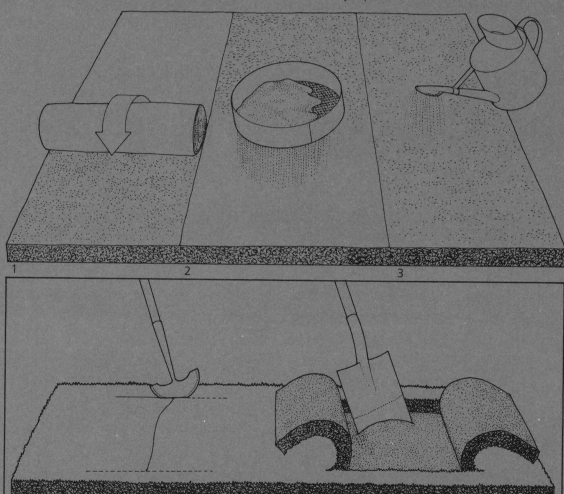

1. Lay roll on prepared bed

2. Cover with fine, sifted soil

3. Water well

Improving an existing lawn

If you have a existing lawn that is far from perfect, there may be a lot that you can do to improve it so that you do not have to re-lay it.

Within limits you can level off an uneven lawn by filling in the depressions and lowering the bumps.

Hollows can be filled gradually by adding about 1/2in (15mm) of sifted soil and peat, repeating once the grass has grown sufficiently to have absorbed this. For just a small area, it should be possible to lift the turf as described for bumps, and remove some soil.

Bumps are best dealt with by making an H-shaped cut over the area with a half-moon edger, then lifting the turf and rolling it back (see illustration). Remove sufficient soil, level the ground, and replace the grass.

Fertilizers and selective weedkillers (see pages 179-180) will then improve the quality of the grass.

A lawn from turf

Preparation does not have to be quite so thorough for turf, but the ground still has to be reasonably level and free from deep-rooted perennial weeds that might grow through the turf.

Turf should always be laid within a couple of days of delivery. If you are unable to do this, unroll the turf and keep it in a shady place and water it regularly if necessary.

Laying turf

Mark out the area to be turfed, using a garden line to keep the edges straight. Mark curves in the soil with a stick, lay the turf *over* this line and trim to size later.

Lay the first row of turf to one of the straight edges. Use a wooden plank to stand on as you work forward to complete subsequent rows, to distribute your weight.

Stagger the turf so that the joints in one row come half way along the joints in the next, like bonded brickwork.

Butt each turf as close as possible to the next one, and firm it down. It is better to make a 'turf beater' out of a slightly wedge-shaped piece of wood with a

handle than to bang it down with the back of a spade.

Make up a topdressing from four parts sand, two parts loam (soil) and one part peat. Pour this into the joints and work it well in using a broom or the back of a rake. This will help the turf to knit together.

Cut curves with a half-moon edger using a hosepipe curved to the shape as a guide. Do not use a spade as it will leave a scalloped edge.

Water thoroughly and keep watered in dry weather until the turf has bonded and grown into the ground below, at which time you can also start to use the grass.

When to lay turf

Mid and late autumn are the traditional times to lay turf, but you can lay it any time during the winter, provided that the ground is not frozen or waterlogged. You can also lay it in the spring but you will have to be prepared to water as often as necessary, which will be frequently if it is a dry spring.

Summer is not a good time as dry weather is likely to prevent the turf from becoming established, and there will be a temptation to use it before the new lawn is really ready to take any wear.

Although turf can be laid at almost any time of the year, provided the ground is not frozen or waterlogged, autumn is the traditional time, with spring a good alternative.

For strength of bond, always stagger turves, like a brick bond, and cut out curves and shapes later.

Try to see the turf before you buy it (which is not always possible). No matter how carefully you lay the turf, the lawn will not look good if it contains unsuitable grasses.

Straight-edged borders against a wall, fence or hedge should not pose any problem, but use a garden line to ensure that the edges *are* straight. Mark out sweeping curves first with a hose-pipe or in sand before you actually cut into the lawn.

Beds within the lawn are more difficult. Even rectangular beds will have to be measured carefully if they form part of a formal design and they will need to be positioned symmetrically within the lawn.

Shapes such as octagons and hexagons need careful calculation and marking out, unless the scale is large enough they can look pretentious. Ovals are particularly difficult unless you are very methodical.

Think very carefully before considering more complicated shapes. Except in a few cases, they do not work as well as simple outlines as they tend to look fussy, and can be awkward to trim and mow round.

Keeping a straight edge

Nothing mars a flower bed more than an untidy edge. Do not be temped to cut the edges with a spade as this may have a curved profile leaving the edge with a slightly uneven outline. A half-moon edger or edging iron will give a neat, straight edge.

Even an edging iron will not produce a straight edge if you judge by eye. Use a garden line as a guide, then a straight-edge piece of wood to trim against, and keep your toes on the strip of wood to provide something firm to work against.

To give the bed a more pronounced outline, try to make a reasonably deep edge, with the soil gradually mounded towards the middle of the bed.

How to mark out an oval

There will be some trial and error before you get the proportions exactly right, but start by marking the top and bottom and the outside edges of the bed. Stretch the string between the top and bottom pegs and between the side pegs. This will form a cross with the lines intersecting in the middle of the bed. Check that the pegs have been positioned accurately by measuring the distance from the centre to them.

Using a piece of string half the *length* of the oval (the distance from the intersected strings to the top or bottom marker), from one of the *side* pegs mark the positions where it touches the long string. Insert the canes here, 1. Cut string equal to twice the distance between one of these pegs and the top or bottom of the oval (whichever is furthest away), 2. Form this string into a loop.

Drape the loop over the inner pegs. Insert a cane within the loop, and, keeping it taut, mark the line that forms the oval edge, 3. On grass mark the line with sand.

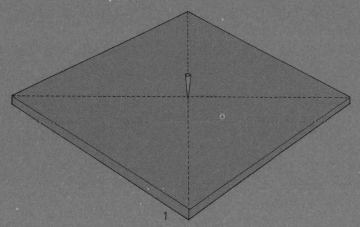

How to mark out an octagon

Start by marking out a square of the required size. This will be dictated by the width of the finished octagon.

Find the centre of the square, which is the point at which two

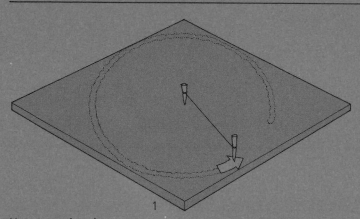

How to make a hexagon

Start by marking out a circle. This is best done by using two canes and a length of string, looped over the cane not tied to it, otherwise the 'winding up' effect will gradually reduce the diameter if you turn it round several times. Push one cane into the ground where the centre

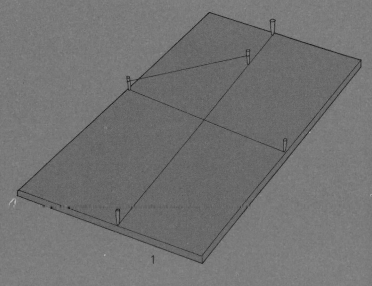

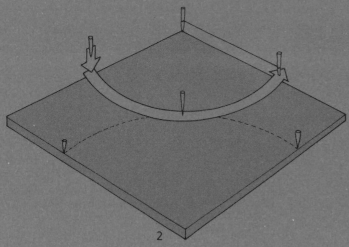

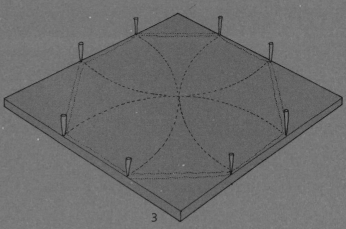

diagonals struck between the corners intersect. Mark this position, **1**.

Using two canes and a piece of string long enough to stretch between a corner of the square and the centre, make an arc with one cane pushed into the ground at the corner. Where the arc touches the sides, push in pegs, **2**. Repeat this from the other three corners.

There will now be eight pegs, which you can join together with a piece of string to provide the octagon, **3**.

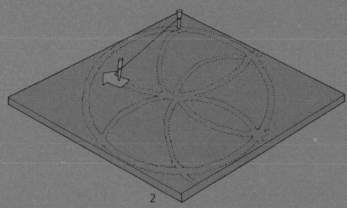

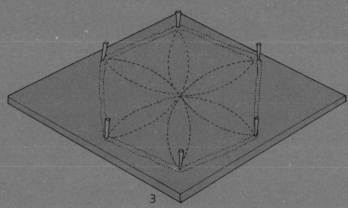

of the circle will be and, keeping the string taut, mark out the perimeter. If you are doing this on grass it will not be possible to mark the arc in the ground, so mark the edge with sand as you work round, **1**.

The radius of the circle, which you already have with your string and two canes, will fit six times round the edge. Start by pushing one cane in where you want a corner, and then push the other cane in where it intersects the perimeter with the string taut. Push in a peg at this point, then continue round the circle in the same way, **2**.

Join the six pegs with string to make a hexagon, **3**.

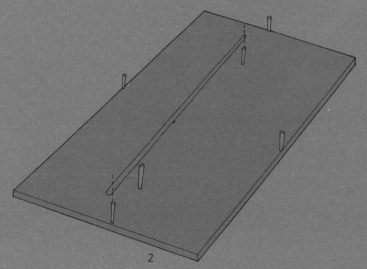

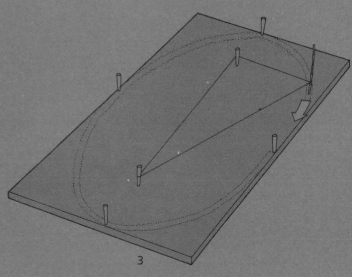

A rock garden is one of the most difficult features to design and construct well unless you have the right site and setting. The ideal rock garden will have plenty of *large* rocks (so large that it will take two or three people to move them into position), a naturally sloping site, and the right background — which is not a garden fence or a view of a house in the background.

At worst, a rock garden can create an effect that looks rather like raisins in a bun. Usually, a well-planned rock feature in a small or medium-sized garden has to be a compromise between these extremes. A 'rock outcrop' bed in a large lawn can be very effective, especially on a gently sloping site.

It is impossible to construct a rock garden to a pre-determined plan — every rock is different, and you can only decide the exact positioning with the rocks in front of you. One famous constructor of rock gardens in the earlier half of this century was described by those who watched him directing his men as being 'like a conductor with his orchestra'. No matter how carefully the outline had been planned before, he would emphasize a point here, choose something lighter there, and shift something slightly to bring out the right tone of the rock.

A book can only describe the principles of construction. The execution has to be individual and unique to a particular garden.

All that is needed for an effective feature is a few rocks placed strategically in an island bed.

The rocks

The choice of rock can set the tone of the feature, and this is particularly important if the rocks are to play a central role in the overall garden design rather than an isolated feature. Colours vary from 'green' and 'blue' slates, to 'red' sandstones and 'white' limestones. Most will tone down as they weather.

The kind of rock that is readily available will depend on where you live. If you set your heart on a type that is quarried hundreds of miles away, you will inevitably have to pay a premium because of high carriage cost.

Generally a locally-quarried stone will fit in most naturally with the surroundings, but sometimes there is no local stone.

Estimating the quantity of rock you will need is extremely difficult. Anyone who does not handle stone regularly will find it hard to visualize the weight of a particular rock, and there is the additional problem of not really knowing how large the pieces will be when they arrive.

Some stone merchants and garden centres will let you go along and select the rocks that you want, and then weigh them for you. Often, though, you will simply have to order rocks by the ton and take whatever sizes and shapes they happen to come in when delivered.

As a very rough guide, a ton of rock will give you about 20 pieces, the size and weight of a hundredweight (50kg) bag of cement.

Much of the rock will be buried beneath the ground, so there will still be considerable guesswork involved in deciding how much you need. However, as a guide, work on the basis of two tons of rock for an area about 10 ft × 10 ft (3m × 3m) if the slope is gentle, and about three tons if the slope is steep.

Large rocks will look most effective, but without help or special equipment you are unlikely to be able to manoeuvre pieces over ½ cwt (25 kg) on your own. If possible choose your own pieces.

Construction

Good drainage is essential. If a mound has to be constructed, this can usually be provided without excavating much of the ground beneath. For a shallow outcrop, though, you should be prepared to excavate the area first, unless the ground is naturally very free-draining. Land drains may be necessary on very wet ground, otherwise excavate to a depth of about 1 ft (300mm), and use a 6 in (150mm) layer of hardcore or stones. If possible, cover this with upturned turves to reduce the chance of the drainage material becoming clogged with soil.

Do not use soil containing roots of perennial weeds. Weeds of any kind are difficult to control in a rock garden, and deep-rooted perennials can be a real problem.

If the topsoil is reasonably light you can simply mix in a generous amount of grit or sharp sand and peat. If the garden soil is heavy, try to use a mixture of three parts garden soil, two parts peat (moss peat is more suitable than sedge peat), and one part coarse sand or grit.

In either case, add about 6½ lb (3 kg) of bonemeal for each cubic metre of soil or compost.

As a guide, for a raised rock outcrop you could need about 1 yard (m³) of compost or soil for a ton (tonne) of rock. You are unlikely to need this amount if the ground has a natural slope.

Constructing a rock garden

Prepare the base and form the soil into the general outline. Leave it for a couple of weeks for weed seeds to germinate and sprout. Remove them by hand or use a suitable herbicide.

Lay out the rocks so you can see the shapes and sizes easily. Choose a large, interesting stone to start with and decide where to place it. You could start at the top, but the bottom is an equally suitable point for your key stone. Excavate enough soil to give the impression that much more of the rock is beneath the ground. The overall effect should be analoguous to the tip of an iceberg. Each rock should tilt backwards slightly, for both stability and appearance.

Bear in mind that any strata lines should run horizontally or at an oblique angle.

Once you are happy with the position of the rock, pack soil beneath and behind it to avoid air pockets.

Choose the next piece of rock, bearing the first in mind. Try to match any strata lines, and colour, if there is much variation, and a size that will look natural next

to the other rocks. If you have a lot of small pieces, these can sometimes be grouped together to make them look like part of one larger piece.

On a steep slope, try to rest each rock on the one below, but be careful not to make them look like a stone or brick wall. Do not be worried about a joint coming directly above the one below – in nature vertical splits often occur down a face.

Use a sack trolley to move rocks, or roll them on a plank over rollers. Do not be tempted to lift and carry them. A wheelbarrow is not really satisfactory because you will have to lift the rocks into it and the weight will make the barrow unstable and may damage it.
Use boards, ropes, levers, and above all help if it is needed.
Below: Island rock beds can be effective but need an open setting to look like natural outcrops.

To look natural, the rocks should follow strata levels with the bulk of each one beneath the surface.

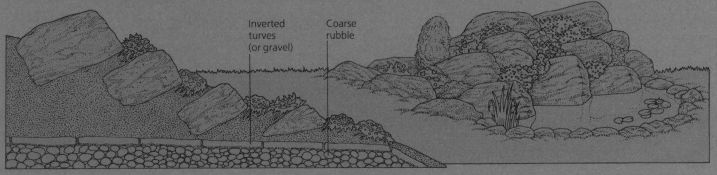

Inverted turves (or gravel)

Coarse rubble

A natural scree is a collection of rocks, small stones and grit that accumulates at the foot of a cliff or mountain. The plants growing there have to survive with the minimum amount of nourishment, and although there is abundant moisture at times, drainage is excellent. Plants growing in a scree are exposed to extremes of temperature and fierce winds. The plants that are naturally adapted to scree life are usually difficult to grow in other conditions in the garden and a scree is often added to a rock garden to accommodate these plants. Ideally, a scree should merge with the rock garden, gradually fanning out from a fissure or gap between the rocks.

For the most favourable growing conditions, the scree should slope at an angle of not less than 20° towards the south. The rocks, small stones and grit that you use to construct the scree should, if possible, be the same sort as the larger rocks used in the construction of the rock garden.

For a scree to look natural, you need quite a large rock garden, and building a scree without a rock garden can look odd.

Screes are a fairly specialist form of gardening, but they can be both attractive and interesting.

Making a scree

Excavate the soil to a depth of about 2 ft (600mm) and place at least 6 in (150mm) of rubble in the bottom. Cover this with a layer of gravel or use inverted old turves.

Use a mixture of three parts soil, two parts coarse sand or grit, and one part peat, to bring the soil back to within a few inches of the finished level. For the top few inches, add an equal part of pea shingle or stone chippings to the previous mixture.

A few rocks will add considerably to the appearance. Do not use too many, and make sure they look as though only the tip of a rock is poking through. The strata should be at the same angle even though the rocks are not close together.

Finish the scree with a layer of pea gravel or stone chippings. In an isolated bed, pea gravel may be adequate, but as part of a rock garden you will need to use suitable stone chippings so the surface does not look incongruous.

If you plan to grow lime-hating plants, avoid limestone chippings; instead use chippings from material like granite.

Planting a scree

Not all alpine plants can be grown in a scree, because of the extremely well drained root run. Particularly suitable species include *Androsace*, many of the dwarf, cushion-forming pinks (*Dianthus*), thrift (*Armeria*), alpine campanulas, and alpine phlox. Try, too, crocus species, dwarf narcissi and dwarf irises.

The most natural site for a scree garden is at the base of a larger rock garden. You could, however, make a small scree bed almost on the level, but it then needs to be quite large to become a worthwhile feature.

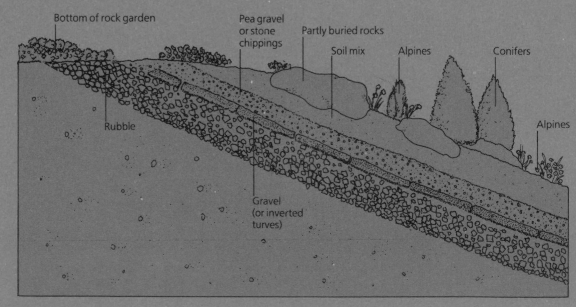

Bottom of rock garden

Pea gravel or stone chippings

Partly buried rocks

Soil mix

Alpines

Conifers

Alpines

Rubble

Gravel (or inverted turves)

A raised peat garden is only worth building if you wish to raise special, lime-hating plants.

Because peat lacks the strength of stone, it will not be possible to gain much height, but as the range of plants that require acid (peaty) conditions is relatively small you should not need to build a large peat bed.

Peat beds are less of a garden feature than a means of growing plants that resent lime in the soil and need the acid conditions provided by the peat. Generally, however, it is better to grow plants that do well in your garden than to concentrate on trying to grow plants that will not thrive naturally. Be particularly cautious about building a peat bed on a chalky slope as the chances are that a lot of lime will be washed into the bed as the moisture drains from the surrounding land. Peat is not suitable for a hot, dry position because once it dries out it can be extremely difficult to moisten again.

You could, of course, provide peat pockets in an ordinary rock garden, but this is seldom satisfactory because the exposed sunny site most rock plants need will not usually suit the peat-lovers, which generally prefer moister, shadier growing conditions.

Aspect is important. It will actually be best in some shade, unlike the normal rock garden for which a sunny site is best. This can make a peat garden a sensible choice where there is too much shade for a rock garden. But dappled shade is best, because then the garden gets reasonably good light without being subject to too much heat from direct sunshine.

Peat blocks are, literally, the building blocks for a peat garden. They are easy to buy if you live in an area where peat is dug, but more difficult elsewhere, although you can sometimes buy them from garden centres.

Constructing a peat bed

As peat blocks are taken from the surface of peat deposits, check that they don't contain roots of perennial weeds, and remove any that you find. If the blocks are dry, start by soaking them. Do not attempt to start building with dry blocks. It may take several hours before they absorb enough moisture. Also make sure that you have a supply of moist loose peat available.

Prepare the site by making sure the drainage is adequate. Heavy ground may need draining first. Although the peat has to be kept moist, it should not be constantly waterlogged. Work a generous amount of peat into the top 9 in (230mm) of soil. Working it to a greater depth will not do any harm, but there is a risk that unless you have a huge supply of peat (which can be costly), it will be distributed too thinly through the soil.

Level or shape the site before you start laying the blocks. Form the contours first, bearing in mind that the 'bricks' will be laid in tiers, and firm the ground where they are to be placed.

Position the lowest tier of blocks first, keeping them level but possibly sweeping in an arc to avoid regimented steps. Put the blocks together closely, and use the damp peat to ram between them for rigidity. Try to make sure that the blocks are firm, and incline them backwards slightly for additional strength.

Top up the level behind the blocks with a mixture of two parts moss peat to one part lime-free soil and one part sand or grit. Then position the new tier of blocks.

On a sloping site it may be useful to build the steps two blocks high at the same time, in which case they should be staggered like brickwork for strength.

Peat beds tend to settle with age and you may have to top them up with another layer of the special soil mixture or some well-rotted leaf mould. Even then, count on a life span of ten years or so, before they need rebuilding.

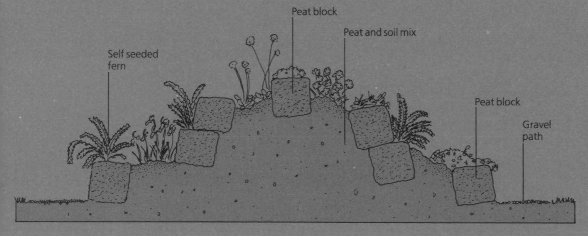

Self seeded fern

Peat block

Peat and soil mix

Peat block

Gravel path

The blocks in a peat bed should be staggered like bricks to provide a strong bond. They should also tilt back for the same reason. It may be necessary to make the walls two blocks thick if the step is more than say two blocks high.

If there is a risk of lime draining in from the surrounding soil, make a trench to take the water away.

In the days before flexible liners or pre-formed plastic and glass-fibre (in America, fibreglass) pools, making a pool was a difficult and unpredictable job as well as being physically hard work. Nowadays you can take the dry components home in the car, and have your pool finished in a weekend.

The fact that these modern materials are easy to use may mean disappointing results. Creating a water-tight pool is easy; getting it to look good is more difficult. Liners are often a conspicious colour that emphasizes any unevenness round the edge or any gap between water level and edging. If the water is clear you will realize how difficult it is to avoid creases and folds that can look ugly. Pre-formed pools are generally small, despite how large they look out of the ground, and you may find that the capacity or depth is inadequate.

Despite these reservations, concrete pools are only worth considering in special cases. They are expensive, hard work to make, need careful reinforcing during construction, and treatment to make the pond safe for plants and fish. They are prone to frost damage and leak surprising easily.

Which material?

Prices will obviously depend on quality and supplier, and relative costs may also vary in different countries but, as a guide, the following materials are listed in order of increasing cost. Pre-formed pools are not included because there are too many other variable factors involved for sensible comparisons to be made.

Heavy-gauge polythene (in America known as polyethylene) (used double thickness). Although this is the cheapest material, bear in mind that you need good quality and twice the amount so that it can be used double thickness. It is easily damaged and may only have a life of a couple of years. This is quite acceptable for a temporary or short-term pool, but otherwise the cost difference is unlikely to be great enough to make it a sensible alternative to laminated PVC, which is a good deal more durable.

Laminated PVC This is a good choice if you need to keep the cost down but want a material with a life expectancy of say five to ten years.

Using a liner

Always work out the liner size carefully before you start. Take the longest point and add *twice* the maximum depth, and also add twice the depth to the width. This will apply even if you have marginal shelves (ledges on which to grow plants that do not like deep water). This allows material for lipping.

Make the pool deep enough so that the fish can survive during the winter, but no garden pool needs to be deeper than, say 2½ ft (750mm). The depth should also bear some relationship to the surface area. As a guide, a pool up to 22 sq ft (2 sq m) should be about 15 in (380mm) deep; up to 100 sq ft (9 sq m), 1½ ft (450mm) while one up to 200 sq ft (18 sq m) would be best about 2 ft (600mm) deep.

Mark out the shape on the ground, using sand or even a hosepipe, **1**. Be prepared to make adjustments if necessary, provided these do not exceed the maximum dimensions allowed for when the liner size was calculated. Make sure there are no tight curves: broad sweeps will look more natural and make the liner easier to instal.

If the pool is being set within an existing lawn, remove the turf for about 1 ft (300mm) beyond the edge of the pool. This will make levelling easier, and the depth of the removed turf will be used for the pool edging afterwards.

Level the area *now* using a straight-edge and spirit-level, **2**. Although levels will have to be checked again later, it is much easier to do any important levelling at this stage once you are taking levels from pegs within the excavated area. You may have to re-define the outline of the pool again before you start excavating.

Remove the soil to a depth of about 9 in (230mm) keeping to the inside of your outline marker. You can always remove a bit more later if necessary. The sides should not be vertical: give them a slope of about 20 degrees, or 3 inches in the 9 inches (75mm in 230mm),

1. Mark out the area then excavate to paving depth

2. Allow for a marginal shelf, and check levels

Laminated PVC with nylon reinforcement The nylon reinforcement will increase the cost significantly but you can expect a life of about ten years. It is tough, but can still be cut with a knife.

Butyl There are different qualities and gauges of butyl, so bear this in mind when comparing prices. The cheaper ones may not be much more expensive than laminated and reinforced PVC. Quality butyl can be expected to last for 50 years.

Butyl is normally black (but see below), and because it stretches it is very easy to use.

Concrete Making a concrete pool is an expensive proposition and should only be undertaken with professional help. The drawbacks have already been described. The main advantage is that once it weathers and loses its 'rawness', concrete generally looks far more natural than most liners.

Butyl with stone-coloured plastic laminate This is very strong, with a life expectancy of 50 years, but you pay a high premium for the coloured finish which may not be an advantage (see below).

What about colour?

Some liners are coloured blue on one side and stone on the other and you may have a choice with the same liner, depending which side you use upwards. These may seem attractive but it is only after using both the black butyl and the coloured PVCs that you realize the visual merits of the former and the drawbacks of the latter.

The coloured PVC liners do not have the same 'stretch' as butyl, so you are bound to have a lot of creases in any pool of irregular shape, though with formal shapes the surplus can be folded into pleats. The creases will almost certainly soon become hidden below water level as soil and other debris washes into the pond, and the green algae that almost always forms covers the liner anyway, in which case any idea of a blue or stone pond will be lost. What will be left unaffected is the area *above* the water, and this will act as a constant reminder that you have a very artificial-looking pond. Remember that water in nature usually looks murky – rarely bright turquoise blue.

On the other hand, black butyl will be inconspicuous above or below the water-line.

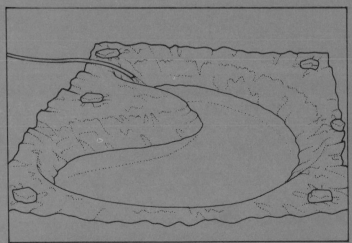

3. Fill the liner, moving the bricks as necessary

4. Paving helps to hide the edge of the liner

although on sandy soil it may have to be more gradual.

Level the bottom, using a straight-edge and spirit level, then mark the edge of the marginal shelf about 9 in (230mm) in from the edge, if you want one.

Excavate the inner area to the final depth, and make sure you do not exceed the depth used to calculate the size of the liner. Again maintain a slope of about 20 degrees for the sides.

Remove any large stones or tree roots that are protruding. If the soil is sandy, that may be sufficient, otherwise spread a layer of sand over the base and the shelf. Old damp newspapers could be used instead, and these are easier to apply to the sides. Polyester matting can also be used to provide a good base for the liner.

Make a final check on levels. If the pool is narrow enough, use a long straight-edge and spirit-level across the pool at various positions. Otherwise drive a peg into the ground in the centre, and take levels all round from this. Any irregularities in level will soon be shown up by the water, and are difficult to correct afterwards.

Position the liner over the pool, making sure it overlaps the widest points equally and, with the liner draped loosely into the excavation, place a few bricks round the edge as anchors.

Run water into the liner, 3. As the level increases, ease the bricks off and reposition them to allow the liner to be taken into the excavation.

Some creases will be inevitable, but for a rectangular pool these can be minimized by making pleats at the corners.

Fill the pond to the edges, which will reveal whether they have been levelled properly. Leave a 4-6 in (100-150mm) lip all round.

Finish the edge with paving or turf, 4. If you want to plant up to one edge of the pool, use inverted turves at the edge, as loose soil will soon be washed into the water. Stone or paving slab edges should be bedded in a mix of three parts sand to one part masonry cement.

Installing a pre-formed pool

The method will vary slightly depending on whether you are installing a vacuum-formed semi-rigid pool or one made from glass-fibre (in America known as fibreglass).

Lay the pool in position the right way up, and use a stick to mark the shape on to the ground, using the outer edge of the rim as a guide (on grass you may have to mark the shape with sand).

For a glass-fibre pool add another 6 in (150mm) all round.

Excavate the soil to the maximum depth of the pool, plus 1 in (25mm) *and* the thickness of any paving material you intend to use round the edge, **1.**

Many pre-formed pools have complex shelves and angles. It is not feasible to excavate these exactly, so take the whole area out to the full depth. You will be able to pack soil beneath the shelves later.

Place 1 in (25mm) of sand at the bottom of the hole and then insert the shell. Use a spirit-level on a straight-edge to check that it is absolutely level before you proceed.

Once it is level, gradually back-fill the cavity with sand or sifted soil, compacting it thoroughly, especially beneath the shelves, **2.**

A semi-rigid pool should be filled to the level of compacted soil as you proceed. For a glass-fibre pool, wait until the job has been finished.

Remember to check the levels periodically as you back-fill in case you have pushed the pool up while compacting the soil.

Raised pools

Raised pools feature in several of the designs illustrated in this book. They have many advantages: there is less soil to excavate; the fish are often easier to spot; there is less risk of anyone falling in, young and old alike; and raised pools can make more of a feature in a formal garden.

Making a raised pool

Prepare a firm foundation—about 5 in (130mm) of concrete on a hardcore base (see page 151) across the full width, but increasing the depth beneath the brickwork (see page 153). If you are using a butyl liner, place a layer of sand over cleared and level ground, using proper foundations just for the wall. To increase the depth of the pond without high walls above ground level, excavate 1 ft (300mm) of soil.

Once the foundation for the wall has set, build a full-brick wall to the required height (see page 157).

If you are using a butyl liner, fold this into the brickwork at the finished water level, before you reach the coping, and mortar the bricks in place on top. Fold in just enough to hold the liner in position; it does not need to span the full width of the wall.

Feed in cable for a submersible pump at this point.

Where bricks are an integrated feature of the overall garden design, it makes sense to top the wall with brick coping. If you plan to render the surfaces, or clad the outside, pre-cast concrete slab coping may be more suitable.

If you do not use a butyl liner, render the inside with a 1 in (25mm) layer of one part cement to three parts of sharp sand, with a waterproofing powder added according to the manufacturer's instructions. The whole of the inside surface must be applied in one session and be smoothed off carefully, eliminating any air bubbles.

A concrete rendering will release lime into the water and this can be harmful to the plants and fish if they are introduced too quickly. You can paint on a neutralizing chemical, otherwise the pool will have to be filled and emptied several times, leaving the final change in for about a week before emptying and refilling once again.

Another option is to use a waterproof rubber paint.

Cascades

Cascades introduce the sound of running water, but to be successful they need careful planning and suitable pumps. Low-voltage submersible pumps are popular but for a fast-flowing cascade a more powerful mains pump in an outside chamber may be better.

Take great care with the levels of each cascade, especially if you want the water to pour over the width of a lip.

Pond liner material can be used, as shown, but if you lack the confidence to try this, you can buy pre-formed glass-fibre (glass-reinforced plastic) cascade trays.

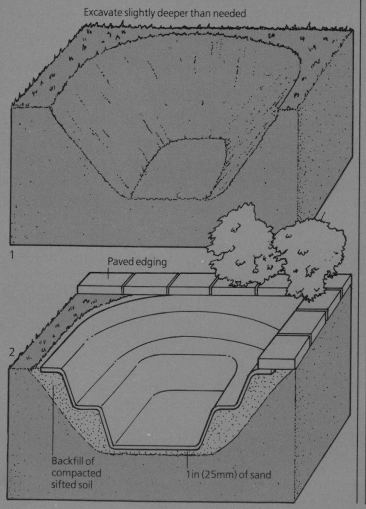

Excavate slightly deeper than needed

1

Paved edging

2

Backfill of compacted sifted soil

1 in (25mm) of sand

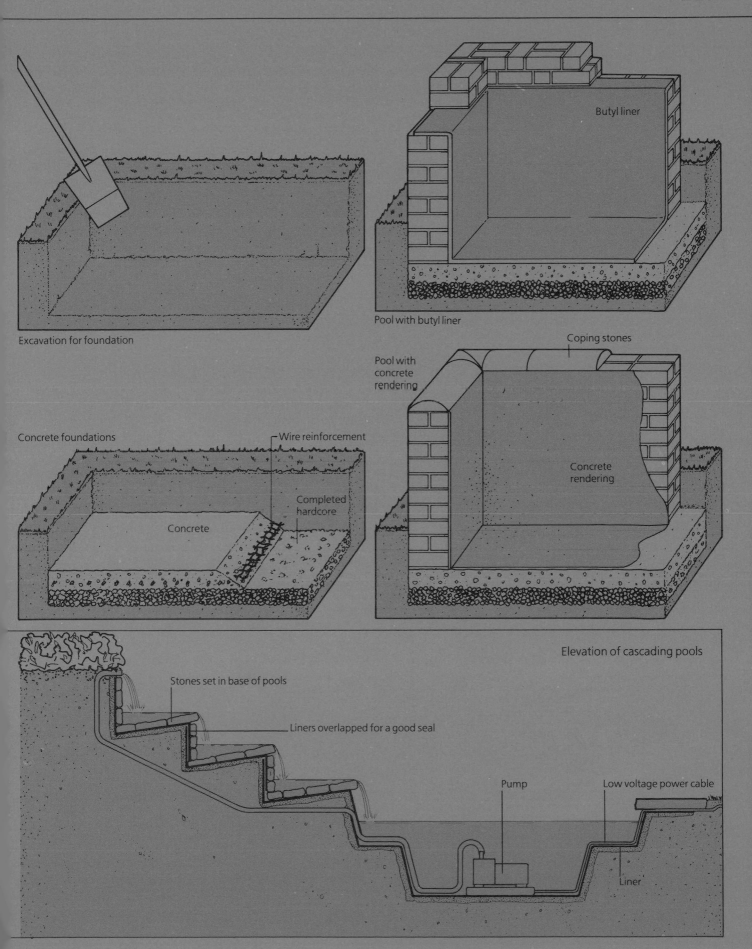

Excavation for foundation

Pool with butyl liner

Butyl liner

Concrete foundations

Wire reinforcement

Completed hardcore

Concrete

Pool with concrete rendering

Coping stones

Concrete rendering

Elevation of cascading pools

Stones set in base of pools

Liners overlapped for a good seal

Pump

Low voltage power cable

Liner

There are many types of wood panel fence, but most are erected in the same way: as panels 6 ft (1.8m) long. A professional who erects a long stretch of fencing may choose to assemble the whole close-board fence on site, nailing individual boards to arris rails, with the horizontal rails fixed to the posts, but for the amateur, fencing panels are generally less trouble.

Erecting fencing panels

Mark the line of the fence with string stretched between the stake at each end, **1**. Then lay the posts roughly in position on the ground, bearing in mind that, if the panels are 6 ft (1.8m) long, the spacing between posts will be that plus the width of the post.

Take out the first hole. As a guide, for a post with about 2 ft (600mm) above ground, a hole about 1 ft (300mm) deep should be adequate, but a 6ft (1.8m) fence will need about 2½ ft of post below ground.

If you have a lot of posts to insert, it is worth hiring a post-hole borer, **2**.

Place the first post on a little hardcore, then pack bricks or rubble around the base to hold the post upright, checking periodically to make sure that it is vertical using a long spirit-level, **3**. If the first post is positioned against the house, you can fix it to the wall with 1/4 in (6mm) diameter rag bolts. Drill through the post first, then use a larger bit to countersink the hole (the bolt head must not obstruct the panel). Make sure the post is vertical and mark the wall through the drilled holes in the post. Remove the post to drill the wall with a masonry bit to take the bolts.

Using the first fencing panel as a guide (lay it on the ground, butting up to the first post), mark the position of the second post. Dig out the second hole and insert the post as before, but this time you will also have to check that they are the same height. If you have a long, straight-edged piece of wood you can use this with a spirit-level, **3**. Otherwise, stretch a piece of string along the length of the fence at the finished height.

Fix the first panel into position, **4** with galvanized nails or screws, or use special brackets sold for the job, which is a better choice if you are likely to want to remove the panel for any reason.

The base of the panel should not be in contact with the soil. Either use a gravel board (a piece of wood that you can replace when it rots, without having to replace the whole panel), or stand it on bricks or blocks, **5**.

Firm the posts once more, checking that they are vertical, and top the hole up with concrete forming a sloping 'shoulder' against the post above soil level, to throw moisture away from the base, **6**.

Nail temporary struts to the posts to keep them in position until the concrete is firm, **7**. Continue along the fence until the last post is in place.
Never attempt to erect a tall or solid fence on a windy day.

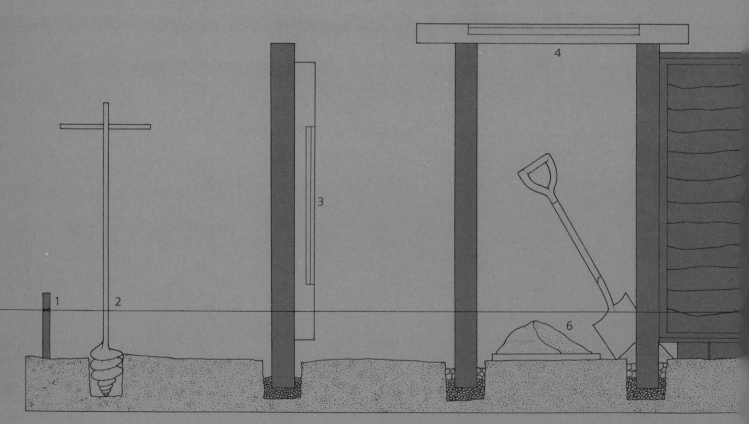

Posts and post supports

A fence will only be as strong as its posts. They should be long enough to be well anchored (see above), but the cross-section of the timber (in America known as lumber) is also important. Sizes generally vary between 2 in × 3 in (50mm × 75mm) and 4 in × 6 in (100mm × 150mm). The taller the fence, the more substantial the posts need to be. The fencing supplier should be able to advise you on the most suitable posts for a particular fence, but if in doubt, err on the large side.

Wooden posts should always be pressure or vacuum impregnated with a preservative by the supplier. If you have to cut the post, though, paint, or preferably soak, the cut surface with a perservative to prevent rot.

A long lasting alternative to timber is concrete. Although you might think of concrete posts as ugly, in reality they can look very neat, since the panels slide into grooves cast into the concrete. Specify if you need corner posts, as these have the grooves cast in adjoining sides. There are other possibilities, including metal posts, but timber or concrete are the most widely available.

Metal post supports

Post supports save the work involved in digging a hole. There is no concrete to buy, carry and mix, and the posts can be shorter, though the cost saved on the post will not offset the price of the support. Above all, they will not rot.

On the debit side you have to make sure that the post is a good fit, and the supports themselves are not always easy to drive in absolutely straight, which is essential. Also, not everyone likes the collar that is visible at the base of the post.

You should be able to buy or borrow a metal fitment to drop into the post-holder while you hammer it in with a sledge-hammer or club-hammer. This can be hard work, and it is also essential to stop frequently to check the verticals with a spirit-level.

There are various types, some of which can be adjusted and tightened round the post.

Other fences

Plastic ranch-style fences These are easy to erect. The exact method of fixing will depend on the make. Follow the instructions provided by the manufacturer.

Chain link fences These are quick and easy to put up, but the posts must be fixed properly. Ideally the posts (usually angle-iron) should be concreted into position, making sure the straining bars are on the right side to take the strain.

Send for a manufacturer's leaflet before ordering as systems vary slightly, and it is impossible to deal with detailed assembly instructions within the limited space available in this book. It is important to order the correct parts.

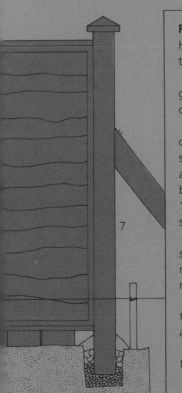

Fixing a gate

Hanging a gate requires patience and precision on the job, and careful measurement is important.

Leave a 3 in (75mm) clearance gap between the ground and the bottom of the closed gate. Start by cutting wedges this thickness.

The space between the posts should be the width of the gate plus 1 ½ in (40mm) on each side of a single gate, but 1 ½ in (40mm) between each gate and post for a double gate, with ½ in (12mm) gap between the two halves, allowing perhaps another 1/5 in (6mm) for wooden gates to allow for swelling.

The type of 'hardware' used (hinge, latches, and so on) will depend on the type of gate and the materials used for both gate and post. The exact method of fitting them varies.

Concrete posts usually have pre-drilled holes. If these are not suitable, bolt lengths of wood to them and screw the hinge fittings into these.

A gate post should have about 2 ½ ft (750mm) in the ground, more for a gate over 5ft (1.5m) high.

Pack moist concrete around the post and use a spirit-level and tape-measure frequently to make sure the position is correct as you proceed. Half fill the hole with concrete, then wait until you are sure the gate hangs well before filling the hole.

The gate will have to be supported with props and blocks for a few days until the concrete has set.

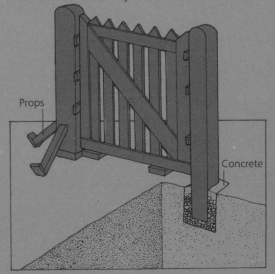

Props

Concrete

Foundations are perhaps the least interesting part of garden construction since they can be very hard work to prepare and construct, and once completed there is nothing to see for all the effort. They can also add significantly to the cost of a job.

There is always a temptation to skimp on foundations and you may have an urge to skip these few pages of the book. But *they are important*, as you will appreciate if your walls begin to crack or your paving sinks because the foundations are inadequate.

A structure of any kind needs a solid foundation to spread the load and carry it down to stable ground. In the case of free-standing walls, a foundation also provides lateral stability.

Because foundations are needed for so many different garden construction jobs, from paths and patios to walls and raised water gardens, the principles are described here. But special techniques, such as foundations for laying 'flexible' paving, are explained on the relevant pages.

How large?

The size of the foundations should be determined by the soil type as well as what it has to support. Some soils are much more stable than others. Clay soils are prone to shrinking and can be particularly troublesome, and for walls over about 3 ft (1m) high on this type of ground, it may be worth seeking the advice of your local building inspector.

Most jobs in the garden are likely to be for low walls or for paving that is only going to take light traffic (front drives are an exception as they may be used by heavy delivery vehicles), so general guidelines should be adequate.

Excavating the ground

If a lot of digging and levelling is needed, it is worth considering professional help. A contractor will have the equipment to do the job quickly and easily, and should be able to take the soil away unless you need it to build up another part of the garden.

If you do it yourself and need to dispose of the soil, it is worth hiring a skip. They usually take about 10 tons which is about 6-8 cu yds (4.5-6 m³) of soil. Working on your own it will probably take you a couple of days to fill the skip. There are, of course, smaller skips.

Getting the level right

If you are laying paving on top of the foundation, bear in mind the thickness of the mortar, as well as the slab or brick. This is important if you want the paving at a particular level.

Start by fixing a datum point. For a patio adjoining the house, the damp-proof course is a sensible

Finding a level

There are several ways of finding a datum level, an essential starting point.

A straight-edge and spirit-level, spanning pegs, **1** are the usual tools. By checking from peg to peg it should be possible to level even a large area by this method.

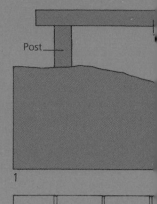

If you are working close to a house it may be possible to use the brickwork as a datum point, **2**. but you must ensure that the finished level will be at least 6in (150mm) below the damp-proof course.

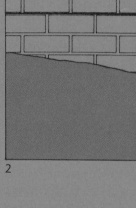

A third method, especially useful for awkward places, perhaps if there is a tree or other obstacle in the way, is to let water find the level, **3**. Use a hose-pipe attached to pegs, and fill it with water. When the water is full to the top of both ends, you have found the level. If necessary, you can measure down from the pegs.

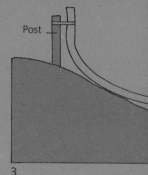

point, provided you remember that any paving must be at least 6 in (150mm) below this level.

For a narrow strip, the easiest way of checking that the ground and foundations are level is to use a spirit-level on a straight-edge spanning two pegs. Start with the top of the first peg at datum level, and leave the second peg slightly high so you can gradually tap it down until the required level is achieved.

Before proceeding, reverse the straight-edge and check again. This will reveal whether the straight-edge is true. You can then work from one peg to the next.

For a larger span you may find it easier to improvize a water-tube level. Fill a length of transparent plastic tubing with water and colour it with ink or dye if you want to make it more visible. Both ends

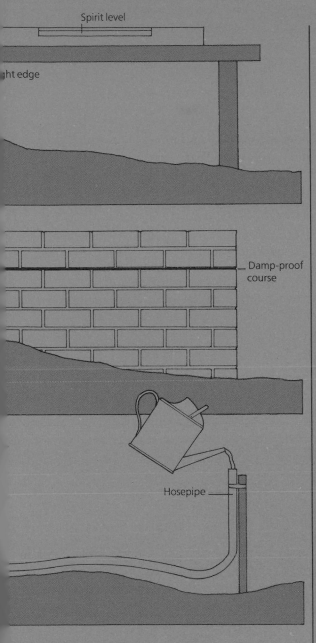

Spirit level

ght edge

Damp-proof course

Hosepipe

'Setting out' for foundations

'Setting out' is a jargon term for marking out the area of the foundation. You could manage to lay a small footing for a wall perfectly well without elaborate marking out, but it is always better to do it properly.

The principles are illustrated in the diagram below. Always set the string on the outside edge of the area to be excavated.

Foundation for a garden wall

The foundation for a wall up to about 2½ ft (750mm) high should be twice the width of the wall itself. As a single brick is about 4 in (100mm) wide, the footing would need to be 8 in (200mm) wide for a half-brick wall (the term for a wall only one brick thick). For a full-brick wall (two bricks across) it will have to be at least 16 in (400mm).

If the wall is higher than 2½ ft (750mm), the width of the foundation should be increased to three times the width of the masonry.

The *thickness* of the foundation need only be about 6 in (150mm) of concrete over 5 in (130mm) of hardcore or hoggin (a mixture of sand or clay and gravel) for a half-brick wall. But increase the concrete to about 9 in (230mm) for a full-brick wall. However, the trench will be deeper than this, as ideally the top of the footing should be below ground level by about one block depth or the depth of three brick courses.

A thicker, deeper foundation could be required on a clay soil.

Going uphill will mean stepped footings. Make sure that the steps equal the height of one course of brickwork or blocks and that there is an adequate overlap between the layers (at least the length of a brick or block).

A ground slab

There are many occasions when a slab of concrete cast *in situ* is required. An *in situ* cast slab is useful for garages and sheds (though often you can manage without this extra job), or as a base for a patio or even a coal bunker.

There are a few basic rules regarding size that are intended to maintain strength and reduce the risk of cracking.

The length should ideally not be more than one-and-a-half times the width, and the maximum dimension should not exceed 13 ft (4m), preferably not more than 10 ft (3m).

If the area is larger than this, cast the base in sections, leaving expansion joints between them.

The thickness of the concrete will depend on use and size. If the sub-soil or sub-base is firm, and the load light, 3 in (75mm) of concrete should be enough, otherwise go for 4 in (100mm). If the area is to be used by heavy commercial vehicles, or if the ground is heavy

must be open when you take the measurement, though you can plug the ends while you are getting the tube into place. The water will always be the same level at each end, so you can easily check the level of pegs at a distance (see illustration), or around an obstacle that might otherwise make levelling difficult.

Patios, drives and other paved areas that are likely to collect rainwater, should be laid with a fall so rain can run off instead of forming puddles.

As a general principle, aim at a fall of about 1 in for every 40 in (25mm for every 1m). This is best done by setting the pegs at 40 in (1m) intervals and using a piece of wood 1 in (25mm) thick to rest on the lower peg each time. If the straight-edge is levelled on top of the 1 in (25mm) shim the fall should be correct.

clay, as much as 6 in (150mm) may be necessary.

The sub-base can be hardcore (building rubble), but it must be broken down into small pieces, and is not as suitable as hoggin or scalpings. Hoggin is usually a clayey gravel; scalpings are usually taken to be 1 in (25mm) stone with dust. One or other should be available from a good builders' merchant.

Finishing is best done with a steel float trowel if you want a smooth finish, but for a large slab, and if a more ridged finish is acceptable, a wooden tamping board may be more convenient. This job is best done by two people, one at each end of the board.

Joints will be necessary if the area is large. Simply divide the area up into smaller sections or 'bays', making each equal in size if possible.

If you are spreading the job over several days, you can let one bay set, then butt the next batch of concrete up to the previous one.

If ready-mixed concrete is being used, then this is not feasible. Cut strips of hardboard to divide off the sections, mounding a little concrete either side to hold them upright, then lay the concrete into the bays on

each side. When using a tamping board, work towards the dividing board from each side alternatively so it is not pushed out of position.

A shed or summerhouse base
Most sheds and summerhouses can be bought with a wooden floor and treated supporting beams. On firm ground this may be adequate, but ideally you should use a concrete slab base even if you stand the timber floor on this. The concrete base should preferably be about 6 in (150mm) above the level of the surrounding ground, to minimize splashing and consequent rotting.

Choosing the right mix
Concrete will only be as good as the mix and the mixing. Unfortunately, the most convenient way to buy concrete to mix yourself – dry, ready-mixed in bags – is both expensive and impractical for all except the smallest jobs; and you may need to make repeated journeys, which will add to the expense and time. Also convenient, within reason, is ready-mixed concrete, and the supplier will make sure the right mix is

Profile boards will help you to set out the work accurately. Mark positions on the boards for both the trench and foundation widths, and the lines for laying the bricks.

Keep the boards in position after excavating the trench and preparing the foundations. Then move the strings across to provide a profile for bricklaying.

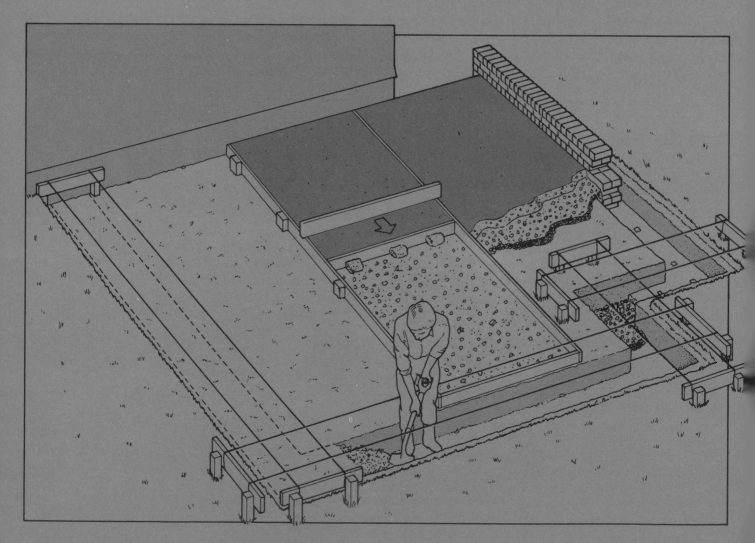

provided if you explain carefully what you want it for. If you order ready-mix concrete, you are committed to doing the job as soon as you get the concrete, regardless of the weather, and will probably need plenty of helpers as you will be working against time. In short, you need to be very well organized.

The third option is to mix it yourself, though there are firms that will bring a mixer on a lorry and do the mixing for you.

If you do your own mixing there are several problems to be overcome if you have not bought concreting materials before: *what* to order, and *how much* to order. The following two mixes should be adequate for any gardening DIY jobs:

For foundations (for walls and as a base for precast paving slabs for instance):
- 1 part cement
- 2½ parts concreting (sharp) sand
- 3½ parts ¾ in (20mm) aggregate
  (instead of the separate sand and aggregate you could use 6 parts combined aggregate). One bag of cement should produce about 6 cu ft (0.18m³) of concrete. Alternatively you may find the following guide to quantities more convenient:

For 100 sq ft (10sq m) of concrete 2 in (50mm) thick:
- 4 × 1 cwt (50kg) bags cement
- 17½ cu ft (0.5 m³) combined aggregate

For 100 sq ft (10sq m) of concrete 3 in (75mm) thick:
- 6 × 1 cwt (50kg) bags cement
- 26½ cu ft (0.75m³) combined aggregate

For 100 sq ft (10 sq m) of concrete 4 in (100mm) thick:
- 7 × 1 cwt (50kg) bags cement
- 35 cu ft (1m³) combined aggregate.

Note: these figures are only an approximate guide, and the amount of cement has been rounded up to the next full bag.

For exposed paving/drives (where the concrete is to form the finished surface):
- 1 part cement
- 1½ parts concreting (sharp) sand
- 2½ parts ¾ in (20mm) aggregate
  (instead of the separate sand and aggregate, you could use 3 1/2 parts combined aggregate). One bag of cement should produce 4 cu ft (0.12m³) of concrete.

Do not use masonry cement for concrete. If in doubt tell the supplier what you want it for.

'Curing' concrete

Concrete needs both time and moisture to set and harden (cure) properly. If it dries out too rapidly it may be weak and will soon start to shrink and crack.

Foundations are normally in a trench and therefore reasonably protected, but a more exposed area of concrete, such as a path or drive, or the base for a patio or shed, should be treated carefully.

Once the surface is hard enough to be marked, cover it with a sheet of polythene (in America polyethylene), weighted at the edges to prevent the wind lifting it. Joints may need taping. Leave it in place for a couple of days.

Do not lay concrete in frosty weather. If it turns frosty shortly after you have laid concrete, try to insulate it with straw or even soil between layers of polythene.

Mixing concrete

By hand

Measure the aggregate and sand in a bucket and make a small heap with it.

Make a depression in the top then tip the measured cement into this. Always measure by volume, using the same container.

Mix thoroughly, turning the heap frequently, until it is an even colour.

Make another depression in the top and add some water. Bring dry material forward into the water. Add more water and turn the mixture until the whole heap is uniform in colour and consistency.

In a mixer

Put half of the measured coarse aggregate and half the estimated amount of water into the drum and let it turn for a while.

Add the bulk of the sand and cement.

Gradually add the rest of the materials, one at a time, and try to keep the mixture fairly moist until towards the end of the mix.

Many of the bricklaying principles apply equally to concrete blocks, but for these there are special considerations, discussed on pages 158-159.

Bricklaying is not difficult, but you do have to be neat and methodical. Short-cuts are tempting, but if you fail to work to proper lines or do not check frequently enough with the spirit-level, there will probably be alignment errors that will mar the finished job, making it look amateurish. If you follow simple rules, though, bricklaying can be an extremely satisfying part of constructing a garden, and you will have acquired a skill that is useful for many other projects.

Ordering the bricks

The job should always be planned carefully on paper. Bricks can be expensive, so you need to calculate the number needed fairly accurately, though you must allow for some breakages, especially if you use a bond that calls for cut bricks.

Allow for the mortar joints in the calculations. In Britain, a standard brick is 8½ in (215mm) long, 4 in (102.5mm) wide, and 2½ in (65mm) deep, but with a ½ in (10mm) mortar joint your calculations should be based on 9in × 4½in × 3in (225mm × 112.5mm × 75mm).

If you are looking for a quick guide to the number of bricks required, a half-brick wall – 4½ in (225mm) wide – will need 60 bricks for every square metre of walling; a full-brick wall – 9 in (450mm) wide – will take 120.

For a low wall of up to say 2 ft (600mm) a single thickness (half brick) will be adequate, but over this you will need a double thickness (full-brick) wall for strength, which will considerably increase the number of bricks required. You could go up to 4½ ft (1.3m) with single thickness by building strengthening piers (thickened sections of wall) about every 10 ft (3m) and at the ends, but this will also require additional bricks.

Walls that are very long, or over 6 ft (1.8m) high, will need some form of reinforcement even though they are full-brick. There are several ways of strengthening such a wall apart from thickening it still further. These include change of direction in the brickwork, the incorporation of buttresses and other reinforcements. However, walls of this height can be dangerous on account of wind pressure and should be designed with professional help.

It is not really possible for an amateur to tell whether a brick is suitable simply by looking at it, though you can get a good idea by trying to scrape it with a coin: if it scratches easily it is probably too soft.

The terms used for the different brick qualities may vary from country to country, but in Britian most 'special quality' bricks (this is a recognized technical term) are suitable whereas soft 'facing' bricks intended for normal buildings are likely to be unsuitable. It is always best to explain what you want them for.

Although most bricks are made from clay, there are other types such as calcium silicate. These tend to be rather pale in colour and have a more 'clinical' look. They can be very effective, but use these only if you are sure they will suit the design. In general it is safer to stick to clay bricks.

Some bricks have holes pierced from one side to the other (pierced bricks), which is a drawback unless you are using some form of coping. 'Frogged' bricks (a 'frog' is a depression in one side) are more common and are perfectly adequate. The frog is normally laid upwards, but for the top row, or where the depression would be visible, simply lay them with the frog down.

The most important quality to look for in a brick is an ability to withstand wetting and freezing from all sides. Bricks used for a house wall are subject to moisture from rain on only one side, and are unlikely to become thoroughly soaked through and then frozen. As a result many bricks used for house building will start to flake or crumble after a year or two in a garden wall or a raised flower bed.

The number you require may influence both your choice of bricks (on cost grounds) and where you buy them.

A few hundred or even a couple of thousand bricks will almost certainly have to be bought from a builders' merchant, but if you need, say, 5,000 or more it is worth phoning a few brickworks to see whether they will quote you a price. The minimum amount that they will deliver depends on the policy of the firm and where you live. You will probably find that even those willing to sell to you direct will need to sell quite a large number to make the delivery worthwhile.

Delivery charges from a brickworks (even a local one) can be substantial, but for a large quantity the lower cost of the bricks themselves can achieve very worthwhile savings.

A local brickworks may not have a wide range of bricks to offer you, but you will almost certainly receive good, authoritative advice about the suitability of the brick for the job.

If you go to a builders' merchant because the quantity of bricks you require is small, you may have to depend on the expertise of the person serving you. Unfortunately there are plenty of builders' merchants who don't have enough knowledge of their products to be able to advise on the different uses of bricks.

When they arrive

Take the trouble to stack the bricks neatly on a level area of hardstanding such as concrete or wooden planks, and cover them with a sheet of polythene. This is to prevent them absorbing too much moisture. If they are saturated when you come to use them they may lack the necessary 'suction' and will 'float' on the water instead of making a firm bond. Saturated bricks are also more likely to bring soluble salts to the surface when they dry resulting in the unsightly white deposit, known as efflorescence, sometimes seen on brickwork.

Preparing the ground

For details of how to construct the foundations, refer to pages 150-153. Use 'profiles' to mark out the area for the foundations. If you make profile boards like those shown, it is best to keep them in place even when you have finished the foundations, because you can use nails driven in at the right position between which to stretch your strings to set the line of bricks.

The finished height of the foundation should be two or three bricks below ground level, so the top of the trench may have to be opened out enough to make bricklaying comfortable.

Wait a week for the foundations to set properly before you start laying the bricks.

Making a start

If you have never laid bricks before, practise with a few bricks and some mortar. This will give you an opportunity to get used to handling the mortar and judging how to get the joints an even thickness of about ½ in (15mm). Try building up a corner, making sure that the bricks are level horizontally and vertically and try to keep the face clean and free of mortar dribbles.

Having a trial run with a corner will also enable you to try out what is often the most difficult part of a bond (see Box right), as many of them call for cut bricks at this point.

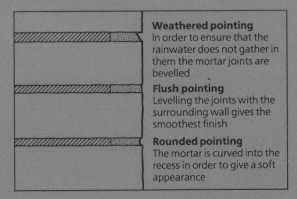

Weathered pointing
In order to ensure that the rainwater does not gather in them the mortar joints are bevelled

Flush pointing
Levelling the joints with the surrounding wall gives the smoothest finish

Rounded pointing
The mortar is curved into the recess in order to give a soft appearance

Mortar and mixing

Do not be tempted to use sand and cement left over from the foundations to make mortar. Mortar requires 'soft' sand, and unless you add a separate plasticizer you will need to buy masonry cement. You can also make a mortar with lime, cement and sand, but for most jobs, soft sand and masonry cement will provide you with the least problems.

For most brickwork, one part masonry cement to four parts soft sand will be suitable, but for sills, copings and retaining walls with dense masonry it may be best to make a stronger mix of 1:3.

Use an old board or a special mixing tray to prepare the mortar. Mix the dry ingredients thoroughly before adding water slowly.

The mortar should be just moist enough to slide cleanly off the trowel or spade without being too runny. It should spread smoothly like butter. Do not mix more than you can use within an hour. Transfer a couple of shovelfuls of mortar to another board that will be convenient to reach as you work.

Coloured mortar can be achieved by adding pigments to the dry cement and these can be bought from builders' merchants. First try a little where it does not matter, to see the effect. If you are using a colour additive, measure the ingredients carefully and consistently to avoid a variation in the finished colour.

Bonding

It is the bonding (the way one brick overlaps its neighbours) that helps to give the wall strength. It also makes a difference to the wall's appearance.

Although there are many possible bonding patterns, only some of the most popular are shown here. These are perfectly adequate for all the bricklaying jobs you are likely to do in the garden.

Stretcher bond is the most straightforward, and is the one to use for a half-brick (single thickness) wall. It is an easy bond to lay, though it can look boring.

English bond can only be used on a full brick wall, but it is easy to lay and is attractive with its alternate courses of headers and stretchers (ends and lengths). To synchronize the 'header' courses, cut bricks in half lengthways (called 'closers') to insert before the last brick at each end.

Flemish bond has a more intense pattern, headers and stretchers alternating within each row. This is a little more trouble to lay, and again it will be necessary to cut bricks, but it is one of the more decorative bonds.

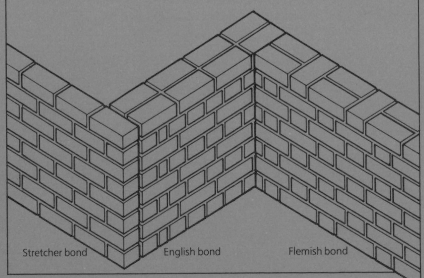

Stretcher bond   English bond   Flemish bond

Laying bricks

Three or four hours before you are ready to lay the clay bricks, dampen them with a hose but do not let them become waterlogged.

Stretch lines from the profile boards to mark where the edges of the bricks will come. Then lay a level bed of mortar on the foundations, and using a trowel, transfer a mark onto the mortar.

If you are laying a curved wall, work from a peg in the centre of the arc and keep the line or tape taut while you work round, transferring the arc with a trowel held close to the line or tape.

Remove any strings once the lines have been transferred, but keep the profile boards in position for the time being, in case you have to refer back to them.

Space the first line of bricks along the row to make sure the spacing will be even. If the wall does not have to be a precise length there should be little problem: just space the bricks at their normal distance. If you have to make the wall fit exactly between two existing structures, though, modifying the jointing spaces slightly may mean you can avoid having to cut bricks.

Build up the corners of the wall first to a height of about six or seven courses, constantly checking alignment with the spirit-level.

To lay a brick, take a slice of mortar, shape the back into a curve, and scoop it up onto the trowel with a sweeping motion. Place a ridge of mortar along about a 1½-2½ ft (450-750mm) run of wall, and spread it out by running the trowel along the centre to make a series of furrows. Then trim any surplus mortar from the edges with the trowel.

Place two sausage-shaped slices of mortar on one

Below: Bricks can be cut very neatly with a suitable power tool that you can hire, but for a garden wall you will probably be able to cope with the number of bricks to be cut by hand.

Score all round, using a bolster and club hammer, then place the brick on a suitable bed (ideally sand, but the lawn will do), and strike the bolster firmly while holding it over the centre of the score line. It should break cleanly. If necessary, trim it further with the bolster.

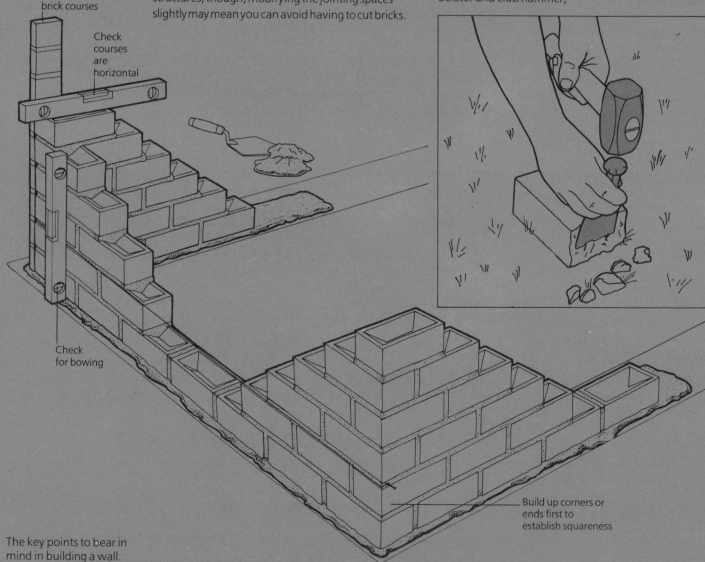

Make a gauge rod to ensure consistent thickness of mortar between brick courses

Check courses are horizontal

Check for bowing

Build up corners or ends first to establish squareness

The key points to bear in mind in building a wall.

end of the brick to be laid, and then press it into place, removing any surplus mortar that is pressed out as you go along using an upward stroke, and being careful not to get mortar on the face of the bricks. Joints should be ½ in (15mm) thick.

Check both vertical and horizontal levels constantly with a long spirit-level. The handle of the trowel can be used to firm or level the bricks.

Once the ends have been built up, complete the courses between them. Use a line fixed to pegs or nails pushed into the mortar joints at the corners, to act as a guide to maintain the correct level for that course. You can manage with string and nails, but if you are doing a lot of bricklaying it is worth buying a special line and pins sold for this job.

When the courses have been built up to the height of the corners, build up the corners again and repeat as before.

Finish the brickwork by 'pointing'. This trimming of the mortar joints can make a big difference to the appearance and finish of a wall. It is best done after an hour or two when the mortar is 'thumb-print' hard. Some of the popular profiles are illustrated on page 155. It is easiest to keep the face of the brickwork clean if a slightly recessed joint is chosen: a square recessed joint, using an old chisel, or a concave finish achieved by drawing a rounded piece of metal (traditionally a bucket handle, but a length of pipe or dowel can also be used)

along the joint. For best results, always smooth the vertical joints first, and then the horizontal.

Keeping the damp at bay
Many perfectly satisfactory garden walls are built without a damp-proof course, but they will be much better with one. Rising damp from the ground beneath may lead to the white deposit known as efflorescence appearing; a damp-proof course will reduce the chances of this happening.

You could use engineering bricks for the lower courses to act as a barrier, but the transition from one type of brick to another is not to everyone's liking. A strip of bitumen felt, made for the purpose and available from builders' merchants, will do the job perfectly adequately. The procedure is to place this over the second course of bricks above soil level and mortar the next layer on to it.

The top of a wall is also vulnerable because the upper surface of most bricks will be less weather-resistant than the face. Coping stones can be used – if these overlap they will also tend to throw water away from the wall – but a coping layer of bricks can be used with the face outwards, and this can also make the wall look more finished.

Ideally, another damp-proof course should be placed beneath the coping, but this is a refinement that you may feel that you can miss out.

Retaining walls
Retaining walls of any size should be inclined backwards slightly. A slope of about ¼ in in 2 ft (6mm in 600mm) should be adequate. To maintain the correct slope, use a piece of wood ¼ in (6mm) thick in combination with a spirit-level.

Walls retaining a substantial bank of soil should have 'weep holes' at the base. The simplest way is to use cut bricks so as to leave half-bricks out every 3-5 ft (1-1.5m) along the base to allow water to drain through. If you want a more finished appearance mortar 2 in (50mm) pipes into the space. Place a layer of gravel about 1 ft (300mm) wide and deep behind the weep holes.

Brick retaining walls should not be higher than 3 ft

(900mm) unless there is concrete behind. Even then, large retaining walls could need reinforcement and it may be best to seek professional advice.

Small, raised beds are not normally subject to the same pressures as a wall retaining a bank of soil, but it is still worth providing some drainage holes even if you only leave the mortar out of some of the joints at ground level.

Both retaining walls and raised beds are best if they are lined. This will reduce the effect of water on the brickwork, which is likely to become attacked by algae or develop a coating of white efflorescence if it is too damp. You should be able to buy a suitable waterproofing paint from a builders' merchant.

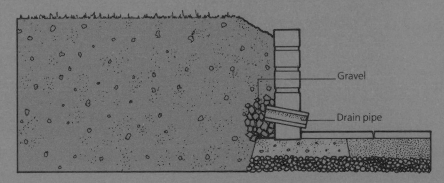

Gravel

Drain pipe

Retaining walls have to slope into the bank for strength. Weep holes are also necessary to avoid a build-up of water pressure. Drain-pipes can be inserted into the base of the wall, ideally with gravel packed behind the wall to prevent the drains becoming blocked.

Concrete sounds unpromising for a wall, but there are many attractive walling blocks in imitation stone, as well as finishes that make no pretence at being anything other than decorative, usually coloured, concrete.

Pierced (screen) block walling is especially useful for a patio surround, but can be equally effective as a boundary between properties.

Concrete 'bricks' and blocks

If you are making a low wall on a patio, you should be able to lay blocks on the paving if this itself has proper foundations. Otherwise the foundations must be prepared as for a brick wall (see pages 150-153).

Blocks of regular sizes should present no problem in either calculating the amount that you need or in laying (follow the principles for laying bricks described on page 156). Designs that include blocks of different sizes or colours should be worked out on graph paper first and the plan should be kept close to hand as a useful reference during building.

Although concrete walling blocks are laid in a similar way to bricks, it is normal to complete one course at a time instead of building up the corners first. It is best to finish the top with a matching concrete coping.

Screen walling

Screen or pierced block walling is 'stacked', so the normal method of bonding does not apply, and the strength has to come from reinforcement.

Although the basic rules for construction described below are simple, errors in alignment seem to be emphasized in screen walling, and you must work very neatly for a good finish.

Where screen walling is to be combined with brickwork or reconstituted stone blocks, check that the dimensions are compatible. Sizes can vary from manufacturer to manufacturer. Bear in mind the depth of the blocks as well as the height and width.

The maximum height that you should consider building a screen block wall is 6ft (1.8m) unless you are prepared to seek professional advice.

Building a screen wall

Prepare the foundations, following the advice on pages 150-153. However, for walls over three courses high you must reinforce each pilaster with an iron bar or angle iron set into the foundation concrete. The position of these will have to be calculated carefully, **1**.

If there is a brick or concrete block base, build this and allow it to set first. On sloping ground, a low wall of brick or blocks is essential to keep the screen blocks out of contact with the soil. The base wall will have to be staggered to take account of the slope.

Lay a row of blocks along the ground first to check the position of the pilasters. Then place a bed of mortar on the foundation or base wall and position the first end pilaster, checking both vertical and horizontal alignment. Place the other end pilaster, and stretch a string between the two to indicate the height, **2**.

Position the intermediate pilasters, which should be at no more than 10ft (3m) intervals.

Place a strip of mortar along the first block to be laid, and butt up to the first pilaster, tapping level with the string line and leaving a mortar joint of about ⅜ in (10mm).

Continue to lay the first row like this, using a spirit-level frequently to check alignment, **3**.

To strengthen the joints on subsequent rows, bridge the adjoining blocks with a wall tie, or a piece of wire-netting, and mortar over this.

When the pilasters have been built three high, pour strengthening mortar into them and round the reinforcement if necessary.

Before the mortar dries, point them, using a piece of dowel or metal rod. Be careful to keep mortar off the face of the blocks.

Top off with coping slabs and pilaster caps.

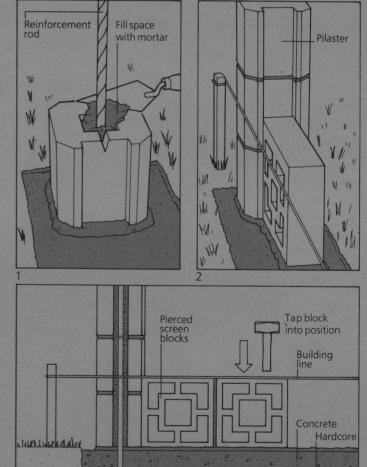

Reinforcement rod

Fill space with mortar

Pilaster

Pierced screen blocks

Tap block into position

Building line

Concrete

Hardcore

Perhaps, more than any other garden feature, patios are the link between home and garden, and are popular even among non-gardeners.

A patio should be more than simply a rectangle of paving. Walls, whether for tall screens or low raised beds (see pages 154-157), will add interest and character, and features such as a built-in barbecue and overhead beams are always worth trying to include.

No matter how you enhance a patio, though, paving will remain the backbone. You simply have to get this right, both visually and structurally.

Precast concrete slabs are the most popular choice for paving, but *bricks* are both traditional and tasteful. They are, however, more expensive to buy and more time-consuming to lay. *Concrete block pavers* are more attractive than they sound, and the interlocking type can make a very strong and neat surface without being obtrusive.

Patio and quarry tiles are expensive, but they provide a touch of class, and are worth considering for a small patio with a barbecue. They are very durable, colourful, and easy to clean.

There seem to be as many ways to lay patio paving as there are different materials and patterns. Some of the most popular methods are described here, but to avoid repetition, the techniques for laying bricks and clay or concrete pavers are described under paths and drives on pages 163-165.

Making a start

Start by clearing the site of rubble and vegetation, then select a reference point from which other levels can be taken. If the patio joins the home, the damp-proof course (dpc) will probably dictate this. The paving should be at least 6 in (150mm) below the dpc – in Britain this is a stipulation of the Building Regulations.

If the damp-proof course is low as is sometimes the case with old property, leave a gap of a few inches between the paving and the wall and provide a small gulley with gravel at the bottom; the water must be able to drain away easily at the end.

Paving should be laid with a slight fall (about 1:40 is usually adequate) *away* from any buildings. The way to prepare concrete foundations is described on pages 150-153, but as a patio is unlikely to be subject to heavy traffic a 3 in (750mm) layer of consolidated hardcore bound with ash, small gravel, or similar material, may be all that is necessary. Alternatively you could use a weak concrete mix (1 part cement to 8 parts ballast or all-in aggregate) to form the sub-base.

If you are preparing proper foundations, it makes sense to bed the slabs on mortar, and again

there are many ways of doing this.

A solid bed of mortar will be strong, but it is difficult to get the slabs straight and to adjust them without lifting and re-laying.

'Spot-bedding' (placing the slab on blobs of mortar) makes it easier to get the slabs level and properly aligned, but the bond is not as strong.

A useful compromise between the two is the 'box and cross' method described below.

If you are using spot-bedding, place a blob near each corner of the slab and one in the centre, and press the slab into position. Slabs less than 9 in (230mm) square are best on a solid bed of mortar.

Overhead beams

Overhead beams will help transform a paved area into something more worthy of the name patio. If clothed with suitable climbers it will give some shade in summer, but more importantly it will help to create the impression of the patio being an outside room, and do much to hold the area together visually.

Wood is the best material, and fairly substantial beams should be used to reflect the architectural lines of an adjoining building.

There are various ways of fixing the joists and beams to the upright, and some of these are illustrated on page 169. To fix the beams to the wall of a building you need to buy joist hangers (builders' merchants sell these). Floor joists are about the right size for overhead beams, so timber of this measure will fit the hangers, which have to be mortared into the wall.

It is best not to attempt to roof over the area with transparent plastic sheets as they will soon be covered with leaves and debris, and when it rains hard the drumming sound can be very annoying.

To set a fall across a path or patio, so as to ensure adequate surface water drainage, use a shim under one end of the straight edge.

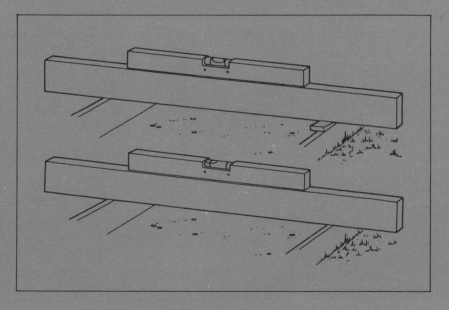

Laying paving slabs

Mix sufficient mortar (1 part ordinary cement to 5 parts sharp sand) for about half an hour's work.

Make sure you start working to straight lines and correct angles. Use a builder's square (see illustration), to make sure your angles are correct. Mark out the area with string. Start laying along the house side (or some other long, straight edge, **1**). Try to avoid having to cut slabs but, if this is not possible, make sure that the cut pieces are at the least conspicuous end. For a large area, once the first row has been laid, build up the corners for several rows before filling between them.

Place strips of mortar about 1¼-2 in (30-50mm) high on the base to form a box shape slightly smaller than the slab. For a small slab this will be sufficient, but for a large slab place two more strips of mortar inside the box to form a cross, **2**.

Place the slab over the mortar and tamp it level with a wooden mallet or handle of a club hammer. Make sure that the slab is bedded firmly and use a straight-edge and spirit-level to check levels in both directions, **3**. To check that the correct fall has been maintained, use a small piece of wood equivalent to

Cutting a paving slab

Most manufacturers produce paving slabs in a range of sizes, so it is usually possible to avoid having to cut slabs. Sometimes, however, slabs have to be cut.

Place the slab on a level bed of dry sand. Then mark a cut line all round the slab.

Using a bolster (sometimes called a brick set) and a club hammer, cut a groove right round the slab.

Work around the slab several times then tap along the waste part of the slab until it cracks along the score line.

the desired fall under the straight-edge. This is easier once a few rows have been laid.

To ensure a neat finish, all the joints should be of equal thickness (about ¼ in (5mm), though it may need to be larger). The easiest way to achieve this is to use a couple of pieces of wood of the right thickness at the edge of each slab. You will need to cut an adequate supply of these beforehand, **4**.

Check alignment after every slab with a straight-

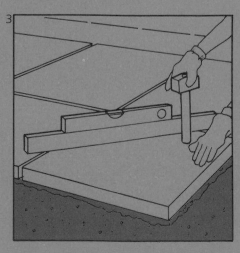

Proportions of a builder's square

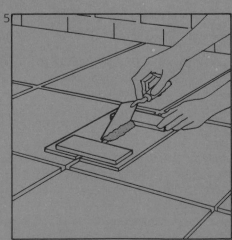

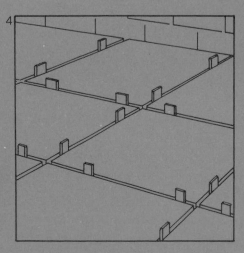

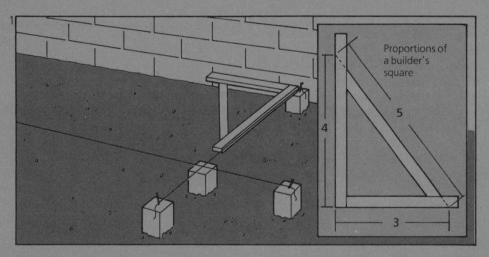

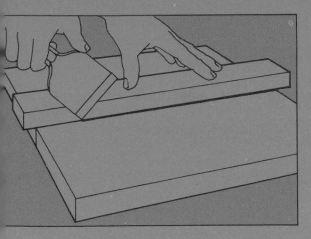

edge that spans at least three slabs. No gap should be visible beneath the straight-edge.

Finish off by jointing with mortar rammed in between the slabs with something like the edge of a piece of plywood, **5**. Try to keep mortar off the slabs — you may find a jig like the one illustrated a useful aid. Use a wet sponge to clean the slabs afterwards anyway, in case any small bits of mortar have dropped or spread from the joints on to them.

The slabs will look better if the joint is recessed by about ⅛ in (2mm), but deeper joints may catch heels.

Bedding on sand

Although it will lack the strength of paving bedded on mortar, you may prefer to use a sand base if the ground is reasonably firm. The basic setting-out, levelling, and order of laying are the same as for bedding on mortar, but a sand base can be used as described for paths on page 164.

Tiling

Patio tiles are brick-red and about 1ft (300mm) square with a half size 1ft × 6in (300mm × 150mm). Quarry tiles come in a greater range of sizes and colours.

For a patio they are best laid on mortar.

Laying tiles

Ideally concrete foundations should be used, but you could lay mortar on firm soil, **1**. If you do this, level the soil to about 1-1½ in (25-40mm) below the finished level, and roll or tamp it firm and flat.

Soak the tiles in water for at least 15 minutes before using them.

Make a mortar mix of 1 part cement to 5 parts sand, mixing no more than you can use in an hour.

Lay a screed with the mortar, using a levelling board between supporting boards at the edges, held in place with pegs, **2**.

Remove several tiles at a time from the water and let surplus moisture drain. Then lay them on the damp mortar, tapping the tiles in with the handle of a hammer or a wooden block, if necessary to level them, **3**. Check levels frequently with a straight-edge and spirit-level.

Grout between the tiles within 24 hours, using a mixture of 1 part cement to 3 parts sand. Make a runny mixture that you can pour into the joints.

Clean up any spills immediately using a damp cloth, and smooth the grouting with a trowel or a piece of dowel.

Do not walk on the tiles for at least three days.

Bricks and pavers

To lay a brick patio, remove enough soil from the area to be covered for the depth of the brick, about 3 in (80mm) of hardcore, and 2 in (50mm) of mortar.

Lay the hardcore first, then mix the dry sand and cement, 1 part of cement to 4 parts of sand. Lay the mix to a depth of 2 in (50mm). Check the levels carefully with a spirit-level and a straight-edge.

Place the bricks in position on the cement mix. When this has been finished, brush dry mortar into the joints. Take care to avoid forming air pockets. Then sprinkle water from a watering-can or a sprayer, and clean off any excess mortar while it is still wet.

For pavers, see the instructions on pages 165-6.

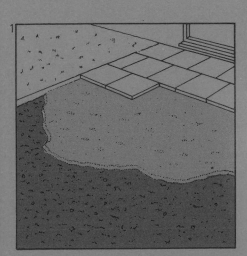

1

2

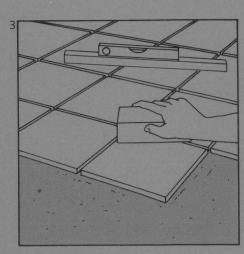

3

A barbecue is not difficult to build, but needs a lot of thought. It ought to be large enought to be practical if you are cooking for a family, but it does not have to look like a monument to be efficient. It will, of course, be the centre of attention when in use but it should not dominate the garden for the rest of the time. For part of the year it will stand cold and uninspiring and even in summer is unlikely to be used every day.

Ideally, it should not be far from the kitchen, for ease of transporting food, equipment, cutlery and so on. A barbecue should be sited well away from overhanging trees, especially holly, which is highly flammable.

A portable barbecue may be perfectly adequate for a family, but a built-in barbecue always looks more impressive.

We have not given brick-by-brick instructions for making a barbecue because the dimensions will depend on the patio, and the availability of the hardware will dictate precise details. Always make sure you have the dimensions of items like the grill and tray before you start. Although you could have these made specially, it is much easier to use a barbecue kit and adapt the masonry to fit it.

You may find that although the kits are made to fit various permutations of standard clay bricks, they may not fit properly if you are using concrete block walling. Rotisseries that are made to clamp over a standard brick may have to be modified for other building blocks.

Brick is a particularly convenient material to work with for a barbecue. Concrete block imitation stone walling is often used for patio walls, and can be made to look as effective and attractive as brick.

If space is really tight, you may be able to fit one in a corner formed by two walls at a 90 degree angle, though facilities are bound to be limited.

You will need somewhere to put the plates, so try to include a shelf, and if you can incorporate a cupboard or two for storage, so much the better. If you entertain a great deal and use a gas-fired barbecue, you will need to have some form of store cupboard to hide the gas cylinders.

In the United States, firepits are sometimes used instead of a barbecue, though they are rare in Britain. These are depressions in the ground lined with firebricks and edged with ordinary brick. You may be able to devise a circular seat to fit over the top when not in use, which will make it a feature at all times.

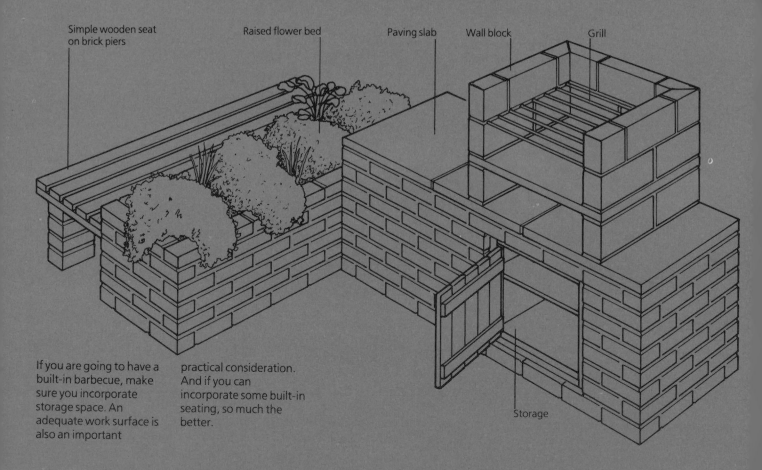

Simple wooden seat on brick piers

Raised flower bed

Paving slab

Wall block

Grill

Storage

If you are going to have a built-in barbecue, make sure you incorporate storage space. An adequate work surface is also an important practical consideration. And if you can incorporate some built-in seating, so much the better.

Paths and drives need a lot of thought, not only in design, but also in choice of materials and method of laying. They are such dominant features that an unfortunate choice of materials or poor construction can mar the whole garden.

Drives

Gravel or paving slabs are both popular choices for a drive, but flexible clay or concrete pavers are well worth considering. Unlike paving slabs, they are easily laid to a curve, and are better than gravel if you want a more formal appearance. However, they will not stand up to heavy vehicles unless bedded on solid concrete. For a straight drive up to a garage, though, paving slabs have the advantage of being more widely available and generally cheaper.

Gravel drives can be very effective, provided they are generously proportioned. They are fairly cheap and easy to lay, but must be prepared properly to avoid ruts and puddles which may become prevalent once weather and traffic take their toll.

Bitumen is not a particularly pleasant material to have in the garden, but it may be worth considering if you want to use it for an inconspicuous area and perhaps to cover an old cracked concrete drive. You must, however, provide a suitable edging for a bitumen path or drive and if you have to buy kerbing, you could find that it costs as much as the asphalt.

Paving slabs are laid in the same way as an area of patio (see pages 160-161), although you will need to increase the depth of the foundations, and to bed them in mortar.

If you have a large area leading to, say, a garage where appearance does not matter too much, it is worth considering concrete. Provided you have the foundations prepared properly first, using ready-mixed concrete delivered to the site should enable you to do the job quite quickly, but you may need some extra pairs of hands to help lay it within the short working time available.

Paths

Paths can be made of all the materials mentioned for drives, however, concrete and asphalt seldom look right.

Flexible pavers can be used, but bricks are probably a better choice for narrow paths within the garden, unless you are specifically matching a larger paved area. The problems of fixing suitable edging pieces and using a flat-plate vibrator (see page 133) are unlikely to make it worthwhile for a narrow path taking little weight. You could probably manage without a vibrator if you use a hammer and a block of wood instead.

Brick paths are easy to lay, and the wide choice of finishes, as well as the many different laying patterns that you could use, mean there is a good chance of finding something that is just right.

Grass paths can be used to link one part of the garden to another, especially lawns, but they must be wide enough to avoid too much wear; ideally there ought to be an alternative route for wet weather.

Stepping-stone paths are more likely to be decorative than purely functional, but they still need to be laid properly if they are not to be dangerous.

Buying bricks

Beware of secondhand bricks unless you know which *type* of brick they are. Many bricks that are suitable for house walls are totally unsuitable for garden walls or paths as they will crumble. If you buy new bricks, always tell the merchant what you want them for, and do not go by appearance alone.

You need a brick that will withstand wetting and freezing (house walls get wet, but from only one side, so they do not become saturated and frozen). In Britain, you will sometimes see clay bricks described as 'special quality' – these are all suitable for the garden. Some 'ordinary quality' bricks can be used, but you will need to check with the manufacturer or supplier.

Engineering bricks are hard and frost-resistant, but some of them could be too slippery when wet.

Avoid bricks that are pierced from side to side, but those with a frog (an indentation on one side) are perfectly suitable as you can lay them frog-down.

Paving materials come in many shapes and forms. Not all precast concrete paving slabs, 1, 2, are rectangular and interlocking pavers, 3, 4, sometimes look better than rectangular ones. Some pavers are made to look as though composed of smaller elements, 5. Bricks, 6, are always popular.
Note: not drawn to scale.

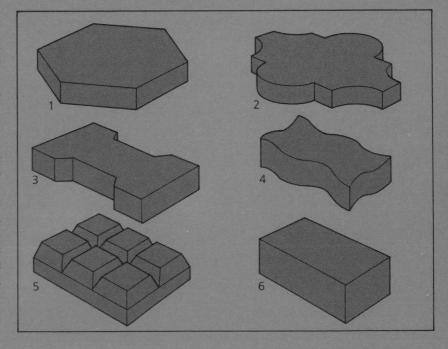

Laying a brick path

Remove sufficient soil to take about 3in (80mm) of hardcore, 2in (50mm) of mortar, and the depth of the brick. If you use sand instead of mortar, allow a 4in (100mm) layer on top of the hardcore if the hardcore is coarse use compacted sand to provide a level surface). If edging bricks are to be used, lay one edge first, setting it in mortar banked up at the side.

Prepare a 2in (50mm) layer of dry sand and cement mix (1 part cement to 4 parts of sand), and bed the bricks on this. As it is important to lay the bricks evenly, use a straight-edge and spirit-level to check levels. Lay the second line of edging bricks as you proceed.

When the bricks are in position, brush a dry mortar mix between the joints, making sure there are no large air pockets.

When the joints have been filled, sprinkle water from a fine rosed watering can, or better still use a fine mist from a compression sprayer. Be sure to clean any mortar off the surface of the bricks before it dries.

How to lay flexible paving

Prepare a good foundation of about 3in (75mm) of compacted hardcore, then for extra strength for a load-bearing drive spread with ¾in (19mm) gravel and vibrate it in to fill in any voids in the foundation.

Even if the main area is to be filled with shaped pavers, prepare the edges by laying rectangular blocks set in mortar.

The finished height of the edging pavers should allow for the depth of the paver plus 2½in (65mm) of sand – you will lay 3in (75mm), but this will vibrate down.

Once any edging pavers have set (ideally leave them for a week), spread *dry* sand over the area, levelled off to a depth of 3in (75mm). It may be necessary to use timber battens (screeding rails) and a piece of softwood of the right size and profile to strike it off level.

Bear in mind that the whole path or drive will need a slight slope *away* from the direction of any building.

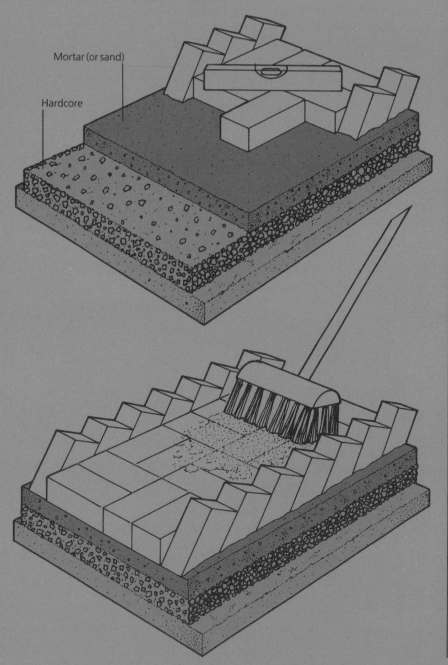

Mortar (or sand)

Hardcore

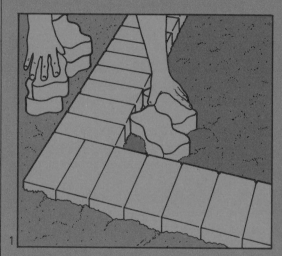

1

2

Start laying from one corner, pressing the blocks close against each other. A typical pattern of laying is shown below, **1, 2.**

Some manufacturers provide special edging pieces to fill in the awkward shapes that you are left with if you use some of the interlocking blocks or pavers. Sometimes you may need to cut blocks to fit, in which case it is well worth hiring a block splitter, **3.**

Spread *dry* sand over the laid paving, and brush it in between the cracks. Then go over it with a plate vibrator, which will force the sand down into the joints. You may need to spread more sand and vibrate again, **4.**

Whether you are laying clay or concrete block pavers, the techniques described here are the same. If you are buying interlocking blocks with separate edge pieces, the supplier will need to know the linear measurement of the edges as well as the overall area to be laid when calculating the number of blocks required.

Laying gravel

Provide a firm base by excavating the ground to take about 3in (75mm) of compacted hardcore and 3in (75mm) of gravel (though for a lightly-used path 2in (50mm) of gravel should be enough).

You will almost certainly need some form of edging to retain the gravel, which should be inserted now.

If using hardcore, use cheap sand to fill in the spaces within the hardcore so you do not lose the gravel. Alternatively, use hoggin (a rough-dug gravel that also contains dirt and clay) instead of hardcore.

Spread half the gravel over the area, building it up slightly in the middle of the path to produce a slight camber.

Rake the gravel smooth and roll it thoroughly. Watering it occasionally will help to ensure good compaction.

Spread the remaining gravel to the required height, maintaining the camber, repeating the raking, watering, and rolling.

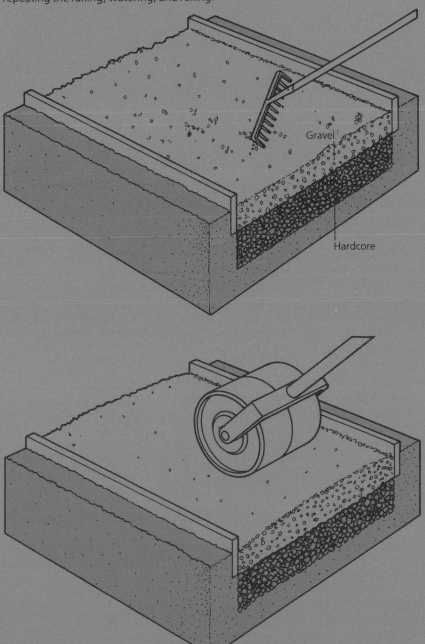

Gravel

Hardcore

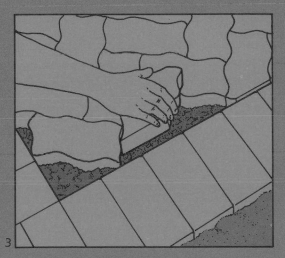

3

4

Laying crazy-paving

Prepare a foundation of about 3in (75mm) of consolidated hardcore, allowing for the thickness of the paving slabs and a 1in (25mm) bed of mortar.

Sometimes an existing path or foundation can be used as the base.

Lay the pieces roughly as you expect to use them, making sure the straight-edged pieces are used for the outsides. Once the large pieces are in position, fill in with smaller pieces. Try to make the joints roughly the same width; very wide joints are unattractive. And because the pattern is so varied, it is best to limit yourself to one type of stone — multi-coloured crazy paving is very discordant in a garden.

Natural stone may be of uneven thickness. Some variation can be taken up by the mortar layer, but very thick stones may have to be split.

Bed the slabs in a mortar mix of 1 part cement to 4 parts of sand, and firm the slabs carefully, checking levels with a spirit-level and straight-edge frequently.

Unless you want to leave the cracks unpointed so you can grow plants in the crevices, fill between the paving with mortar. Wipe off the surplus from the paving before it has a chance to set. When it is almost dry, clean the edges with an old knife or wire brush.

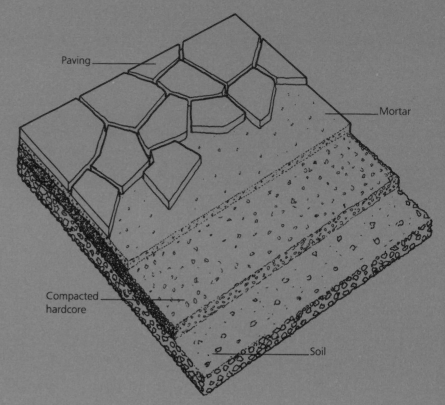

Garden steps

Most well-designed gardens involve some change of level, and steps usually form the practical and visual link.

The range of materials and the different changes of level, from shallow to steep, mean there are many possibilities, but you should always be guided by practical considerations.

As a general rule, the tread (the distance from the front to back of each step) should be about 18in (450mm), and 1ft (300mm) should be regarded as a minimum. The risers should be at least 4in (100mm) but not greater than 7in (180mm) for comfort and safety. About 6in (150mm) is right for most garden steps.

It is a good idea to let the tread overhang the riser below it by about 2in (50mm). This tends to cast a shadow that looks good, and generally helps to define the steps and makes them safer.

Width is also important. Even an ambling path intended to be taken by one person at a time ought to be at least 3ft (1m) wide, while paths that form important links where a couple of people might approach together should be a least 5ft (1.5m) wide.

There are too many permutations to make detailed instructions for any one type of step that is applicable to many situations, but the illustrations below demonstrate the principles that should enable you to construct steps to suit a particular need.

Calculating the dimensions

There is a simple formula to work out suitable tread and riser dimensions. You first choose the height of your rise, then to find the suitable depth for the tread multiply the height of the rise by two, and deduct the figure from 26 in (660m) for depth of the tread.

Therefore, if the rise is 6 in:
6 in × 2 = 12 in
26 in − 12 in = 14 in
The tread should then be 14 in.

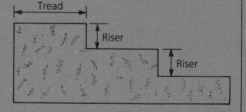

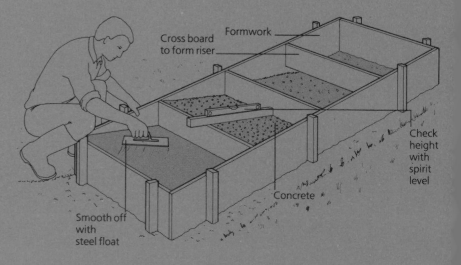

Laying concrete

Excavate for the foundation (see pages 150-153) and use old wood as shuttering, levelled to the correct height. Allow for a fall for drainage by using a wedge under one end of the straight-edge (see page 159).

Divide the path or drive into manageable sections about 3ft (1m) long with shuttering (formwork).

Use a concrete mix of 1 part cement to 6 parts combined aggregate, and shovel it in leaving it a little higher than the shuttering.

Lay about 3ft (1m) at a time, striking the concrete level with a tamping board used with a sawing motion. On a wide path you will need a person at each end of the tamping board.

On a long path, lay alternate bays. Once the concrete is hard enough, remove the shuttering between each bay and pour concrete into the space.

If you are using ready-mixed concrete, where it will not be possible to work in 3ft (1m) bays, insert pieces of hardboard at intervals to act as expansion joints. The hardboard is left in position afterwards, so make sure it fits exactly and is flush with the surface. Never lay concrete in frosty weather and if you are working in hot weather, cover the newly laid concrete with wet sheets to keep it from going off too quickly.

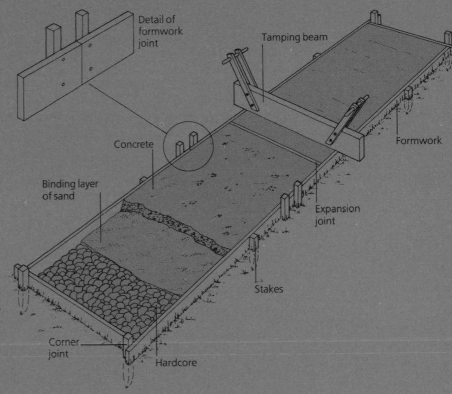

Detail of formwork joint

Tamping beam

Concrete

Formwork

Binding layer of sand

Expansion joint

Stakes

Corner joint

Hardcore

Brick steps

Paving slabs

Railway sleepers

Sawn logs

Split stone

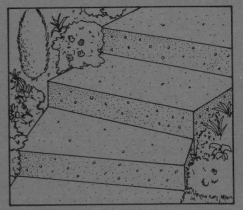

Cast concrete

There is a fundamental choice to be made before you start to build a pergola or other wooden framework for plants: whether to go for a rustic appearance or whether to use sawn wood. For wooden beams over a patio (see page 159), sawn timber is clearly a more suitable choice than rustic poles. But for a traditional pergola covering a walk, the choice of material is likely to be influenced by the general style of the garden. A traditional 'cottage garden' atmosphere clearly calls for rustic-work, but a modern garden, with clean-cut lines, perhaps much of it paved, will almost certainly look better with sawn timber.

Sawn wood has the advantage of being easy to come by and is visually compatible with modern building materials. It has a much firmer outline that makes for a stronger design element. Rustic poles are generally less substantial in appearance; their use should really be confined to informal, cottage-style gardens, though if all you want is a decorative support for your roses, they are an acceptable choice.

Sizes and proportions

Any structure that will actually bridge a path must be high enough to allow sufficient clearance *when it is covered with plants.* Unless you are using sawn timber purely as an architectural feature, the ultimate aim should be to have the pergola clothed with climbers. These will not simply grow up and over, but will almost certainly cascade down a little too. Although much will depend on the climber, it is wise to allow 1½ ft (450mm) above the height of a person to be sure of comfort.

The higher the structure the wider the spans, the more important it is to use substantial timber or poles, for strength as well as appearance. Once clothed with plants in full leaf there will be a great deal of wind resistance that may cause problems in a gale, unless the structure is strong.

SOME RUSTIC JOINTS

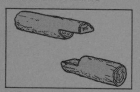

Halving joints to join lengths end to end

Vertical post notched into cross beam

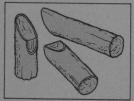

Birdsmouth notch to fix diagonal to vertical post

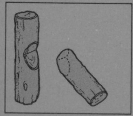

Mitred corner joint with diagonal shaped to fit

A rustic pergola gives scope for individual design —but keep it simple

Making a rustic pergola

Strip the bark from the bottom 1½-2 ft (450-600mm), to go into the ground, and stand the poles in creosote or some other preservative and allow them to absorb as much as possible. If you can leave them for a week, so much the better.

Then lay out the proposed design on the ground, so you can decide which pieces are to be used where. This will make best use of the poles. Only start cutting poles once you have worked out the best position for each piece.

Insert the uprights firmly. Rest the base of each pole on a piece of broken brick, wedge more bricks round the pole to hold it upright, then pour concrete round, finishing with a slight shoulder just above soil level to encourage water to run off. The pole may be too uneven to use a spirit-level to check that it is vertical, in which case you will have to judge by eye.

Cut the tops and long side pieces first, measuring carefully. The exact joint used will depend on the design, but some basic joints are shown here. Cut notches by sawing down to the correct depth, then use a chisel to remove the unwanted portion. Sloping struts are best marked with a pencil while holding the piece in position, but even so there will probably have to be some trial and error. If both ends slope, get one right first before cutting the other end.

Nail the joints with galvanized nails. Unfortunately, the nails can be difficult to drive home because there is insufficient resistance to work against, so get someone to hold a club hammer at the other side for additional support.

Avoid having a rustic arch that sticks up with no apparent purpose in the middle of the garden. It needs to be flanked on either side by a rustic trellis or screen, so the whole outline blends together. If you really do want a rustic arch on its own, try to find a suitable position somewhere along the side of the house, rather as you might use a gate to separate parts of the garden, so the building provides a sense of proportion.

Rustic pergolas

Work out your plan on paper first so you can decide on the poles required. Keep the design simple: it is better to use a few, substantial sections than a lot of insubstantial ones. The design below might help as a starting point, but you will almost certainly need to modify the design to suit your own garden.

If possible, choose the poles yourself (try a good garden centre or a fencing contractor), even though you will almost certainly need to have them delivered.

Using sawn timber

You can buy pergola kits, and you may find this a useful solution if time is at a premium. Making your own from scratch, however, enables you to adjust the dimensions to suit specific needs.

Brick piers always look impressive, but they make it a much more ambitious project. Generally, wooden posts are perfectly acceptable, but they should be at least 4 in (100mm) square. For the overheads, 6 in × 2 in (150mm × 50mm) wooden beams are usually perfectly adequate; but where the structure is to adjoin a house, for example, it is better to have something that looks more substantial, such as 9 in × 2 in (225mm × 50mm) beams. Where the beams are to adjoin the brickwork of a house, use a metal joist hanger let into the brickwork.

Always try to visualize a pergola clothed with plants – and bear in mind the extra wind resistance they will present

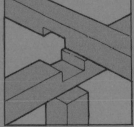

Detail of joint at head of posts in pergola on the left

Making a sawn timber (lumber) pergola

Always start by treating the timber with a wood preservative. (Creosote is best avoided if you are going to grow your plants against the uprights fairly soon after erecting.) Surfaces cut during construction will have to be treated as you work.

Fix the uprights in position as described for rustic poles, using a spirit-level on a straight-edge between each post to make sure the tops are level. If you are fixing one end of the beams against a wall, the exact height will be determined by the level of the mortar joint into which the beam hanger is inserted.

Assemble the overhead part of the structure 'dry' on the ground, cutting the pieces to size and making all the necessary joints but not actually fixing them.

Halving joints are particularly useful for this type of assembly.

For fixing the overhead part to the uprights, it is worth cutting out half the thickness of the rail with a saw, then using a chisel to remove the notch to slip over the post.

While the overhead pieces are on the ground, take the opportunity to drill small starter holes for the screws; this is much easier than drilling at a height.

When fixing the overhead in position, always use galvanized nails or zinc-plated screws.

If the pergola is long you will have to join rails. This should be done over a post. Screw or nail through the rails into the post.

When making foundation for posts bevel the concrete to throw water away from the post

Full instructions for erecting your shed or greenhouse will almost certainly come with the building, and, as the exact method will vary according to the make, the methods described here are only intended to show what is likely to be involved.

It is also useful to be aware of the various options *before* you buy.

In some countries, sheds, summerhouses and greenhouses may need planning permission from the local authority, though generally they will be exempt if they are of moderate size and situated to the side or rear of the house. Remember, though, that a greenhouse should not be sited in the shade cast by a house. If in doubt about the need for planning permission, it is always worth checking.

Some companies will erect the building for you, but there should be a cost saving if you do it yourself. It is an easy job if you have an extra pair of hands to help.

Sheds and summerhouses

For a concrete shed – which should not be dismissed outright, as some look very much like brick from a distance – a concrete base is essential. The dimensions must be right, however, so ask the supplier for a foundation specification before you take delivery, then you can see what is involved and have the base ready.

A concrete shed can be very heavy work to erect and the sections will be difficult to lift and manoeuvre, even with help. Unless you have the necessary muscle-power, it is well worth considering having a concrete structure erected for you.

A timber shed, by comparison, is easy to put up yourself. If the ground is firm you should not need a concrete base as the floor can rest on bearers (stout wooden timbers, well treated with preservative). The shed manufacturer can supply these.

You will need about three rows of bearers for a shed 6 ft (1.8m) wide, four rows for a shed 8 ft (2.4m) wide.

Floors are sometimes quoted as an extra, but, unless you are using a concrete base, they should be regarded as essential.

The buildings should come complete with roofing felt, glass, and items like nuts and bolts to complete the job. Always use rust-proof bolts and nails. The sections are simply bolted together, which is very easy if you have someone to help support the panels.

Normally you start by laying the base then add one end and one side. Once these have been assembled, the remaining side and end are bolted on, followed by the roof.

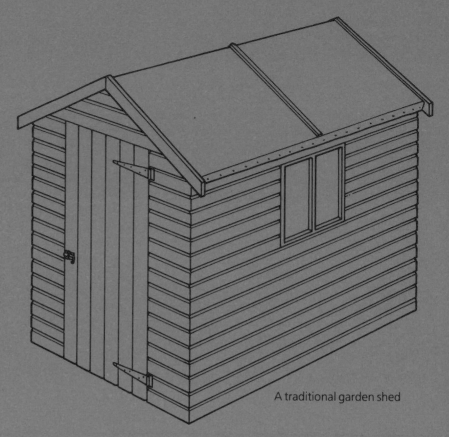

A traditional garden shed

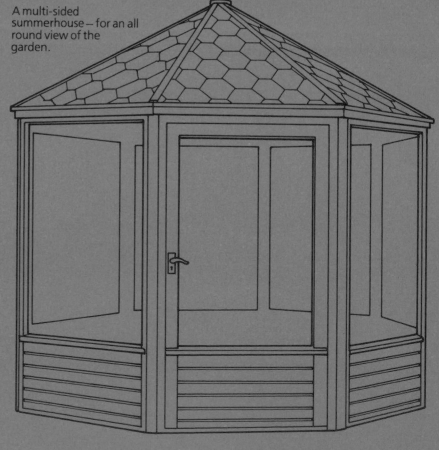

A multi-sided summerhouse – for an all round view of the garden.

Erecting a greenhouse

Timber greenhouses are usually very easy to erect as they generally come in sections that you screw or bolt together, rather like a garden shed.

Aluminium greenhouses are not difficult to erect but an aptitude for jigsaws and a liking for construction kits will help. The greenhouse will probably arrive as bundles or boxes of sectional pieces, nuts, bolts, and glazing strips. Instructions should always be provided, but if for any reason they are missing, make sure you obtain a copy before you start. Some of the pieces can be difficult to identify without a profile key.

The method described on this page is based on a typical aluminium alloy greenhouse, and although details will vary according to make, most are erected in a similar way.

Bases and foundations

If you want to make your own base, which is more usual with wooden greenhouses than metal, you will have to make proper foundations and build a low wall as described on page 156. Before you attempt this, however, check all dimensions carefully with the manufacturer.

On unstable ground you can make a simple base by excavating a trench about 1 ft (300mm) deep, filling with hardcore and topping with paving slabs or concrete.

For an aluminium greenhouse it is almost certainly worth buying the manufacturer's base, which is sometimes included in the basic price, but often quoted as an extra. Many have ground anchors supplied, and these are simply dropped into a hole and surrounded with concrete.

Erecting an aluminium greenhouse

If you are using the manufacturer's base, assemble it, following the instructions. Alternatively, prepare your own base. In either case it is critical that the base is absolutely square. Measure across the diagonals – they should be exactly the same.

Although some bases are supplied with ground anchors to concrete in, some have screws to fix into a concrete base that has been drilled and plugged.

Some sections can be assembled on the ground first. The only tools you are likely to need are a spanner (wrench) and screwdriver, but it is worth using a spirit-level to ensure that everything is properly aligned.

Sections are easily bolted together, although for some of them, especially the roof, you will probably need someone to help support the section.

Glazing is easy with modern glazing strips and clips, but use gloves when handling panes of glass, and do not attempt to glaze on a very windy day.

Press the glazing strip firmly into the correct channel, simply cutting it to the correct length with a knife. Insert the glass between the glazing bars, leaving an equal gap either side, and insert the spring wire glazing clips; they should snap into position if you press the sides apart.

The upper panes should overlap the lower ones by about 3/8 in (10mm), and special clips are supplied to support the upper panes, but you may have to bend them to the right profile.

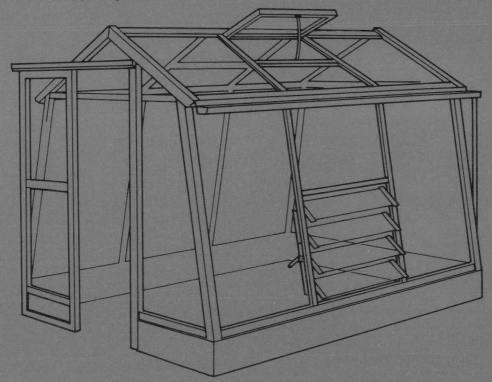

A Dutch-light greenhouse, designed to make the best use of available light. A greenhouse like this is intended primarily for border crops – if you plan to grow mainly pot-plants on benches other types are better.

If you have spent a lot of time and expense on designing and constructing the hard landscaping side of the garden, it would be a pity to spoil the result by taking the plants for granted.

A plant that is looked after during the critical years of establishment will usually easily outperform one that is planted carelessly and has had to compete with weeds for nutrients and water.

Trees and shrubs

Trees and shrubs grown in containers can be planted at any time of the year, provided the ground is not frozen or waterlogged. But if you plant during a dry period, be prepared to water regularly until established.

Bare-root and 'balled' plants (those lifted from a field but with the root-ball held together in a piece of hessian or plastic) are best planted while dormant—from late autumn to early spring, provided the weather is suitable.

Evergreens should not be moved during the winter, and autumn or spring are the best times.

Planting a tree or shrub

Dig a hole large enough to take the roots fully spread; even a container-grown plant should have a hole large enough to be able to spread out some of the roots.

If planting in grass, remove a circle of turf about 3 ft (1m) in diameter first.

Check the depth of the hole by placing the plant in it. The soil-level should be the same as the old soil mark on the stem, but if this is not visible, aim for about 1½-2in (40-50mm) of soil above the highest root.

Fork over the bottom of the hole, and add a sprinkling of bonemeal or a general fertilizer. If the soil is sandy or heavy clay, add a generous amount of peat or garden compost.

Insert a stake if necessary. This should not be necessary for shrubs or for small trees up to 4 ft (1.2m) tall, provided the ground is firmed properly after planting. If a gap at soil level does appear because of wind-rock, a bamboo cane should be sufficient support.

Trees above 4 ft (1.2m) will need a stake but it does not need to be massive, or very tall. The stake should not be higher than crown level, and there is no advantage in having it more than one-third the height of the tree.

If using a stake, nail the tree tie to the stake before you put it in the hole as it will be easier to knock in the nails. One tree-tie may be enough, if the stake has to be a little way from the stem because of the root-ball of a container-grown plant.

If a bare-rooted tree or shrub is being planted spread the roots evenly around the hole. If the plant is container-grown, loosen and tease apart any roots

Planting a tree

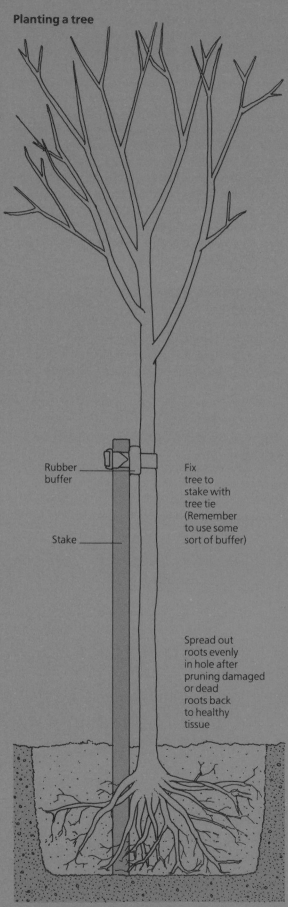

Rubber buffer

Stake

Fix tree to stake with tree tie (Remember to use some sort of buffer)

Spread out roots evenly in hole after pruning damaged or dead roots back to healthy tissue

that have started to wind around at the bottom.

For bare-rooted plants, sprinkle some soil between the roots, then move the plant up and down gently to settle the soil around them. Check the planting level again and return the remaining soil, enriched with fertilizer and compost or peat if necessary.

Firm the soil around the roots, using your foot if necessary. But to avoid compacted soil, gently fork or hoe the ground afterwards to leave a fine surface.

Secure the tree to the stake if it needs one.

Water thoroughly if the weather is dry, and continue to do so during dry periods until the plant has become established.

Competition from weeds will severely check growth. A plastic or other mulching square will do a great deal to help establishment and growth, but if you do not like the look of this, apply a mulch of compost, peat, or pulverized bark at least 2 in (5.m) thick. Always mulch over damp soil.

Herbaceous plants

Although container-grown plants can be planted at any time, the most sensible period for herbaceous plants is either autumn or spring.

If your border has been thought out properly, and you have not bought the plants on impulse, you should have the plan on paper. Lay the plants out on the ground first, according to your plan. This will ensure that you have the right ones in the right place *before* you start to plant.

Planting herbaceous plants

Remove the plants from their container one at a time, as you plant, so the roots are not exposed to drying winds and cold air unnecessarily. Plants received by post will probably arrive with their roots wrapped in damp newspaper or moss and polythene (polyethylene). If this is the case, remove them from the outer wrapper as soon as possible, but do not unwrap the roots until you are ready to plant. Remove immediately any leaves or stems that are clearly diseased or have been damaged.

Make the planting holes large enough, in well prepared ground. Plants that come without a ball of soil should have the roots spread out. Return the soil and firm in with your fist or foot.

If the ground is dry, puddle water into the hole before planting and water well afterwards.

Remember to label each plant.

What to look for when you buy

Quality *is* important with plants. Those that are well-grown, and whose growth is not checked, may save a year's growth over a poorer specimen that was the same age and size when it was planted.

Remember also that quality can vary, whether you buy by mail order, collect from a nursery, or go to a garden centre. There is a lot to be said for collecting the plants and seeing what you are buying – then you have only yourself to blame if the plants are poor!

Rock plants

Look for plants that are well established in their pots, but avoid any that seem to be pot-bound, with too many roots growing out of the pot, and a solid mass of roots if you tap it out of the pot.

Do not buy if the compost has been allowed to dry out. If the label is very weathered it may have been sitting there too long. Clear, accurate labels are usually a good sign.

Herbaceous border plants

Unfortunately, strain is important with many herbaceous plants, and seed-raised plants may be variable in quality, but you are unlikely to know this by looking at the plant. Generally, it is best to avoid vague labelling; again, clear, accurate labels which name the variety (where applicable) are usually a sign that the plants have been cared for.

When you buy in spring, there may not be much growth, but you can usually tell if the plant is established in its container. Avoid any that are not.

Border plants are sometimes sold with roots bound in damp peat or moss. These are usually cheaper and perfectly satisfactory, provided growth is not too advanced.

Trees and shrubs

Balled plants should only be bought if the root-balls (which will be wrapped in hessian or a plastic mesh) are plunged in damp peat or soil to prevent them drying out. Make sure the ball feels firm and not loose and crumbly.

Bare-root plants are still worth buying provided you plant in the dormant season and the roots have not been allowed to dry out. Only buy if there is a good, relatively undamaged root system, and the plants have been kept plunged in moist peat or similar material.

Container-grown plants should be well established in the container. Lift gently by the stem and, if the plant begins to lift free of the compost, put it back right away and leave it there. A little mossy growth or even some weed growth can be an indication that the plant is well established, but weed-free compost may simply mean that a weedkiller has been used.

A *few* roots growing through the container is a good sign, but avoid plants with a mass of roots that have embedded themselves in the standing ground.

Balled plant

Container grown plant removed from pot

Although raising all your own plants is a nice idea, it is an unnecessary constraint. Unless you are really good at long-term planning and begin years before you start the garden construction, you will have to live with a bleak garden while the plants grow large enough to make an impact. Even then, you will probably have to buy in some plants to provide the cuttings.

Although propagating all the plants yourself is not a sensible proposition, raising some of them is perfectly feasible and a practical way of keeping down the cost.

Many of the more rampant rock garden plants are easy to raise from seed and *Alyssum saxatile*, *Aubrieta deltoidea* hybrids, and *Cerastium tomentosum* are examples. These will make respectable plants the year after sowing and could be used to give cover and colour while you raise some of the choicer alpines from seed, some of which can be quite tricky to germinate and are slower-growing.

Many herbaceous plants, such as hollyhocks (*Althaea rosea*), dianthus, and lupins, are very easy to grow from seed and should flower in the second season. Some of the modern strains of these perennials will flower the first year if sown early enough. If you know that you will be planting an herbaceous border next year, you should be able to propagate a wide range of border plants from seed that will be as large as those you would buy as plants next year. You will still have to buy some, of course, but you may be able to reduce the number by about half.

All the biennials, such as foxgloves (*Digitalis purpurea*) and sweet-williams (*Dianthus barbatus*), are easily raised from seed sown during the summer.

There is also a vast range of hardy and half-hardy annuals that can be raised as gap fillers (see page 121), which will be invaluable in providing fairly instant interest while the slower-growing plants are becoming established.

Division is an excellent way of increasing your stock of herbaceous plants and many alpines. If you have these plants already, or have friends willing to split some clumps (which is desirable once

---

Sow the seeds outdoors on a well-prepared seed-bed, using a garden line or pegs and string to ensure the drills are straight. Always sow thinly to avoid overcrowding or a lot of thinning. This form of regimented sowing is most suited to vegetables.

Plants from seed

The vast majority of seeds that are sold commercially are relatively easy to germinate, but some do need special treatments or techniques. It is impossible in this short space to suggest methods for individual plants, other than by way of example. Most seed catalogues and packets give some advice, but for some of the tricky ones this information often falls short of what is desirable. If you suspect that a particular plant might be difficult, split the packet into several lots and try a different method for each one.

Hardy annuals These are the easiest, and the most dependable. By their very nature they *have* to germinate readily because annuals have no other way of perpetuating themselves. As gap fillers they have the considerable merit of flowering within a few months of sowing, which is just what you want for a bare area.

Always sow in drills, even if the drills cover an irregular area, in which case they are best at an angle, because this will make identification and weeding easier. As an approximate guide, cover the seeds with

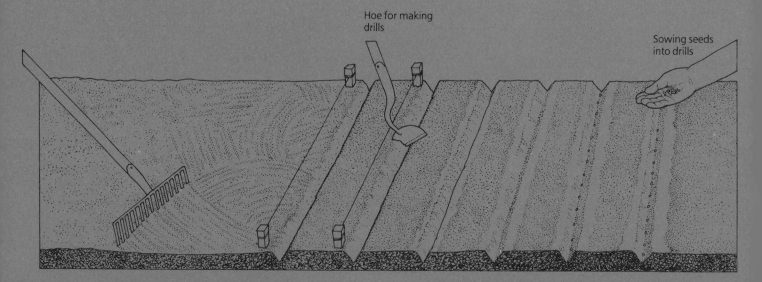

Hoe for making drills

Sowing seeds into drills

they become large), this is one of the best ways of filling your border because you can use quite large pieces for a more established look, or use a lot of small pieces to fill a large area.

Cuttings are generally a longer-term project, although if taken from herbaceous plants, they will make good plants for the following year. Woody subjects are generally slow to make plants of respectable size. You could, though, buy the stock plant and use it for instant impact in an area you want to clothe in the shortest possible time, and use some shoots to provide cuttings to fill out another part of the garden where immediate results are less important.

In the meantime, if you have some form of boundary, perhaps an old fence, you could save the expense of buying a lot of hedging plants by purchasing a few stock plants and using them for cuttings or for layering to bulk up the numbers.

Layering is also worth considering for many shrubs, especially if you already have some desirable plants that are suitable. Within a year you could have a plant almost as large as some of those that you might buy from a garden centre.

Techniques such as grafting and budding are really beyond the scope of most people simply trying to bulk up their plants. It is best to regard these methods as interesting experiments to try for their own sake.

A word of warning
In the enthusiasm to raise your own plants, it is easy to lose sight of your original planting plan. There is a temptation to settle for inferior varieties, or perhaps use seed-grown plants that may not be as good as named varieties propagated vegetatively. If you have plants in your garden that are not in your plan, or friends offer you something not planned for, it takes determination to exclude them if they are unsuitable.

The answer is probably to go ahead and use them now, as gap fillers, *provided you are willing to sacrifice them later* as you acquire the plants of your first choice.

their own depth of soil; with fine seeds this means no covering at all.

If the ground is dry, water the drills *first* as watering after sowing will probably wash the seeds away. Although some can be sown in autumn, they are generally sown in spring for use as temporary gap fillers.

Provided the soil is warm enough, they should germinate within a week or two, but during that time ensure the soil is kept moist. Water with a fine mist so the soil does not form a hard cap which will make it difficult for the seedlings to emerge.

Keep weeded, and then thin in stages, starting early.

Half-hardy annuals This term generally covers tender perennials that are treated as half-hardy annuals, and even a few hardy perennials that perform best given half-hardy annual treatment – the popular snapdragon or *antirrhinum* is an example.

In favourable areas, a few of the tender plants can be treated like hardy annuals. French marigolds, *Tagetes patula*, for example can sometimes be sown outdoors in late spring or early summer, where they will flower, albeit a bit later than normal.

The normal treatment for half-hardy annuals is to sow them in a greenhouse or as second-best by a light window indoors, from mid winter to mid spring. The majority of half-hardy annuals will germinate most readily in a temperature within the range 68-86°F (20-30°C), but follow the seedman's instructions. A steady temperature is not always a good thing, and some respond much better to a fluctuating temperature.

A few seeds may need special treatment. Those with very hard seed coats may germinate better if carefully chipped or nicked to allow moisture to penetrate; some need exposure to light to germinate well (*impatiens*, *lobelia*, and *petunia* are examples); a few are inhibited by exposure to light (*Eccremocarpus scaber* for instance).

Always sow thinly in pots or boxes in sterilized compost – most plants will not mind whether it is loam-based or peat-based. Prick off, as soon as the first pair of true leaves has formed.

Trees and shrubs It is probably wise to buy your tree and shrub seeds from a specialist seedsman. Success may depend on how fresh the seed is. The temperature for germination need not be high, so a garden frame will be adequate for most species. There may be dormancy problems, and it may be worth trying pre-chilling (see border plants and alpines) and perhaps fluctuating temperatures.

Raising plants from seed

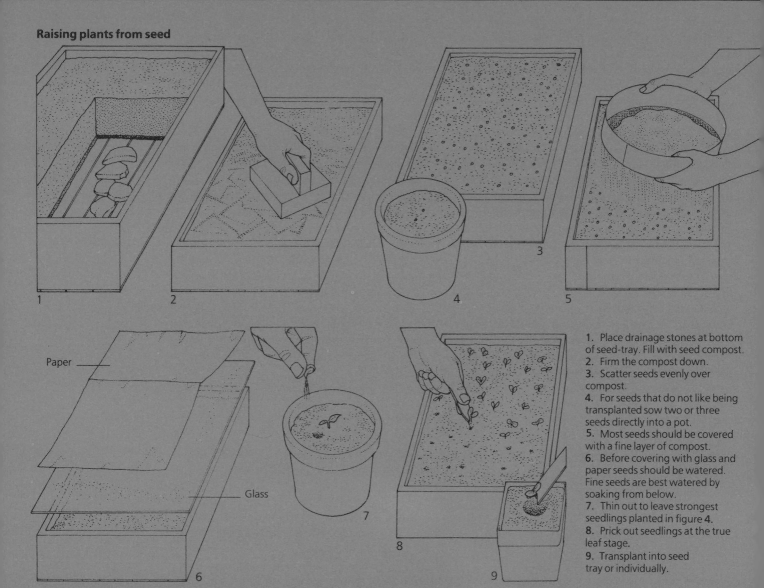

1. Place drainage stones at bottom of seed-tray. Fill with seed compost.
2. Firm the compost down.
3. Scatter seeds evenly over compost.
4. For seeds that do not like being transplanted sow two or three seeds directly into a pot.
5. Most seeds should be covered with a fine layer of compost.
6. Before covering with glass and paper seeds should be watered. Fine seeds are best watered by soaking from below.
7. Thin out to leave strongest seedlings planted in figure **4**.
8. Prick out seedlings at the true leaf stage.
9. Transplant into seed tray or individually.

Border plants and alpines

Some of these should germinate readily with no special treatment, but many need special measures to break dormancy.

One of the traditional methods was to place the seeds in layers of moist sand and leave them outdoors for the winter, then sow in spring. You can save time, in many cases, by placing the seeds in a refrigerator for about two weeks before sowing. The seeds should be placed on moist blotting paper or towelling and covered with another piece in a covered dish. Do not let the seeds dry out. Sow normally after pre-chilling.

A few seeds with hard glossy coats may benefit from chipping or nicking, though this must be done very carefully so the seed inside is not damaged.

Some border and alpine plants may take more than a year to germinate, so do not throw the trays or pots out too hastily.

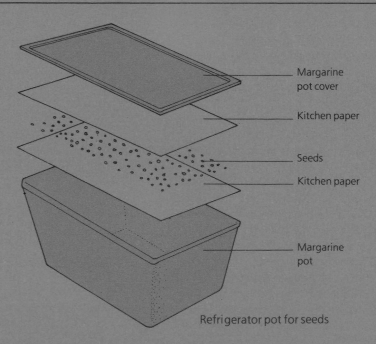

Refrigerator pot for seeds

Division

Old clumps of herbaceous plants will benefit from division, whether you want new plants or not. If you want to increase your stock, the method is the same but relatively young plants may be used (commercially, plants only one or two years old are used).

It is possible to divide the plants throughout the growing season, but the best time is usually after flowering, though late-flowering plants such as Michaelmas daisies (New York asters) are best divided in spring.

Most plants can be divided by lifting the old clump and dividing it with two digging forks placed back-to-back to prize apart a tough clump, or with two hand forks. With an old clump the woody centre is usually discarded and only the younger outer pieces replanted.

Some plants, like hostas, have fleshy crowns, and you will need to cut these with a knife, making sure that each piece has at least one bud.

Many alpines can be divided and those that are likely to be successful are the ones with a clump-forming habit and fibrous roots. Do not try to divide any plants that have a long, fleshy tap root.

Some alpines (*androsace* and *sempervivums* for instance) and herbaceous border plants (such as herbaceous *potentillas*) produce offsets or runners that can be detached.

Semi-woody plants such as *cortaderias* and *phormiums*, can also be divided.

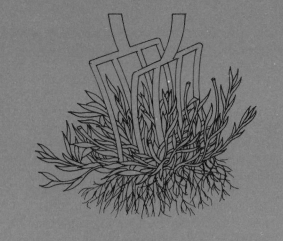

Dividing lifted root clump with two forks

Dividing roots with a knife

Layering

There are several forms of layering, including tip layering, air layering, and specialized techniques such as stooling and French layering. But normally, simple layering is perfectly adequate for most of the plants you are likely to want to propagate this way in the numbers that you are likely to require.

The best time to layer most shrubs is late winter or early spring.

If you want to produce a lot of material for layering, prune some low branches on an established plant to stimulate vigorous growth in the spring. If you only need one or two plants, though, you will probably be able to find some suitable shoots without waiting.

Select a strong, actively growing shoot that is already close to the ground, and trim off side shoots below the growing point to make layering easier. Remove any leaves that would be buried, and pull the stem to the ground so you can mark the position where the stem will touch the ground 6-12 in (150-300mm) behind the tip. Use a spade to make a shallow trench 3-6 in (80-150mm) deep, with a straight side away from the plant and a sloping side towards the parent plant.

Bend the stem at right angles, about 9 in (230mm)

behind the tip but be careful not to break it, and peg it into position with an old-fashioned clothes peg or a piece of bent wire, then return the soil. It may be necessary to tie the tip to a cane to keep it in an upright position.

A few difficult plants may layer better if the stem is wounded by either partial slitting and twisting, or by removing a thin strip of bark at the point close to where the shoot is pegged down.

Plants layered in late winter or early spring should have rooted by the autumn, though obviously much depends on the species. It is usual to sever rooted plants in late summer or early autumn.

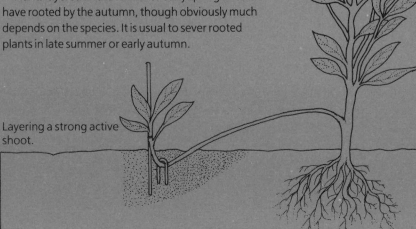

Layering a strong active shoot.

Cuttings

The vast majority of trees and shrubs can be raised from cuttings. Commercially, many cuttings are rooted on propagating benches, often with the aid of mist propagation. Clearly if you have to spend money on such expensive equipment for the sake of a few extra plants for your garden you might as well buy the plants. Advanced techniques are worthwhile if you need to raise a large number of plants regularly, or simply like the challenge of striking cuttings of difficult subjects.

The methods described here use nothing more scientific than a hormone rooting powder and perhaps a fungicide, but you should be able to raise most garden shrubs this way with a little patience.

Taking the cutting Most cuttings are either basal, nodal or heeled (see illustration). There are other types, but most shrubs will root from one of these three methods even though they may root from other types too. Some plants will root regardless of where you make the cut.

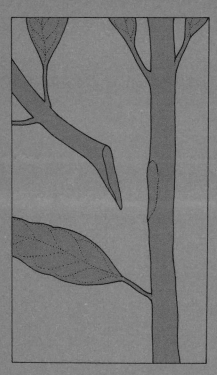
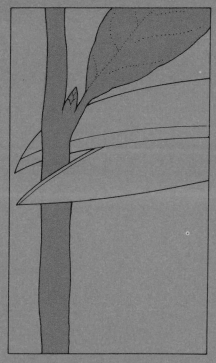

Above: Heeled cutting

Above right: Nodal cutting

Basal cuttings are simply sliced through, close to where the shoot joins the parent plant; heeled cuttings are pulled off with a downward motion so that a tail of older wood is peeled off with it; nodal cuttings are cut at right-angles to the stem at the slight swelling that can usually be seen just below a leaf.

Avoid old shoots that are not growing actively, and also very vigorous sappy ones. And always take your cuttings from healthy plants. The young growth from recently pruned plants is often very successful.

The length of the cutting will depend on the plant,

but generally 2-6 in (50-150m) is about right for semi-hardwood shrub cuttings, and perhaps 9 in (230mm) for some hardwood cuttings.

Softwood cuttings are taken from young shoots early in the season, and although sometimes used for woody plants such as fuchsias, these are generally confined to herbaceous perennials.

Semi-hardwood, or semi-ripe cuttings as they are also known, are popular for evergreen trees and shrubs. They are taken just as the young shoots of the current season start to harden up at the base.

Hardwood cuttings are used for many deciduous trees and shrubs, and are usually taken between mid autumn and late winter.

Prepare the cutting by removing the lower leaves and then immersing the cutting in a fungicidal solution to reduce the chances of it rotting (wear waterproof gloves when you do this).

There is some evidence that wounding the stem may also help some difficult subjects to root, so if you have had difficulty in the past, try removing a slice of outer bark on one side of the bottom few centimetres of the cutting.

Many cuttings will root without the aid of a rooting powder or solution.

Rooting in open ground If you choose a sheltered spot, away from tree and shrub roots, and free from perennial weeds, many tree and shrub cuttings will root perfectly well outdoors. If the soil is heavy, use sand and peat to improve conditions. Simply open up a slit with a spade, making one side vertical, the other sloping (the depth will depend on the cuttings), and sprinkle sharp sand along the bottom before inserting the cuttings in an upright position. Aim to have about two-thirds of the cutting buried, with one-third above the ground. Return the soil and firm gently.

The plants will probably have rooted within a year.

Rooting in a garden frame If you root your cuttings in a frame, make sure it is protected from direct sunlight, and do not let it become overheated in summer.

It is normal to insert the cuttings directly into the soil, though if the frame is on a solid base, you will have to use containers but you must make sure these never dry out.

Pot and bag method

This is well worth considering if you want to root just a few cuttings. Insert them round the edge of the pot of rooting compost and enclose in a clear plastic bag. Make sure the bag does not touch the cuttings and use canes or wire if necessary to keep it clear. This method is particularly useful for soft or semi-hardwood cuttings.

Never let direct sunlight shine on the bag, but keep the pot in a reasonably light position.

Weedkilling may seem to have little to do with garden planning and construction, but modern herbicides can make a huge difference to the ease with which some types of garden can be maintained. The careful use of suitable weedkillers before and after planting an area can substantially influence the establishment and subsequent performance of the plants.

Weedkillers should always be treated with respect and caution. In the wrong place they can cause immense harm, and spray-drift, or even vapour on a hot day, may damage plants along with the weeds. Such problems are the result of abuse or carelessness, however, and should not deter you from using herbicides. They are a real boon to a busy gardener and perfectly safe if instructions are followed to the letter.

Affect on design

Gravel areas can be a permanent headache if you are unable to control weed growth. With suitable non-creeping weedkillers you can treat the areas to be kept clear even though you might have shrubs and other plants growing there too. One treatment a year is likely to be sufficient.

Paths are often a problem, especially if there are joints, cracks, or edges in which weeds can take a hold. These are both fiddly and time consuming to try and weed by hand, and you may be tempted to avoid some types of path for this reason, but there are weedkillers such as simazine that will keep them clear for a year at a time.

Shrub borders can be a nightmare to weed, if you let some of the tenacious perennial weeds become established. Yet once you have cleared the ground, a herbicide that kills weeds as they emerge should keep it maintenance-free for most of the season, provided you do not disturb the soil. Even quite large borders can be established and kept weed-free with the minimum of time and effort, though at some financial cost.

Neglected gardens can be cleared with total weedkillers that will kill existing plant growth yet leave the soil safe to plant in a matter of days or months depending on the chemical. Even really neglected areas can be brought back into cultivation in a fraction of the time that would be feasible without the use of weedkillers.

Reclaiming established plants that have weeds entangled within the roots would have been extremely difficult years ago; today there are selective weedkillers you can use to remove grasses from other plants like shrubs, (such as alloxydim sodium) and others that can be painted on the leaves of weeds entwined within a desirable plant, which will then be translocated to the roots to kill the weed while leaving the other plant unharmed. Simazine, dichlobenil and propachlor, for instance, can be used around established shrubs, roses and some fruit trees.

A weedy rockery can also be salvaged even though deep-rooted grasses and other weeds might have penetrated beneath the rocks as well as through the root-balls of your rock plants.

Selective weedkillers for lawns, for example, ioxynil and MCPA are now a well-established part of routine garden maintenance. Nevertheless, it is not sensible to decide on a large area of lawn just because you can keep it free of broad-leaved weeds with chemicals. The larger and more informal the lawn, the less important weeds are likely to be, especially if the area is mainly recreational. Applying selective weedkillers regularly to a large expanse of lawn could also become prohibitively expensive and time-consuming. If you hope to keep a *large* lawn looking like a classic bowling green, bear in mind that broad-leaved weeds will not be your only problem; you will also have to cope with moss and other difficulties.

Selective weedkiller applied by touch stick

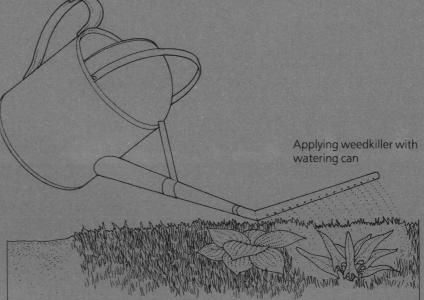

Applying weedkiller with watering can

Priorities

This section of the book could easily leave you with the feeling that you need to have a store of chemical potions to be sure of success. You can manage without any of them, as they simply do more quickly and with less effort what you could achieve by traditional hand weeding. And that will cost you nothing more than effort and time.

Chemicals are most useful for clearing the ground to plant and keeping it clear for those crucial months when the plants are becoming established, reducing competition from weeds for moisture, nutrients, and sometimes light. Once the plants are beyond that stage you could try using ground cover plants (see page 98) to reduce the need to weed. In many gardens, mulching and hoeing will be all that is needed to keep the weeds within bounds.

Mulching

A mulch can be decorative as well as useful. A mulch of compost, peat or pulverized bark, at least 2 in (50mm) thick, and put over moist ground, will control weeds and conserve moisture. Black polythene (polyethylene) or other sheet material will also achieve this, and can be well worth considering around newly-planted trees and specimen shrubs. Tests have shown that those mulched with black polythene (polyethylene) can grow up to 30-40 per cent faster than those that are merely kept weed-free, and this is mainly because water loss from the soil is reduced.

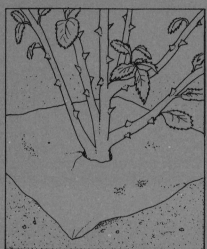
Polythene mulch

Compost mulch

If you do not want to use chemicals

Everything that can be done with herbicides can also be done by hand weeding, but it may take a great deal of time and determined effort.

Annual weeds are easy to kill with a hoe, but timing is important. Always hoe all weeds off before they flower and seed: this is the only way to reduce the weed population over the long term.

Deep-rooted perennial weeds are difficult to control by hoeing, though most will succumb if you keep hoeing the new growth off when it reaches about 2-4 in (50-100mm). For the really stubborn ones you will have to resort to forking the ground over and pulling the roots out by hand.

Flame guns have a limited use for killing off the top growth. They are unlikely to get rid of deep-rooted perennial weeds, and you can hardly use them close to desirable plants.

Do not overlook the role of mulches (see above) and ground cover plants (see page 98).

WHICH HERBICIDE TO USE WHERE

Paraquat + diquat * (can replant within days) *or* glyphosate

Glyphosate

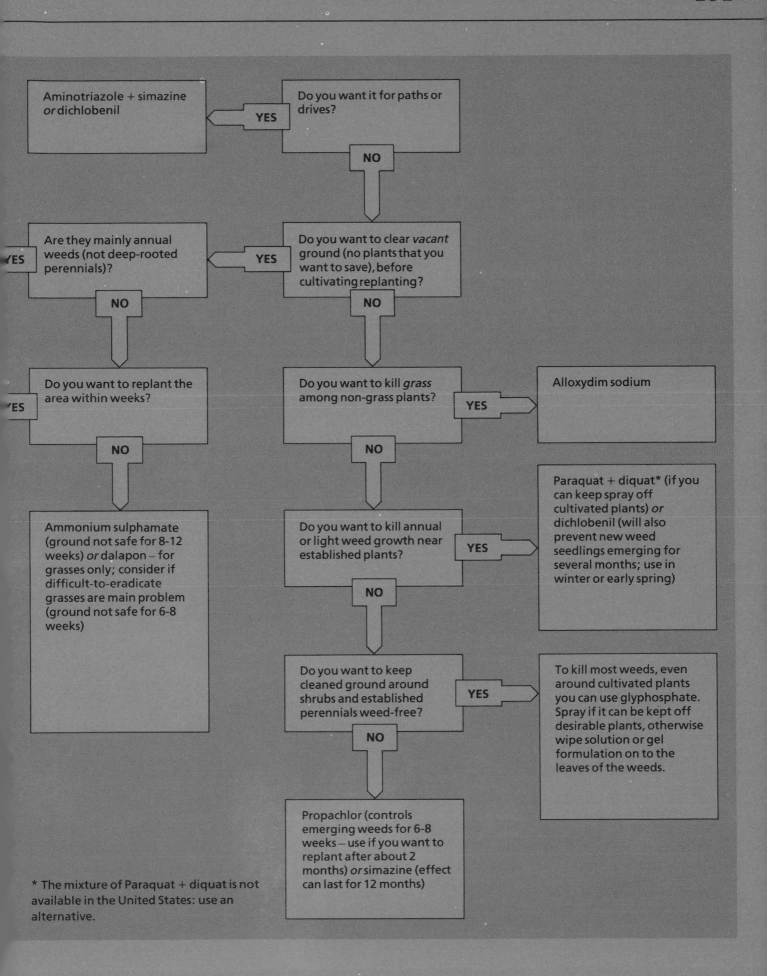

Aminotriazole + simazine *or* dichlobenil

Do you want it for paths or drives? — **YES**

NO

Are they mainly annual weeds (not deep-rooted perennials)? — **YES**

Do you want to clear *vacant* ground (no plants that you want to save), before cultivating replanting? — **YES**

NO

NO

Do you want to replant the area within weeks? — **YES**

Do you want to kill *grass* among non-grass plants? — **YES** → Alloxydim sodium

NO

NO

Ammonium sulphamate (ground not safe for 8-12 weeks) *or* dalapon – for grasses only; consider if difficult-to-eradicate grasses are main problem (ground not safe for 6-8 weeks)

Do you want to kill annual or light weed growth near established plants? — **YES** → Paraquat + diquat* (if you can keep spray off cultivated plants) *or* dichlobenil (will also prevent new weed seedlings emerging for several months; use in winter or early spring)

NO

Do you want to keep cleaned ground around shrubs and established perennials weed-free? — **YES** → To kill most weeds, even around cultivated plants you can use glyphosphate. Spray if it can be kept off desirable plants, otherwise wipe solution or gel formulation on to the leaves of the weeds.

NO

Propachlor (controls emerging weeds for 6-8 weeks – use if you want to replant after about 2 months) *or* simazine (effect can last for 12 months)

* The mixture of Paraquat + diquat is not available in the United States: use an alternative.

PLAN SYMBOLS

The following pages contain symbols that you can use to help design your garden. Once you have measured your existing plot, established a basic grid for your new design, and decided in principle how you would like it to look, you can use these symbols to visualize how different arrangements will work. You can either trace out or photocopy the symbols and then cut them out in order to lay them on your basic garden plan.

This collection is, of course, by no means exhaustive, but does contain all the basic shapes and features that you might use. They should be used in conjunction with the plans in Part Two. Do not feel restricted by what is included here, but regard these symbols as a source of inspiration; for example the curved raised bed will stand in for a circular pool or a sandpit.

These symbols have been drawn to the scale of 1:50. Use the scale below to work out on your plan the size of objects you want to include which are different from these.

SEATS

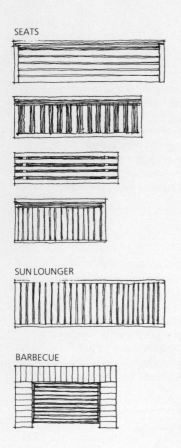

SUN LOUNGER

BARBECUE

TABLE AND BENCHES

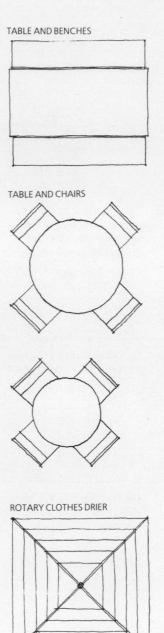

TABLE AND CHAIRS

ROTARY CLOTHES DRIER

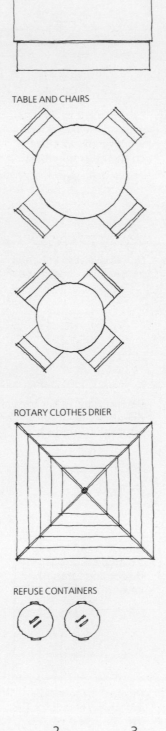

REFUSE CONTAINERS

PLANTS IN CONTAINERS

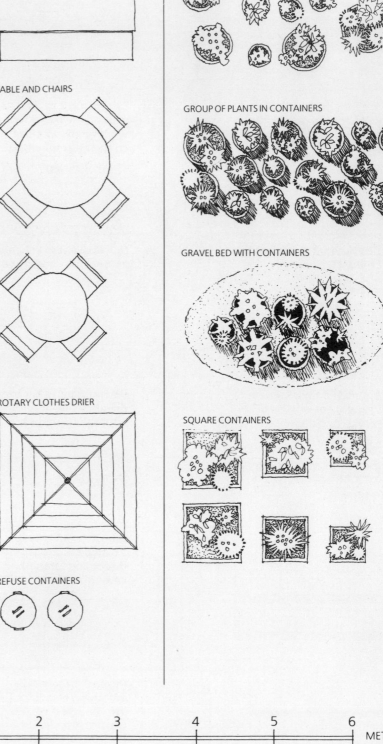

GROUP OF PLANTS IN CONTAINERS

GRAVEL BED WITH CONTAINERS

SQUARE CONTAINERS

```
0        1        2        3        4        5        6
|--------|--------|--------|--------|--------|--------|   METRES

0  1  2  3  4  5  6  7  8  9 10 11 12 13 14 15 16 17 18 19 20
|--|--|--|--|--|--|--|--|--|--|--|--|--|--|--|--|--|--|--|--|  FEET
```

Note: all symbols (except textures) have been drawn to the Scale 1:50.

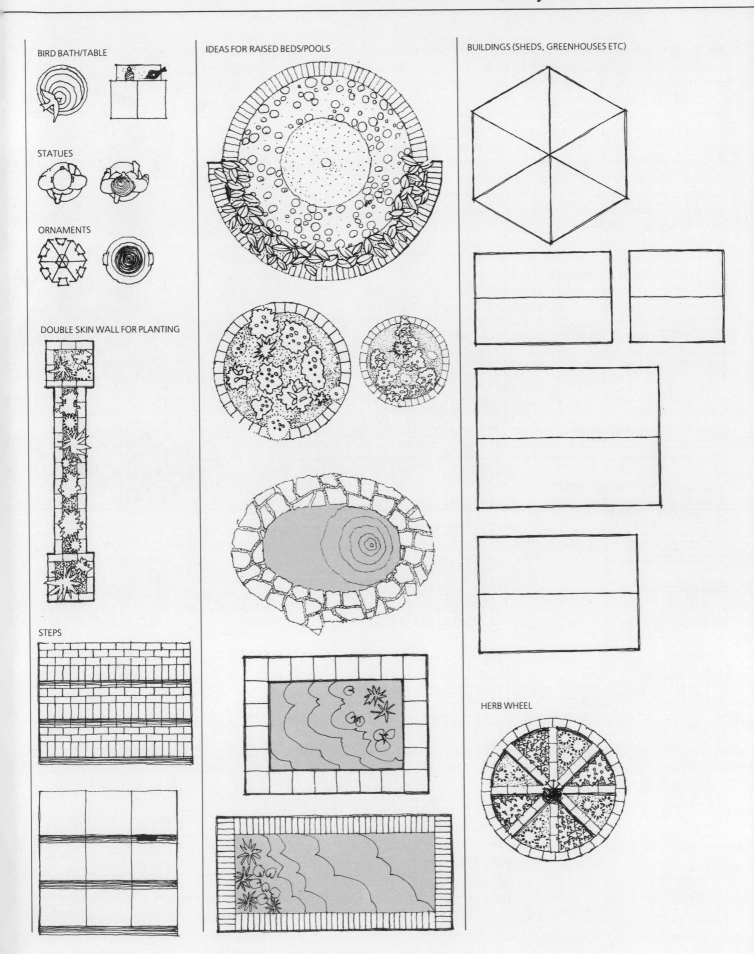

BIRD BATH/TABLE

STATUES

ORNAMENTS

DOUBLE SKIN WALL FOR PLANTING

STEPS

IDEAS FOR RAISED BEDS/POOLS

BUILDINGS (SHEDS, GREENHOUSES ETC)

HERB WHEEL

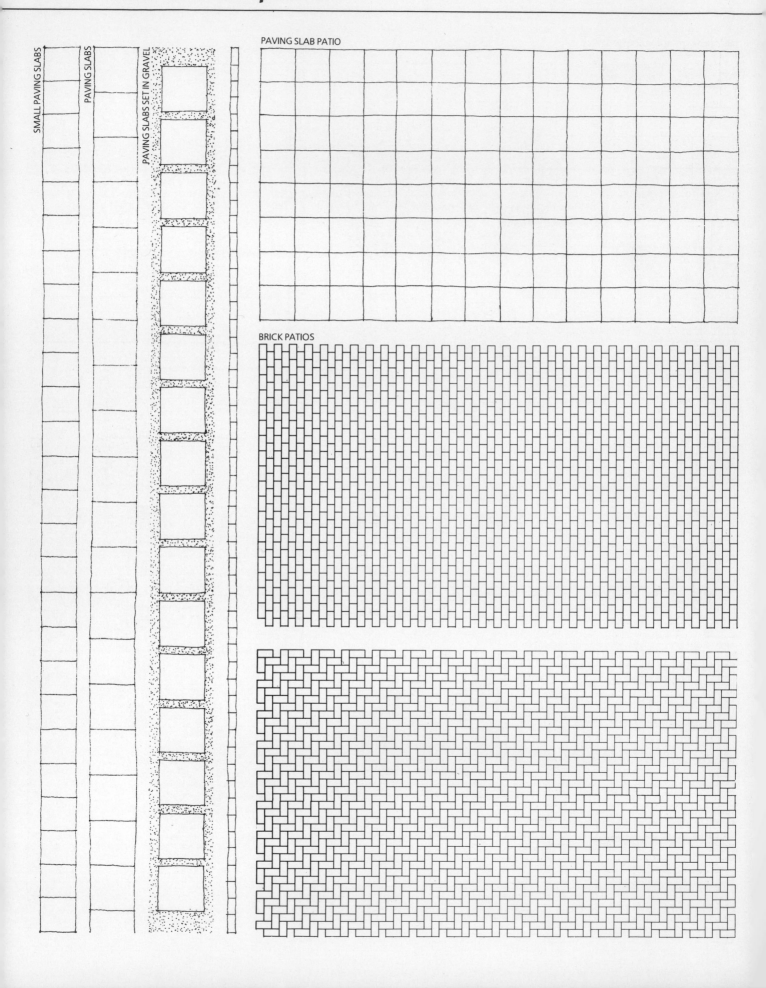

SMALL PAVING SLABS

PAVING SLABS

PAVING SLABS SET IN GRAVEL

PAVING SLAB PATIO

BRICK PATIOS

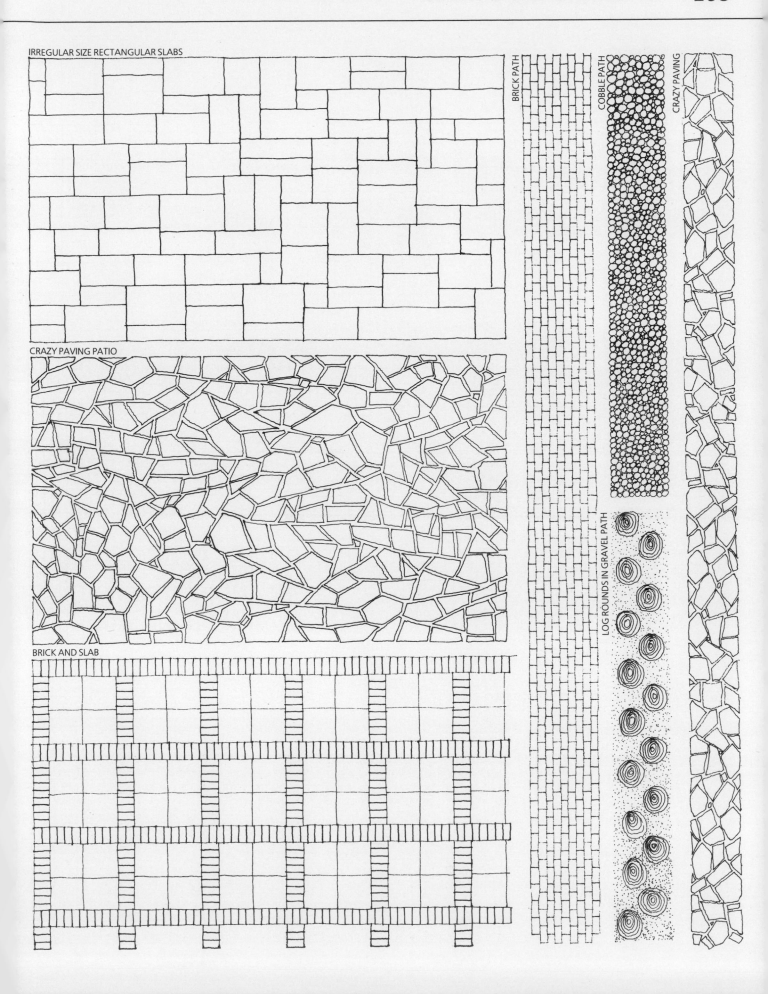

IRREGULAR SIZE RECTANGULAR SLABS

CRAZY PAVING PATIO

BRICK AND SLAB

BRICK PATH

COBBLE PATH

CRAZY PAVING

LOG ROUNDS IN GRAVEL PATH

TREES/SPECIMEN SHRUBS

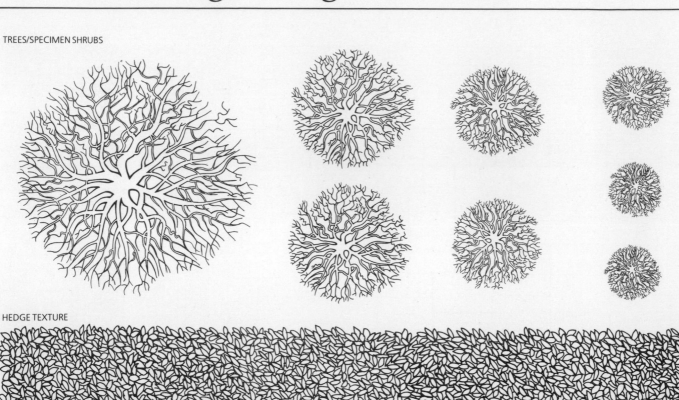

HEDGE TEXTURE

LONG GRASS

GRASS

SHRUB BORDER

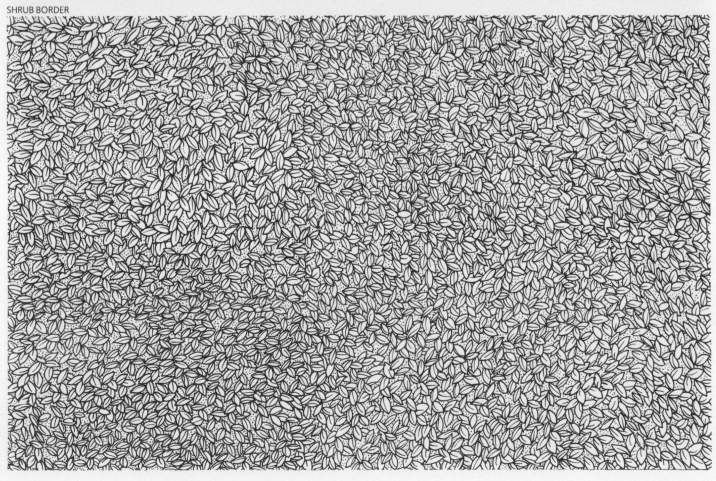

GRAVEL

WATER

HERBACEOUS BORDER

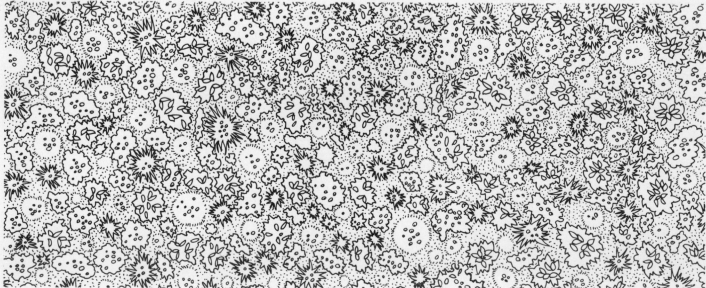

LINEAR MEASUREMENT

1 centimetre	0.39 inch
1 metre	39.4 inches
1 metre	3.28 feet
1 metre	1.094 yards
1 inch	25.40 millimetres
1 inch	2.54 centimetres
1 foot	30.48 centimetres
1 foot	0.305 metres
1 yard	91.4 centimetres
1 yard	0.914 metres

THICKNESS

Millimetres	Inches (Approx)
0.8	$\frac{1}{32}$
1.5	$\frac{1}{16}$
3.0	$\frac{1}{8}$
5.0	$\frac{3}{16}$
6.0	$\frac{1}{4}$
9.0	$\frac{3}{8}$
12.0	$\frac{1}{2}$
15.0	$\frac{5}{8}$
18.0	$\frac{3}{4}$
22.0	$\frac{7}{8}$
25.0	1 inch

AREA MEASUREMENT

1 sq centimetre	0.155 sq inches
1 sq metre	1.196 sq yards
1 sq inch	6.452 sq centimetres
1 sq foot	0.093 sq metres
1 sq yard	0.836 sq metres

CAPACITY

1 litre	1.76 pints
1 litre	0.22 gallons (Imperial)
1 litre	0.264 gallons (US)
1 pint	0.568 litres
1 gallon (Imperial)	4.546 litres
1 gallon (US)	3.786 litres

WEIGHT

1 gramme	0.0353 ounces (ozs)
1 kilogramme	35.27 ounces
1 kilogramme	2.205 pounds (lbs)
1 tonne	0.984 ton
1 ounce	28.35 grammes
1 ounce	0.0283 kilogrammes
1 pound (lb)	0.454 kilogrammes
1 ton	1,016 kilogrammes
1 ton	1.016 tonnes

The author has tried to include a wide variety of different gardening styles and designs in this book – something that is only possible by building on the inspiration and effort of others. He wishes to thank the following, whose gardens have been included, albeit modified in some cases, as examples in the garden plans in Part Two:

Probus County Demonstration Garden (nr Truro Cornwall) 52, 53, 56, 57
Mr and Mrs White 54, 54
Julian Treyer-Evans 58, 59
Mr and Mrs J. Pitchford (design: Julian Treyer-Evans) 60, 61
Horticultural Therapy, Frome 64
Pat Higgins 65
Mr and Mrs A. McIntosh 66, 67
Mr and Mrs G. Hudson 68, 69
Landscape students and staff of Merrist Wood Agricultural College 71
Mr and Mrs P. Goldstein (design: David Stevens, construction Mike Chewter) 72, 73
Mr and Mrs R. Lycett 74, 75
David Stevens (design) 76
David Stevens (design) 77
F.W. Woolworth (design: David Stevens, construction Jack Sexton 78, 79, 88, 89
Stapeley Water Gardens (water garden feature) 81
Mr and Mrs A. Wallis (construction: Mike Chewter) 82, 83
David Stevens (design) 84
David Stevens (design) 85

Thanks are due also to the following, whose gardens have been illustrated elsewhere in the book: Mr and Mrs L. Cliffe 101; Barry Gray 33b; Mr and Mrs P. Holland, design John Brookes 33t, 50; Mr and Mrs Martin Furniss 13tr; Mr and Mrs S. Rimmer 9; and Mrs J.H. Robinson 10r. Thanks are also due to the many unknown gardeners of the above, to whom the author is equally grateful, and to Sue and Colin Goff, Mrs E. Mann, Mrs E. Leete and Mr and Mrs P. Johnstone, for their help in research. The author is especially grateful to David Stevens for his considerable help and advice with the garden plans.

Swallow books would like to thank Letraset Ltd for their permission to reproduce their symbols which appear on page 186. Consult your local dealers to see the full range of Letraset products.

Photographs
All photography by Peter McHoy except as listed below:
Liz Eddison/Trannies 26, 27, 41b, 128
The Iris Hardwick Library of Photographs 42, 43
Tania Midgley 2–3, 11tr, 126
David Stevens 76, 77, 84, 85
Michael Warren/Photos Horticultural 6–7, 22–3, 35, 90–1, 132–3

Illustration
Steve Cross 28, 30, 31, 49, 142, 143, 146, 147, 152, 155, 158, 159, 160–1, 162, 163, 164–5, 166, 167, 170–1, 172, 173, 178, 180
Andrew Farmer 156, 168–9
Elsa Godfrey 135r
Rob Shone 36, 37, 134, 135l, 136, 137, 138–9, 141, 144–5, 148–9, 150–1, 157, 174, 176, 177, 179
David Tetley/Lewis, Jones and Tetley 18, 19, 24, 25, 52–3, 54–5, 56–7, 58–9, 60, 62–3, 64, 65, 67, 68–9, 70, 71, 72–3, 74–5, 76, 77, 78–9, 80–1, 82–3, 84, 85, 88–9, 182–9

Swallow Books would like to thank WHS Distributors for permission to reproduce the illustrations on pages 147b, 155l, 156, 166b, 167t, 168, 169

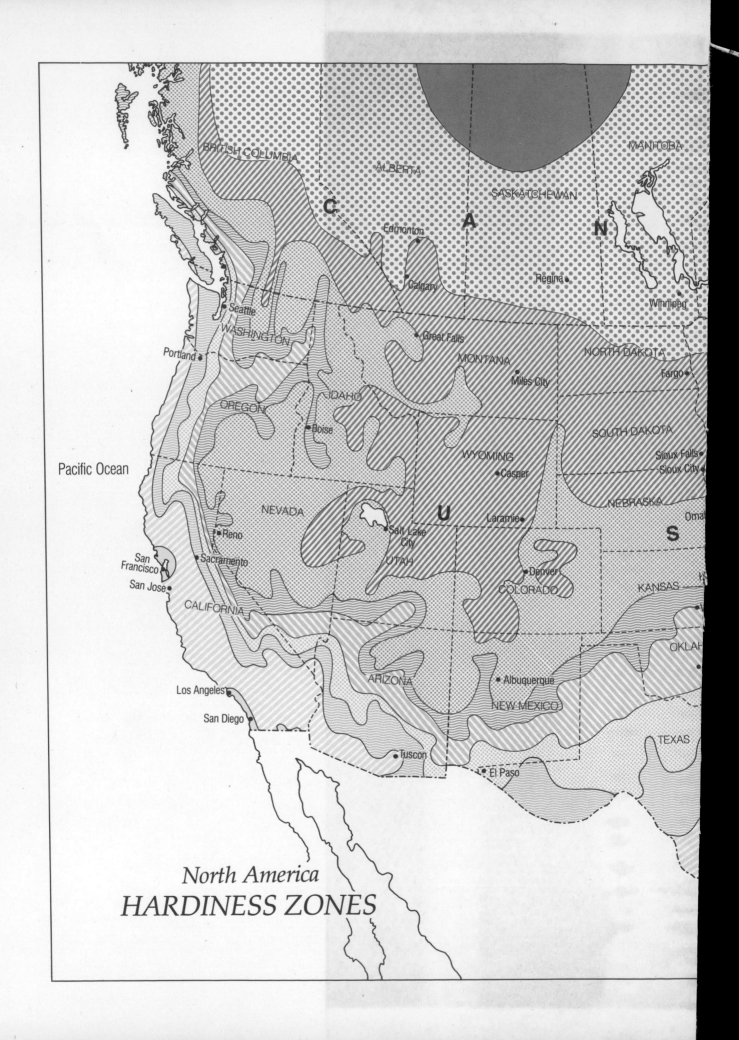

North America
HARDINESS ZONES